SELF AND WORLD

Self and World

QUASSIM CASSAM

OXFORD
UNIVERSITY PRESS

OXFORD
UNIVERSITY PRESS

Great Clarendon Street, Oxford OX2 6DP

Oxford University Press is a department of the University of Oxford
It furthers the University's objective of excellence in research, scholarship,
and education by publishing worldwide in

Oxford New York

Athens Auckland Bangkok Bogotá Buenos Aires Calcutta
Cape Town Chennai Dar es Salaam Delhi Florence Hong Kong Istanbul
Karachi Kuala Lumpur Madrid Melbourne Mexico City Mumbai
Nairobi Paris São Paulo Singapore Taipei Tokyo Toronto Warsaw

with associated companies in Berlin Ibadan

Oxford is a registered trade mark of Oxford University Press
in the UK and in certain other countries

Published in the United States
by Oxford University Press Inc., New York

© Quassim Cassam 1997

The moral rights of the author have been asserted

Database right Oxford University Press (maker)

First published 1997
First published as paperback 1999

All rights reserved. No part of this publication may be reproduced,
stored in a retrieval system, or transmitted, in any form or by any means,
without the prior permission in writing of Oxford University Press,
or as expressly permitted by law, or under terms agreed with the appropriate
reprographics rights organization. Enquiries concerning reproduction
outside the scope of the above should be sent to the Rights Department,
Oxford University Press, at the address above

You must not circulate this book in any other binding or cover
and you must impose this same condition on any acquirer

British Library Cataloguing in Publication Data

Data available

Library of Congress Cataloging in Publication Data
Cassam, Quassim.
Self and world / Quassim Cassam.
Includes bibliographical references.
1. Self (Philosophy). 2. Self-consciousness. 3. Self-perception.
I. Title.
BD450.C29 1996 126—dc20 96-21021
ISBN 0-19-823540-2
ISBN 0-19-823895-9 (Pbk.)

Printed in Great Britain
on acid-free paper by
Biddles Ltd
Guildford and King's Lynn

PREFACE

My deepest intellectual debt is to P. F. Strawson, whose writings have had a profound influence on my thinking about a wide range of philosophical issues. I first became seriously interested in philosophy when I read his book *Individuals* as an undergraduate, so it is fitting that Strawson's work should figure so prominently in what follows.

In *The Bounds of Sense*, his brilliant commentary on Kant, Strawson claims that to be self-conscious one must conceive of oneself as a corporeal object among corporeal objects. This claim, together with Strawson's arguments for it, was the focus of the research leading up to this book. Although I have my doubts about these arguments, there is hardly a single page in the present work which has not been shaped by my engagement with them.

My central thesis is that it is not possible to give an adequate account of self-consciousness without acknowledging the importance of certain forms of bodily self-awareness which have received surprisingly little attention in the analytical tradition. My interest in the topic of bodily self-awareness was first stimulated by my colleague Michael Ayers, from whom I have learned a great deal over the years. His influence on this book, both through his writings and through his comments on an earlier draft, has been very considerable.

I have profited from many vigorous discussions with John Campbell, whose scepticism about my approach to self-consciousness has helped me to sharpen up my arguments. I am also grateful to an anonymous reader for Oxford University Press, and to Naomi Eilan, whose incisive comments on earlier drafts of the first four chapters were enormously helpful. Bill Brewer's comments on an earlier version of the discussion of immunity to error through misidentification in Chapter 2 led to a significant change in the argument of this chapter. My response to Reductionism about persons in the final chapter owes much to discussions with Derek Parfit.

This book first began to take shape in 1993 in a class given at the University of California, Berkeley, and in subsequent classes in Oxford. I am grateful to the audiences on these occasions for some extremely stimulating responses, and to audiences in Birmingham, Cambridge,

London, Oxford, Reading, Sheffield, and Stirling for many other helpful comments.

I would also like to thank the following:

The editor and publishers of the *Review of Metaphysics* for permission to use material from my paper 'Kant and Reductionism', *Review of Metaphysics*, vol. 43 (1989): 72–106, in Chapter 2.

MIT Press for permission to use material from my paper 'Introspection and Bodily Self-Ascription', in J. Bermúdez, A. Marcel, and N. Eilan (eds.), *The Body and the Self* (Cambridge, Mass., 1995), pp. 311–36, in Chapter 2.

The Indian Council of Philosophical Research for permission to use material from my paper 'Transcendental Self-Consciousness', in P. K. Sen and R. R. Verma (eds.), *The Philosophy of P. F. Strawson* (New Delhi, 1995), pp. 161–78, in Chapter 3.

Blackwell Publishers Ltd. for permission to use material from my paper 'Self-Reference, Self-Knowledge, and the Problem of Misconception', *European Journal of Philosophy* (December 1996), in Chapter 4.

CONTENTS

I

SELF AND WORLD

1. *Introduction*

A remarkable feature of many philosophical accounts of the nature of self-consciousness has been their commitment to the idea that the self is, in some important sense, systematically elusive.[1] The supposedly elusive self is the thinking, experiencing self, and the perspective from which this self has seemed so elusive is that of introspective self-awareness. As Hume puts it in his *Treatise of Human Nature*, 'when I enter most intimately into what I call myself, I always stumble on some particular perception or other . . . I can never catch myself without a perception, and can never observe anything but the perception' (Hume 1978: 252). From this, Hume concluded that the self is nothing but a bundle or collection of different perceptions, and that the identity which we ascribe to the mind of man is only a fictitious one (p. 259).

Later, in an appendix to the *Treatise*, Hume expressed dissatisfaction with his own account of the self on the grounds that it failed to 'explain the principles, that unite our successive perceptions in our thought or consciousness' (p. 636). This point was taken up by Kant, who argued that for different perceptions or 'representations' to be united in one consciousness, it must be possible for their subject to attach the representation 'I think' to each of them (B131).[2] The 'I think' is 'the one condition which accompanies all thought' (A398), and is a representation which cannot itself be accompanied by any further representation. A self-conscious subject is one who is at least capable of consciousness of its own identity as the subject of different representations, but self-consciousness is not and cannot be a matter of one's being perceptually or 'intuitively' aware of the subject of one's representations as an *object*. As Kant puts it, 'this identity of the subject, of which I can be conscious in

---

[1] See the brilliant parody in Ryle 1994 of traditional philosophical arguments for what he calls the 'systematic elusiveness of "I"'.

[2] All references in this form are to Kant (1929).

all my representations, does not concern any intuition of the subject, whereby it is given as object' (B408). Instead, Kant proposes that consciousness of self-identity is to be understood as involving consciousness of the identity of the *representation* 'I' which 'accompanies . . . with complete identity, all representations at all times in *my* consciousness' (A362–3). It remains to be seen what this proposal amounts to, but the claim that self-consciousness is not awareness of the subject of one's representations as an object represents one point of contact between the views of Kant and Hume on this most intractable of philosophical problems.

What would it be for one to be conscious of one's thinking, experiencing self 'as an object'? Kant implies that such awareness would have to consist in one's being aware of the subject of one's representations as a persisting immaterial *substance*. Awareness of oneself as a substance would need to be awareness of oneself as the persisting subject of different representations which 'inhere' in one's substantial self only as 'determinations' or 'accidents', but Kant follows Hume in arguing that 'no fixed and abiding self can present itself in the flux of inner appearances' (A107). It follows from this that although the 'I' that thinks 'can always be regarded as *subject*', this does not mean that 'I, as *object*, am for myself a *self-subsistent* being or substance' (B407). This point was subsequently taken up by Schopenhauer, who even went so far as to describe the suggestion that a subject should become an object for itself as 'the most monstrous contradiction ever thought of'.[3]

One reaction to these arguments would be to agree that there is not and cannot be any such thing as introspective awareness of the subject of one's representations as an immaterial substance, but to point out that there is another possibility, namely, that we are aware of ourselves as abiding *material* substances, as physical objects among physical objects.[4] This may be described as a *materialist conception of self-consciousness* or as *materialism about self-consciousness*. One question about this proposal concerns its understanding of the concept of 'awareness'. More will be said about this below. Another question concerns its understanding of the concept of a 'physical object'. It may be assumed that what makes an object a physical object is its possession of a range of Lockean primary

---

[3] Quoted by Christopher Janaway (1989: 120).

[4] Michael Ayers endorses this conception of self-consciousness in Ayers 1991. He claims that 'our experience of ourselves as being a material object among others essentially permeates our sensory experience of things in general' (1991: ii. 285). For a related line of thought, see Strawson (1966: 102).

qualities, including shape, location, and solidity.[5] In this sense, horses and tables are physical objects, holograms and shadows are not. To the extent, therefore, that one is aware of one's thinking, experiencing self as shaped, located, and solid, one is aware of oneself as a physical object. According to the conception of self-consciousness to be defended in the chapters that follow, it not only makes sense to suppose that one might be aware of the subject of one's representations 'as an object' in this sense, it is also plausible that introspective awareness of one's thinking, experiencing self as a physical object among physical objects, is a *necessary* condition of self-consciousness.[6] This is enough to undermine the suggestion that the self is elusive.

Why should the materialist conception of self-consciousness ever have been thought to be problematic? One explanation is this: if one is committed to denying that thinking subjects can actually be physical objects, it might seem difficult to accept that the sense in which one is aware of one's thinking self 'as an object' is that one is aware of it as a physical object. This explanation might lead to the proposal that in order to argue for materialism about self-consciousness, no more is required than to argue for a materialist conception of the self, according to which thinking selves are themselves physical or bodily entities. Since there is no reason to suppose that bodies are peculiarly elusive, if thinking subjects are bodies, there should be no reason to suppose that they are peculiarly elusive. This will be referred to as the *simple proposal*.[7]

Unfortunately, the simple proposal is so simple as to be wholly inadequate in a number of important respects. In the first place, questions about the nature of self-consciousness are epistemological questions, whereas questions about the nature of the self are metaphysical. The significance of this distinction is that, as Descartes himself insisted, an

[5] Locke's primary qualities are solidity, extension, figure, motion or rest, and number. These qualities of a body are 'utterly inseparable from the Body, in what estate soever it be' (1975: 134). Locke also claims that solidity 'seems the Idea most intimately connected with, and essential to Body' (p. 123). For further discussion of the concept of a physical object, see Joske 1967, Peacocke 1993, and Chapter 2 below.

[6] Strawson claims that it is a necessary condition of personal self-consciousness that 'each of us is a corporeal object' (Strawson 1966: 102). My main concern is not with the question of whether self-consciousness requires that each of us is a corporeal or physical object, but with the question of whether it is a necessary condition of self-consciousness that we are *presented* to ourselves as physical objects among physical objects. It is a further question whether it follows from the fact that one's thinking self is presented to one as corporeal that it is corporeal.

[7] A version of the simple proposal is outlined by Roderick Chisholm, who writes that 'if we are identical with our bodies and if, as all but sceptics hold, we do perceive our bodies, then, whether we realize it or not, we also perceive ourselves' (1994: 94).

immaterialist about the self—someone who believes that thinking selves are non-physical—is not obviously committed to denying that thinking subjects are *presented* to themselves as physical. Indeed, it appears that the point of Descartes's insistence that one is not in one's body as a pilot is in a ship is, precisely, to draw attention to the fact that there is an important sense in which our thinking selves are presented to themselves as *bodily* subjects of consciousness, not just as subjects who happen to be associated with bodily entities.[8] For the immaterialist about the self, such awareness of one's thinking subject as corporeal embodies an illusion about the actual nature of this subject, but there is no need to suppose that the nature of the self is wholly transparent to one in ordinary self-awareness.[9] By the same token, even if the subject of one's representations is in fact a flesh and blood physical object, this seems to leave open the possibility that, as Sydney Shoemaker puts it, 'when one is introspectively aware of one's thoughts, feelings, beliefs and desires, one is not presented to oneself as a flesh and blood person, and does not seem to be presented to oneself as an *object* at all' (1984a: 102). In other words, one respect in which the simple proposal is far too quick is in arguing directly for an epistemological conclusion from a metaphysical premiss.

It might be objected that this somewhat abstract criticism of the simple proposal fails to explain precisely how a materialist conception of the self is supposed to leave it open whether we are introspectively aware of ourselves as physical objects. This objection calls for the following response: introspective self-awareness is not just awareness or consciousness of what is in fact the subject of one's thoughts and perceptions. If this were the case, then someone who thinks that subjects are bodies would be committed to regarding awareness of the bodily self in a mirror as a form of introspective self-awareness, and this cannot be right (cf. Shoemaker 1994b: 123). Nor will it do to exclude such cases by defining introspective self-awareness as awareness of the self 'from the inside', for the distinction between awareness 'from the inside' and 'from the outside' cannot bear much weight. Rather, introspective self-awareness must be understood as awareness of oneself '*qua* subject' (McGinn 1993: 48;

[8] See Descartes's Sixth Meditation in Cottingham, Stoothoff, and Murdoch 1984: ii. 56, and his letter to Princess Elizabeth, dated 28 June 1643, in Cottingham, Stoothoff, Murdoch, and Kenny 1991: 226–9.

[9] As one commentator puts it, Descartes's view was that 'however vividly our inner experience might tell us that we are embodied creatures, our reason . . . tells us that we are "thinking things", entirely incorporeal and essentially distinct from the body. The result is a deep tension between what our reason tells us and what our ordinary everyday experience tells us' (Cottingham 1986: 132).

cf. Shoemaker 1994a: 119).So the sense in which a materialist conception
of the self leaves it open whether we are introspectively aware of ourselves as physical objects is this: even if a given physical object O is in
fact the subject of one's representations, and one is aware of O as a physical object, it does not follow that one is aware of O *as* or *qua* subject of
one's representations. This suggests the following account of how it is
that a materialist about the self might still be persuaded to agree that the
self—even a bodily self—must be elusive from the perspective of introspective self-awareness: when one reflects on what it would be to be
aware of anything '*qua* subject', it should become apparent that if O is a
physical object which one is aware of as such, then it is a conceptual truth
that O cannot at the same time present itself to one *qua* subject of one's
representations. The suggestion, then, is that it is a monstrous contradiction that a subject should ever become an object for itself, because
awareness of something as an object, and awareness of it *qua* subject, are
mutually exclusive modes of awareness.

The plausibility, or otherwise, of this argument is largely dependent
on what it takes to be involved in object-awareness and awareness of
something '*qua* subject'. These are matters about which a great deal will
be said later in this chapter and in Chapter 2, but for present purposes
the important point is this: to the extent that the central thesis of the
chapters that follow is the thesis that awareness of oneself as a physical
object among physical objects is a necessary condition of self-consciousness, it will not be enough to defend this thesis simply by arguing that it
is a necessary condition of self-consciousness that one is aware of what is
in fact the subject of one's representations as a physical object. What
needs to be shown is that a self-conscious subject must be aware of itself
qua subject as shaped, located, and solid.

Another difficulty with the simple proposal is this: it needs to be
acknowledged that a good number of those who have been exercised by
the supposed elusiveness of the self have argued from this elusiveness to
what might be called the Exclusion Thesis, the thesis that the thinking,
experiencing self is not an object among others in the world.[10] If the self
is not an object among others in the world, then it is certainly not a physical object among physical objects. So if one were to argue for the claim
that the self is not elusive from the perspective of self-consciousness
from the premiss that the self is in fact a physical object in a world of

---

[10] There are illuminating discussions of this line of argument in Rosenberg 1986: ch. 1,
and Janaway 1989: chs. 4 and 12.

such objects, one would be assuming the falsity of the very thesis—the Exclusion Thesis—which, for some, is the single most important consequence of the elusiveness of the self.

How is the Exclusion Thesis supposed to follow from the claim that we cannot be introspectively aware of ourselves as objects? According to what might be called the *Self-Consciousness Argument*, only what can be presented to itself as an object can *be* an object among others in the world. So the thinking self, in virtue of its peculiar elusiveness from the perspective of self-consciousness, is not, as Husserl puts it, a 'piece of the world' (1991: 25). Just as the simple proposal draws an epistemological conclusion from a metaphysical premiss, so the Self-Consciousness Argument draws a metaphysical conclusion from an epistemological premiss.

It might be objected that the Self-Consciousness Argument fails because its transition from an epistemological premiss to a metaphysical conclusion is unacceptably idealist. As Christopher Janaway puts it:

We have agreed . . . that the subject is not, and cannot be, straightforwardly an object for itself. But if we want to conclude that the subject is therefore not an object in the world at all, we must introduce the premiss that something can only be an object in the world if it is an object for the subject . . . But if we are not idealists, and do not force together in this way the notions of an object existing in the world and an object for the subject, there is no ground for the conclusion that the subject is not a part of the world. (1989: 308)

This response to the Self-Consciousness Argument is unobjectionable as far as it goes, but by the lights of the account of self-consciousness to be defended here, it does not go far enough. The problem with the Self-Consciousness Argument is not just that it is unacceptably idealist but that its epistemological premiss is false; contrary to what this premiss claims, we can and must be presented to ourselves, *qua* subjects, as objects among others in the world—not as immaterial thinking substances but, to repeat, as physical objects among physical objects.

In defending this materialist conception of self-consciousness in the chapters that follow, great care will need to be taken to avoid giving the impression of begging an important question by arguing against the Exclusion Thesis from the premiss that thinking selves are in fact physical entities in a world of such entities. Unlike the simple proposal, the proposal to be defended here is that the need for us to be presented to ourselves as corporeal is a consequence of certain constraints suggested by the concept of self-consciousness rather than a straightforward conse-

quence of a materialist conception of the self. Nor should it be claimed
that the fact that we are presented to ourselves as corporeal entails that
our thinking selves are in fact corporeal; at the very least, further argument would be required to show that introspective self-awareness does
not embody an illusion about the actual nature of the subject of one's
representations. The main aim of the chapters that follow is to defend a
materialist account of self-consciousness rather than a materialist
account of the self, although there is no reason why a materialist account
of self-consciousness should not figure among a range of metaphysical
and epistemological considerations in support of a materialist account of
the self. If such an account is correct, and the 'I' that thinks is in fact
shaped, located, and solid, then things are just as they seem in introspective self-awareness.

The Self-Consciousness Argument is not the only possible argument
for the Exclusion Thesis, and this thesis is itself less than clear; for what
exactly does it mean to say that the self is not an object among others in
the world or, as Wittgenstein puts it, that it 'does not belong to the world'
(1961: 5.632)? The plan for this chapter is therefore as follows: in the
next part, a more precise account will be given of the meaning of the
Exclusion Thesis, and an attempt will be made to disarm an argument
for this thesis which, though related to the Self-Consciousness
Argument, is not exactly the same as this argument. In the final part of
this chapter, an outline will be given of three major arguments against
the epistemological premiss of the Self-Consciousness Argument and in
support of a materialist conception of self-consciousness. These arguments will be developed in detail in the next three chapters.

Before concluding this introduction, it would be worth saying something about the wider significance of materialism about self-consciousness, apart from its bearing on the Exclusion Thesis. A striking feature of
current philosophy of mind is that few of its practitioners have much
time for Cartesian dualism. Yet this retreat from dualist accounts of mind
or self has not always been accompanied by a willingness to accept that
self-consciousness involves being presented to oneself as a physical
object.[11] For example, Shoemaker's claim, quoted above, that we are not
introspectively aware of ourselves as flesh and blood objects, occurs in

---

[11] A notable recent exception is Michael Ayers, who describes Shoemaker's account of
introspection as 'evidently fallacious' (Ayers 1991: ii. 287), and claims that the physical or
material self is the 'presented subject of experience and action' (p. 286). For a more detailed
discussion of the dispute between Shoemaker and Ayers, see Cassam 1995a.

the context of an argument whose main aim is to defend a materialist account of the self. The fact that one of Shoemaker's main targets is Cartesian dualism therefore makes it all the more paradoxical that Descartes should have been far more receptive than Shoemaker to the idea that we are at least *presented* to ourselves as corporeal. In this context, therefore, one way of understanding the point of much of what follows would be to see it as attempting to show that while Descartes may have had an ultimately incoherent conception of the nature of the 'I' which thinks, his apparent acknowledgement that we are introspectively aware of ourselves as bodily subjects of consciousness is much closer to the truth about the nature of self-consciousness than the views of some twentieth-century materialists about the self.

Although the force of the conception of self-consciousness to be defended here has not been acknowledged by some epistemologists and philosophers of mind who do not have the slightest sympathy for Cartesian dualism or the Exclusion Thesis, others have been much more receptive to the idea that self-consciousness involves physical self-awareness. In the analytical tradition, some of the most important arguments for this view of self-consciousness have been developed by P. F. Strawson and others influenced by him (see Strawson 1966: 162–9; Evans 1982: 205–35; McDowell 1994: 99–104). In order to understand these arguments, however, mention must be made of a crucial ambiguity in talk of self-consciousness involving 'awareness' of oneself *qua* subject as a physical object among physical objects. On one interpretation, such awareness would be a matter of one's *conceiving* of oneself *qua* subject as a physical object. This might be called the *concept version* of materialism about self-consciousness. On another interpretation, it would be a matter of one's being sensibly or, in Kant's terminology, *intuitively* aware of oneself *qua* subject as a physical object.[12] This might be called the *intuition version* of materialism about self-consciousness. Crudely, to conceive of something as a physical object is to think of it as such, but to be intuitively aware of something as a physical object is to experience or perceive it as shaped, located, and solid. Much more will be said about this distinction in later chapters, but it is important to note at this stage that for the most part writers in the Strawsonian tradition have argued for the concept version of materialism about self-consciousness (see, for example, Evans 1982: 163; McDowell 1994: 103; and Cassam 1989: 89).

---

[12] Kant defines 'intuition' as that through which 'a mode of knowledge' is in immediate relation to objects. Intuition takes place only in so far as an object is given, and 'objects are given to us by means of sensibility' (A19/B33).

In contrast, writers on self-consciousness in the so-called 'Continental' tradition have been much more concerned with what is, in effect, the intuition version of materialism about self-consciousness. For example, it would be difficult to read writers such as Husserl, Sartre, and Merleau-Ponty without being struck by the importance which they attach to forms of bodily self-awareness which, in the present terminology, amount to intuitive awareness of oneself as a bodily or corporeal subject of consciousness. Yet, according to some writers in this tradition, in being intuitively aware of oneself as a bodily subject one is not thereby intuitively aware of this subject as what Sartre describes as 'a thing among other things' (1989: 304). As with Schopenhauer's account of self-consciousness, the worry seems to be that there is a conflict between awareness of something *qua* subject and awareness of it as an object among others, so the body which is the presented subject of one's perceptions is a 'phenomenal' rather than an 'objective' body.[13]

In terms of the above distinction between concept and intuition versions of materialism about self-consciousness, the main aim of much of what follows will be to argue for an intuition version which rejects this Schopenhauerian dualism of subject and object. While acknowledging the depth and importance of the Strawsonian contribution to our understanding of the nature of self-consciousness, it will be argued that there are serious difficulties with the idea that a self-conscious subject must, as John McDowell puts it, '*conceive* of itself, the subject of its experience, as a bodily element in objective reality—as a bodily presence in the world' (1994: 103). At the same time, it will emerge that in being intuitively aware of itself as a bodily subject of consciousness, a self-conscious subject can and must be presented to itself, *qua* subject, as a thing among other things, as a physical object that is straightforwardly a 'piece' of spatio-temporal reality.

2. The Exclusion Thesis

What is to be made of the thesis that the self is not an object among others in the world? On one interpretation, suggested by Kant's account of what it would be to be aware of oneself 'as an object', the Exclusion Thesis simply amounts to a denial of the substantiality of the self. On a

---

[13] See Merleau-Ponty 1989: 105–6 for the distinction between 'objective' and 'phenomenal' body.

traditional conception of substance, substances are the ultimate subjects of predication, and, as Hume puts it, 'may exist separately, and have no need of anything else to support their existence' (1978: 233). The central contrast is between substances and 'modes' or 'accidents', which are logically and ontologically dependent on substances.[14] Horses and tables are substances, nations and the colour of a particular horse are not. Contrary to what Descartes maintained, substances must also be material, since it is not possible to give a satisfactory account of what the singularity and identity of immaterial substances would consist in. On this interpretation, to be a substantial presence in the world is to be a physical or bodily presence in the world, and the Exclusion Thesis is simply committed to denying that thinking selves are present in the world in this sense.

The problem with this reading of the Exclusion Thesis is that it implies that the Humean claim that the self is a bundle of perceptions is compatible with the Exclusion Thesis, since bundles of perceptions are not substances any more than nations are.[15] Yet perceptions are at least temporal if not spatial beings, so if selves are bundles of perceptions, they would still be (non-substantial) elements of temporal reality. Since, on a proper understanding of the Exclusion Thesis, the bundle theory of the self does not go far enough in the direction of excluding thinking selves from the world, this thesis is not *just* the denial that thinking selves are substances. On a Kantian reading of the Exclusion Thesis, the spatio-temporal world is the phenomenal world, and the point of saying that the 'I' which thinks is not an object among others in the world is to deny that it is *in any sense* an element of the phenomenal world, 'whether it be as substance or as accident' (B420).

On one reading of Kant's idealism, he is committed to the existence of a distinction between two worlds, the phenomenal world and a non-spatio-temporal 'noumenal' world. This might prompt the thought that the exclusion of the self from the phenomenal world leaves open the possibility that it is an 'object' in the noumenal world. This suggestion will not be pursued here. While it may do justice to some versions of the Exclusion Thesis, it will be assumed that according to this thesis the self is neither a phenomenal nor a noumenal 'entity'. For Kant, the self that does not belong to the phenomenal or noumenal world is the 'I' of the 'I think', and the ontological status of this 'I' is, if anything, somewhat akin

---

[14] See Ayers 1991: ii. 110–28 for an illuminating account of the notion of substance.
[15] Cassam 1993b discusses the significance of this point for Derek Parfit's neo-Humean account of personal identity in Parfit 1987.

to that of a universal. As W. H. Walsh remarks, the Kantian 'I' is something abstract, a 'universal core which can be presumed to be the same in
all of us' (1975: 57). The full force of this conception of the self that
does not belong to the world will become evident shortly, but even this
preliminary account serves to bring out the extremely radical nature of
the Kantian version of the Exclusion Thesis. It is this version with which
the present chapter is primarily concerned.

It has to be said that the Kantian Exclusion Thesis is not a thesis the
attractions of which are immediately obvious. This may be illustrated by
reference to what will be referred to here as the *robust response* to it. The
robust response points out that subjects of thought and experience are or
include persons, and that persons in the ordinary sense are surely 'worldly' beings. It may be a matter for further debate what the identity of a
person consists in, but it is surely not a matter for debate that persons are
elements of spatio-temporal or, at any rate, temporal reality. So unless
proponents of the Exclusion Thesis are prepared to argue that persons
are not thinking, experiencing selves, it would appear that this thesis
must be rejected.

If the robust response is along the right lines, it makes it difficult to
understand the distinguished support which the Exclusion Thesis has
received in the Kantian tradition. There are those who will not be troubled by this, but this is to risk failing to give the Exclusion Thesis its due.
As with other influential but apparently improbable theses in philosophy,
it is not enough simply to 'refute' the Exclusion Thesis, even if there are
reasons for thinking that such a refutation is possible. On quite general
methodological grounds, it is reasonable to expect from a proper
response to the Exclusion Thesis at least some explanation of its force
and influence. It is difficult to believe that the robust response passes this
test. Indeed, it makes it virtually incomprehensible that the Exclusion
Thesis should ever have been taken seriously, and this supports the view
that the robust response needs to be approached with caution.

On one interpretation, it is simply impossible to grasp the point and
significance of the Exclusion Thesis without understanding its connections with other aspects of Kant's transcendental idealism. The role of
idealism in the Self-Consciousness Argument for the Exclusion Thesis
has already been remarked, but it might be held that it is *transcendental*
idealism in particular which is required to make sense of this thesis.
Transcendental idealism is the thesis that space and time are only the
sensible forms of our intuition rather than properties of things as they
are in themselves, and that the mind or self is the 'source of the laws of

nature' (A127). The self is therefore not a piece of the world because, to put it crudely, that which 'makes' the world cannot simply be an element in the world which it makes.

It cannot be denied that a complete account of the attractions of the Exclusion Thesis would need to make reference to considerations such as these, but it is not the aim of the present discussion to provide such an account. The present aim is the more limited one of uncovering and disarming a cluster of *neo*-Kantian arguments for the Exclusion Thesis which have influenced a number of philosophers who are not otherwise attracted by the metaphysics of transcendental idealism. Despite the fact that these neo-Kantian arguments are, as will be argued here, unsuccessful, it is at least possible to understand why they might nevertheless have been *thought* to provide a case for the Exclusion Thesis which is both unaffected by the robust response and which does not require any commitment to full-blooded transcendental idealism.

One neo-Kantian argument for the Exclusion Thesis is the Self-Consciousness Argument, about which more will be said in the next section. While this argument may not carry any commitment to specifically Kantian doctrines about space, time, and nature, it is still an idealist argument. A neo-Kantian argument for the Exclusion Thesis which is less obviously idealist is what might be called the *Abstraction Argument*. This argument suggests the following way of dealing with the robust response: suppose that persons in the ordinary sense are corporeal entities, and include human beings.[16] Since human beings are substances in space and time, they are 'objects' in the 'world'. To this extent, the robust response is right to insist upon the 'worldly' status of persons. Moreover, this conception of *persons* as corporeal objects is not one which the Abstraction Argument is concerned to dispute. The sense in which, according to this argument, the robust response misses the point of the Exclusion Thesis is that the 'self' which is claimed not to belong to the world is not the personal or human self. To this extent, the Exclusion Thesis is committed to a form of dualism, though it is not dualism in the Cartesian sense. For Husserl, it is the 'transcendental Ego' that is not a piece of the world. Crucially, the transcendental Ego is not 'the man who, in natural self-experience, finds himself as a man' (Husserl 1991: 25). Wittgenstein also claims in the *Tractatus* that the 'self' which does not belong to the world is the 'philosophical self', and argues that 'the philosophical self is not

---

[16] This is Strawson's account of persons in Strawson 1959: ch. 3. See also Wiggins 1980: ch. 6.

the human being, not the human body, or the human soul, with which psychology deals, but rather the metaphysical subject, the limit of the world—not a part of it' (1961: 5.641). Since the philosophical self is not the personal or human self, the observation that persons or human beings are pieces of spatio-temporal reality is besides the point.

In order to understand the precise sense in which the neo-Kantian position is 'dualist', a rough indication is needed of what might be meant by phrases such as 'philosophical self' or 'metaphysical subject'. It has already been remarked that the 'self' in the context of the Exclusion Thesis is the thinking, experiencing self. This fits Wittgenstein's characterization of the subject that does not belong to the world as 'the subject that thinks or entertains ideas' (1961: 5.631). Similarly, Kant's 'transcendental subject' is 'the I or he or it (the thing) which thinks' (A346/B404). This might prompt the following reaction from champions of the robust response: this response can only be accused of missing the point if, in claiming that it is the metaphysical rather than the personal self that does not belong to the world, the Exclusion Thesis is able to give an account of how the metaphysical self differs from the personal self. To say that the metaphysical self is 'the subject that thinks or entertains ideas' does not advance matters because this characterization also fits persons perfectly. If, as Locke argued, a person is 'a thinking intelligent being, that has reason and reflection' (1975: 335), and the transcendental subject is the 'I or he or it (the thing) which thinks', then the transcendental subject is a person.[17] In that case, how can the observation that persons belong to the world be dismissed as irrelevant from the perspective of the Exclusion Thesis?

A Kantian answer to this question would presumably be to insist that while the philosophical self is indeed the subject that thinks or experiences, it is the *transcendental* rather than empirical thinking subject. Reference to persons is irrelevant in this context not because persons are not thinking intelligent beings but because they are only subjects in the

---

[17] This argument is similar to Snowdon's argument for the claim that Locke is committed to regarding some animals as persons. As Snowdon remarks, 'if we ask to what entities the functional predicate (person), as elucidated by Locke applies, the answer we all want to give is—a certain kind of animal, namely human beings. They are animals which reason, reflect, and talk of themselves!' (1990: 90). By parallel reasoning, the Kantian 'I' must be a person if a person is, as Kant puts it, 'that which is conscious of the numerical identity of itself at different times' (A361). This might explain why Kant does not, as might have been expected, directly challenge the conclusion of the Third Paralogism, according to which the soul is a person. Instead he focuses on the question of whether self-consciousness establishes the 'objective permanence of myself' (A363).

empirical rather than transcendental or metaphysical sense. On its own, however, the repetition of qualifications like 'transcendental' and 'metaphysical' can scarcely be said to clarify matters. What is required is a detailed account both of the point of these qualifications and of the relationship between the so-called 'metaphysical' thinking subject and empirical thinking subjects. In the absence of such an account, the robust response is within its rights to insist that the subject that thinks or entertains ideas *does* 'belong to the world'.

The moral of this discussion is that while the robust response may well be too robust, it does succeed in focusing attention on the difficulty of arriving at a settled interpretation of the Exclusion Thesis. Just as this thesis is supported by a wide range of different considerations, so there are several different routes to, and explanations of, the concept of the 'metaphysical' or 'transcendental' subject. The Abstraction Argument is one such route or explanation, which it is possible to extract from Kant's account of the 'transcendental subject of apperception' and, more recently, from Nagel's account of the 'objective self' (Nagel 1986: ch. 4). The key to these accounts is the idea that the self which does not belong to the world is, in McDowell's words, 'an *abstraction* from the ordinary substantial persistence of the living subject of experience' (1994: 103, my emphasis). To anticipate, it will be argued that once it is understood that the idea of the philosophical self is arrived at by this sort of abstraction, the claim that this self is not a piece of the world becomes less surprising and, in a way, less interesting than it might have seemed at the outset.

To the extent that the Kantian rejoinder to the robust response turns on a distinction between the empirical and transcendental subject, this explains the suggestion that the Exclusion Thesis is committed to a form of dualism. Unlike Cartesian dualism, however, the dualism of the Exclusion Thesis is not a dualism of two substances.[18] Cartesian dualism is the view that a person is a compound of body and immaterial soul. While it is the substantial immaterial soul that is supposed to be the I or he or it (the thing) which thinks, the Cartesian still conceives of this soul as being, in Rosenberg's words, 'within the ontological fabric of the world *per se*' (1986: 14). In contrast, the dualism of the Exclusion Thesis is a dualism of person and (metaphysical) subject, where the latter is neither a (corporeal or incorporeal) substance nor a 'mode' or 'accident'. It is this distinctively post-Kantian dualism that needs explaining.

One way of developing such an explanation would be to reflect on

[18] Janaway makes this point in 1989: 126.

Kant's account of the 'I think'. A more detailed account of Kant's conception of the 'I think' will be given in Chapter 4, but as far as the relationship between persons and the transcendental subject is concerned, it would be worth remarking at this stage that according to Kant the use of personal pronoun in the 'I think' does not refer an individual person. Kant's own way of capturing this point is to deny that the 'I' of the 'I think' is 'a concept of any object' (A382). Instead, he characterizes it as the 'mere form of consciousness' (A382), as meaning a 'something in general (transcendental subject)' (A355) which 'announces itself as a universal proposition valid for all thinking beings' (A405). In other words, the difference between the concept of a person and the 'concept' of the transcendental subject is the difference between the concept of an object among others in the empirical world and the 'concept of a mere something' (A355).

Kant is not entirely consistent in characterizing the transcendental subject as a 'something in general'. Elsewhere, for example, he identifies the transcendental subject with the self as it exists in itself (A492/B520), and it is not clear that this comes to the same thing. Moreover, even to the extent that Kant's account of the 'I' of the 'I think' is supposed to cast light upon the relationship between persons and the transcendental subject, it might be objected that this account is incoherent. For when a person attaches an 'I think' to one of her representations, it would seem that her use of the personal pronoun must be governed by the rule that this pronoun refers to its user on each occasion of its use.[19] So if the subject who attaches an 'I think' to a representation is a person, then this use of 'I' must refer to a person. In that case, how can the 'I' of the 'I think' simply mean a 'something in general (transcendental subject)'? There is also a question about the 'numerical identity' of the 'I', which Kant describes as one and the same in all consciousness and as 'a priori certain' (A113). If numerically distinct empirical subjects attach an 'I think' to their representations, then it would seem that their uses of 'I' must differ in reference and so must express different Fregean 'modes of presentation'.[20] In that case, how can the 'I' be one and the same in all consciousness?

Short of arguing that the 'I think' is not available to persons, it would seem that the only way of making any progress with these questions

---

[19] This aspect of the first person pronoun is emphasized in Strawson 1994 and Campbell 1994: ch. 3.

[20] For a fuller explanation of this point see Peacocke 1983: 108.

would be something along the following lines: suppose that one person thinks 'I think p', and that a different person thinks 'I think q'. The perspective of transcendental apperception is one which abstracts from the reference of these uses of 'I' and focuses instead on the fact that these are still thoughts of the same *type*.[21] In Kant's terminology, the 'mere form of consciousness' (A382) is the same in both cases, despite the difference in empirical reference. It is this identity of form which, unlike the identity of the self *qua* Cartesian thinking substance, can be known with a priori certainty,[22] and consciousness of which is partially constitutive of transcendental self-consciousness. Since the 'form' of the 'I think' is not itself the concept of a worldly object, it makes no sense to describe the 'I' of the 'I think', *qua* 'mere form of consciousness', as a determinate referring expression. On the other hand, to the extent that the 'I' of transcendental apperception gives expression to the 'bare *form* of reference' (Strawson 1966: 166), it can be provided with an 'object' in a purely logical or formal sense. This object is the 'transcendental subject'. On this reading, the transcendental subject is, as it were, the 'logical subject' of the universal proposition 'I think', and this is the sense in which it is the concept of a 'mere something'. The fundamental error of rational psychology is to misinterpret knowledge of the logical identity of this extensionless logical subject as knowledge of the numerical identity of the subject of different 'I think' instances as a substantial object in the world.

This 'form of consciousness' reading of transcendental apperception raises several questions of interpretation which cannot be resolved at this stage. In particular, it remains to be seen whether anything can ultimately be made of the idea of a purely 'logical' subject of the 'universal representation of self-consciousness' (B401). What is already clear, however, is that *if* the 'form of consciousness' reading is along the right lines then the identification of person and transcendental subject would involve something like a category mistake. For although persons belong to the empirical world, the 'mere form of consciousness' is something abstract and 'beyond' space and time somewhat in the way that universals, as traditionally conceived, are 'beyond' space and time. So if the 'transcendental subject' is, as one might put it, simply the logical correlate of the form

---

[21] Graham Bird also draws attention to what he calls 'Kant's use of "abstraction" as a method in his descriptive metaphysics' (1996: 249 n. 9).

[22] Something along these lines is suggested by Dieter Henrich's remark that 'Cartesian certainty . . . only extends to the fact of a particular "I think" and to the form of "I think" as such which is necessarily thought in this particular "I think"' (1989: 277). Henrich's account of the form of the 'I think' is, however, somewhat different from mine.

of consciousness in general, then the sense in which the concept of this subject is arrived at by abstraction from the ordinary substantial persistence of the living subject of experience is that it is effectively the concept of the form of such a subject's consciousness and so is, in this sense, the concept of something abstract. The fact that this abstract formal 'subject' does not belong to the world would have no bearing upon the worldly status of any individual thinking subject.

Another way of fleshing out the Abstraction Argument for the Exclusion Thesis would be to remark that the 'form of consciousness' reading fails to do justice to at least one important aspect of Kant's theory of apperception, namely, the idea that apperception is, as Henry Allison puts it, not just a transcendental principle or reference point but a 'real mode of self-consciousness' (1983: 273). To be more precise, 'apperception' is 'consciousness of the activity of thinking', and the distinction between empirical and transcendental apperception is one between 'consciousness of the activity as it functions determinately with a given content and the thought of the same activity, considered in abstraction from all content' (p. 274). In the light of this account of 'transcendental apperception', Allison proposes the following account of the concept of the 'transcendental subject': as there can be no activity without an agent, consciousness of the activity of thinking involves consciousness of the existence of an active thinker. Since in transcendental apperception 'one explicitly abstracts from everything empirical', this thinking subject 'can be characterized only as a "something in general = x"'. The thought of this subject is 'nothing more than the empty thought of a logical subject', and it is this merely 'logical' subject that is the 'transcendental subject of apperception' (p. 281). The concept of this transcendental subject is therefore 'the concept of the bare form of a thinking subject (a logical subject of thought or "subject in general"), which is all that remains for thought when abstraction is made from the content of inner sense' (p. 283). It is this 'logical subject' that the rational psychologist mistakenly identifies with a separately existing noumenal subject.

As Allison emphasizes, it is always possible to give a perfectly good *empirical* answer to the question 'what is the I which thinks?' by assigning the activity of thinking to 'a subject in the world with a body, memory, and history', but this answer is unavailable from the perspective of transcendental apperception, which 'yields only the bare thought of a subject that must be presupposed as a condition of thinking' (Allison 1983: 290). Like Wittgenstein's 'metaphysical subject', Allison's transcendental subject of apperception is 'the knowing subject considered *qua* knower' (p. 291). To say that the transcendental subject—the I or he or it (the thing) which thinks—is not an object in the world is to be committed to the view that it cannot be equated with the noumenal self since, in Allison's words, 'the concept of the latter is the concept of an object in the world (the "transcendental object of inner sense"), albeit one that can only be known in a unique, nonsensible manner' (p. 291).

While the differences between the 'form of consciousness' reading and Allison's account of the transcendental subject should not be underestimated, the respects in which they are in agreement are of greater significance in the present context than the respects in which they differ. Firstly, it is agreed by both interpretations that the transcendental subject is neither the phenomenal nor the noumenal self. Secondly, for both interpretations, the concept of the transcendental subject is arrived at by abstraction from empirical considerations. Finally, both interpretations make sense of Kant's claim that the fundamental error of rational psychology consists in 'confusing the possible *abstraction* from my empirically determined existence with the supposed consciousness of a possible *separate* existence of my thinking self.' (B428). If the perspective of transcendental apperception is committed to abstracting from the content of thinking and from one's empirically determined existence, then it is hardly surprising that the concept of the 'transcendental subject of apperception' can only be the concept of the bare *form* of a thinking subject. Just as, for the 'form of consciousness' reading, the transcendental subject is not an object among others in the world because the 'mere form of consciousness' is not such an object, so Allison's transcendental subject cannot be regarded as an object among others in the world because the bare *form* of a thinking subject cannot be regarded as such an object. In both cases, it is the abstraction from the ordinary substantial persistence of the living subject of experience that holds the key to the exclusion of the transcendental subject from the world.

It might appear that the reliance upon this sort of abstraction in explaining the concept of the transcendental subject is a peculiarity of Kant's position and therefore of little wider significance, but such an impression would be mistaken. Substantially the same pattern of argument is discernible in the writings of others who have some sympathy for the Exclusion Thesis. There is an excellent example of this in Thomas Nagel's account of the 'objective self' in *The View From Nowhere*. Nagel explains that the idea of the objective self has something in common with Wittgenstein's 'metaphysical subject' and Husserl's 'transcendental Ego', but that there are also important differences between his position and those of Wittgenstein and Husserl. Firstly, Nagel's argument for the objective self does not rely upon transcendental idealism. Secondly, Nagel's account stops short of excluding the objective self from the world entirely. Rather, 'the objective self is the last stage of the detaching subject before it shrinks to an extensionless point' (Nagel 1986: 62 n. 3). To this extent, it is important that Nagel's position is described as one which is closely related to the Exclusion Thesis rather than as one which is actually committed to this thesis.

The key to the idea of the 'objective self' is the notion of an objective conception of the world. This is a conception of the world as 'simply existing, seen from no particular perspective, no privileged point of view—as simply there, and hence apprehensible from various points of view. This centerless world contains everybody, and it contains not only their bodies but their minds' (Nagel 1986: 56). It is important, however, that the objective conception '*has* a subject' (p. 64), and the objective self is the subject of an objective conception of the world. Thus, each of us, 'in addition to being an ordinary person, is a particular objective self, the subject of a perspectiveless conception of reality' (pp. 63–4). Although TN's objective self views the world through TN's perspective, it can seem that any relation which this objective self may have to the person TN 'must be accidental and arbitrary' (p. 55). TN's objective self has direct access to TN's experiences but it treats them as being on an equal footing with those that it learns about only indirectly (p. 62). This helps to explain how the thought 'I am TN' seems so remarkable and nontrivial; as Nagel puts it, 'because TN possesses or is an objective self, I can state a significant identity by referring to myself indexically under that aspect as "I", and again under the objective aspect of the publicly identifiable person TN' (p. 64).

There is a great deal here that is less than clear, but there are still some striking similarities between Nagel's route to the objective self and the accounts given above of Kant's route to the idea of the 'transcendental subject'. Just as the transcendental subject is the merely 'formal' or 'logical' subject of transcendental self-consciousness, so the objective self is, as Nagel puts it, the 'logical focus' of an objective conception of the world (1986: 64). In the same way that the perspective of transcendental apperception yields only the bare thought of a subject that must be presupposed as a condition of thinking, so the perspective described by Nagel yields, as one might put it, only the bare thought of an 'I' that must be presupposed as the ('logical') subject of an objective conception. In both cases, the idea of an 'I' that seems incapable of being an object

among others in the world is arrived at by abstracting this 'I' from the
point of view of an ordinary person (p. 62). Indeed, Nagel goes so far as
to write that the fact that it is possible to abstract or detach an objective
self from the person TN does not show that this self is a 'distinct thing'
(p. 61). Yet he goes on to maintain that 'the objective self functions independently enough to have a life of its own' (p. 65), and that while talk of
the objective self as a distinct part of the mind should not be given a
metaphysical interpretation, 'this way of speaking is not altogether inno-
cent' (p. 66).

This might prompt the following objection to Nagel's account: if his
objective self is not an entity that is distinct from the person TN, and
TN is contained in the world, then TN's objective self is contained in
the world. If, on the other hand, the objective self is simply an abstraction from the person TN, then it makes no sense to suppose that such an
abstraction can function independently enough to 'have a life of its own'.
Nagel's claim that his position stops short of excluding the objective self
from the world altogether seems to be the result of wavering between
these two options. *Qua* 'logical focus' of an objective conception, the
objective self cannot be more than an extensionless point; *qua* something
that is not distinct from the person TN, the objective self is as much a
piece of the world as TN is. There is simply no space for the idea of an
objective self that is *neither* an object among others in the empirical world
nor an extensionless point, a *mere* abstraction.

This objection leads on to a more general difficulty with the
Abstraction Argument for the Exclusion Thesis. The Exclusion Thesis
seems so interesting and disconcerting because of the impression that
the self which it claims not to be a part of the empirical world is the *individual* subject of thought and experience, but when the Kantian position
is understood in this way, it faces a serious challenge from the robust
response. In contrast, if the transcendental subject is an essentially
abstract 'logical' or 'formal' subject, then its exclusion from the empirical
world is no more surprising than the exclusion from the empirical world
of anything else that is essentially abstract or formal. The dilemma, in
other words, is that the Exclusion Thesis is, on this reading, either incoherent or platitudinous. The first horn of this dilemma points out that if
the Exclusion Thesis concerns the 'individual' thinking subject, then it
ought to be possible to specify criteria of singularity and identity for this
subject. Yet the specification of such criteria must draw upon the spatiality of the self, and the spatial self is, as Strawson puts it, 'a corporeal
object among corporeal objects' (1966: 102). The other horn points out

that to regard the transcendental subject as something like a universal, of which individual living subjects are instances (cf. Janaway 1989: 128), would be to deprive the Exclusion Thesis of the very feature which gives it the greatest interest.

The above discussion of Kant, Allison, and Nagel suggests that this is not a dilemma which the Abstraction Argument is able to escape. As has already been remarked in connection with Kant's position, the fact that the universal representation of self-consciousness, or the bare form of a thinking subject, is not an object among others in the world seems to have no bearing upon the worldly status of any individual thinking subject, since individual subjects and the *form* of a thinking subject belong in different ontological categories.[23] By the same token, the fact that the objective self is simply the 'logical focus' of an objective conception of the world means that it should come as no surprise at all to discover that it is difficult to think of this self as, in Nagel's words, 'contained in the world' (1986: 55). It would appear, therefore, that for all its limitations, the robust response succeeds in putting its finger on a fundamental problem for the Exclusion Thesis. It is one thing to criticize the robust response for failing to do justice to the fact that the 'self' which is claimed by the Exclusion Thesis not to belong to the world is the 'philosophical self', but to regard the philosophical self as an abstraction from the individual subject that thinks or entertains ideas is to change the subject in more than one sense. The tantalizing suggestion that the individual subject that thinks or entertains ideas is not an object among others in the world is as mysterious now as it was at the outset.

3. The Self-Consciousness Argument

In the light of these difficulties with the Abstraction Argument, it would be appropriate at this point to return to the Self-Consciousness Argument. It has already been argued that this argument certainly involves some form of idealism, though it is less obvious that it involves specifically Kantian doctrines about the nature of space and time. The concern of the present section is not to challenge the idealism of the Self-Consciousness Argument but to challenge its epistemological premiss, which has influenced a surprising number of non-idealist philosophers. While the failure of the present discussion to address specifically tran-

---

[23] Karl Ameriks (1982: 54) makes a closely related point.

scendental idealist arguments for the Exclusion Thesis means that it is incomplete in one respect, the recognition that there are powerful independent objections to transcendental idealism diminishes the importance of this point. In any event, the fact that the epistemological premiss of the Self-Consciousness Argument has influenced many non-idealist philosophers is itself a good enough reason for spelling out objections to it.

The epistemological premiss states that the subject cannot, *qua* subject, be an object for itself. To be an object for oneself in this sense would be for one to be introspectively aware of oneself as an abiding substance, but no fixed and abiding self can present itself in the flux of inner appearances. It might be wondered, however, whether this argument is really decisive. Kant himself insists that, even if 'everything that is in inner sense is in constant flux' (B291), the representation of abidingness need not be an abiding representation.[24] In that case, is it not still possible that the flux of representations that are the objects of introspective awareness present themselves to one as representations of an abiding, substantial subject? Kant's response to this line of attack would presumably be to appeal to what might be called his *circularity argument*. According to this argument, even if one were somehow aware of an abiding object in the flux of inner appearances, one could not be aware of this object *qua* subject. The elusive self is the *knowing* self, and 'I cannot know as an object that which I must presuppose in order to know any object' (A402).

Why is it not possible to know as an object that which must be presupposed in order to know any object? For Kant, knowledge of an object requires both an intuition and a concept of it. So knowledge of the thinking 'I' as an object would require both an intuition and a concept of it. This suggests two versions of the circularity argument, a concept and an intuition version. In connection with the suggestion that the 'I' can conceive of itself as an object among others, the circularity argument objects that in order to conceive of anything as an object, the 'I' must already be there doing the conceiving (cf. Allison 1983: 292). To the extent that the 'I' is the presupposed *subject* of conceptual activity, it cannot make itself the object of its own conceptual activity. As Kant puts it, the I or he or it

---

[24] To be more precise, Kant writes that 'the representation of something *permanent* in existence is not the same as *permanent representation*' (Bxli). Yet Kant himself is arguably guilty of precisely this confusion in his account of the representation of substance.

(the thing) which thinks 'is known only through the thoughts which are its predicates, and of it, apart from them, we cannot have any concept whatsoever, but can only revolve in a perpetual circle, since any judgement upon it must already make use of its representation' (A346/B404). In connection with the idea that the 'I' can intuit itself as an object among others, the circularity argument objects that in order to intuit anything as an object, the 'I' must already be there doing the intuiting. Since the 'I' is the presupposed *subject* of intuition, it cannot make itself the object of its own intuition.

In a sense, this distinction between two versions of the circularity argument does not really advance matters, for it now needs to be explained why the subject of thought or intuition cannot make itself the object of its own thought or intuition. For example, a robust response to the circularity argument would be to point out that persons are thinkers and perceivers and that persons can certainly perceive themselves and think of themselves as objects among others in the spatio-temporal world. The impression that the self systematically steps out of cognitive reach certainly needs explaining, but the explanation may be that this impression embodies a linguistically generated illusion. An explanation along these lines is provided by Ryle, as part of his account of 'higher-order actions'—those the descriptions of which involve the oblique mention of other actions. The utterance of an 'I' sentence may be part of a higher-order performance, such as 'self-commentary' or 'self-admonition', and a 'higher-order action cannot be the action upon which it is performed' (Ryle 1994: 39). In this sense, a higher-order action is 'logically condemned to eternal penultimacy', yet 'nothing that is left out of any particular commentary or admonition is privileged thereby to escape comment or admonition for ever. On the contrary, it may be the target of the very next comment or rebuke' (p. 40).

It might be objected that all of this misses the deeper point of the circularity argument. Kant is quite prepared to accept that the thinking being 'as man' is an object of the outer senses (B415), and the robust response to the circularity argument is right to argue that there is no reason in principle why a particular thinking being 'as man' cannot become an object of his own outer sense. The difficulty in such cases is that even if the man is the I or he or it (the thing) which thinks, one's intuitive awareness of the person that is the subject of one's thoughts cannot be awareness of this subject '*qua* subject'. It would appear, therefore, that the circularity argument reduces to the point, already discussed in the introduction, that awareness of something 'as an object' and '*qua* subject' are mutually exclusive modes of awareness. As McGinn puts it:

> When I think of myself that which thinks occurs as subject; thus I never become merely an object of my own apprehension. The self always, and systematically, steps out of cognitive reach. Even if the reflecting self and the self reflected upon are numerically identical, I can never stand back and apprehend this identity, since I shall always occur as a subject in my reflections, as well as an object. *Qua* subject I can never become an intentional object to myself. Yet it is *qua* subject that I have my essence. (1993: 48)

The most important questions raised by the circularity argument are therefore these: what is it to be aware of something '*qua* subject', and what is it about awareness of something *qua* subject which means that this mode of awareness cannot be reconciled with object-awareness? If there is a conflict between these modes of awareness, what exactly does this conflict consist in?

One possibility is this: awareness of something *qua* subject of one's thoughts is, by definition, a form of awareness which does not require the identification of a presented object as oneself. In Shoemaker's terminology, awareness of oneself *qua* subject must be such that, upon the basis of such awareness, it is possible to make first-person statements that are 'immune to error through misidentification' relative to the first-person pronoun (see Shoemaker 1994a: 82). More precisely, to say that the judgement '*a* is *F*' is immune to error through misidentification relative to the term '*a*' is to say that the following is not possible: the thinker knows some particular thing to be *F* but makes the mistake of judging that *a* is *F* because, and only because, she mistakenly thinks that the thing she knows to be *F* is what '*a*' refers to. In contrast, awareness of something 'as an object' requires an identification of it and so is necessarily identification-dependent. Thus, if one is aware of what is in fact the subject of one's thoughts 'as an object', then it follows that such awareness cannot be awareness of it '*qua* subject', since it would not allow for the making of first-person judgements that are immune to error through misidentification relative to 'I'. *This*, it might be held, is the sense in which the self is systematically elusive from the perspective of self-consciousness.

This argument raises a number of difficult questions which will be addressed in the chapters that follow. For example, how plausible is its conception of awareness of oneself '*qua* subject'? How can the claim that object-awareness is necessarily identification-dependent be reconciled with the immunity to error through misidentification of some perceptual-demonstrative judgements? Is it not question-begging to define the notions of 'object-awareness' and awareness of oneself '*qua* subject' in such a way that the two forms of awareness become mutually exclusive? It will be argued in the second half of the next chapter that these are not questions to which the circularity argument is in a position to provide satisfactory answers. In particular, it will emerge that the very idea of a purified form of self-awareness which has a unique claim to the label 'awareness of the self *qua* subject' is itself an unacceptable abstraction from a more plausible and full-blooded concept of self-awareness which provides little or no support for the circularity argument.

To the extent that these objections to the circularity argument are successful, they help to undermine the epistemological premiss of the Self-Consciousness Argument in a way that confirms the earlier impression that the standard non-idealist reaction to the latter argument is too concessive. As has already been indicated, however, the remaining chapters will not simply confine themselves to establishing the inconclusiveness of certain familiar arguments for Kant's epistemological premiss. They will also argue, more positively, that intuitive awareness of the self, *qua* subject, as a physical object is actually a *necessary* condition of self-consciousness. While there are difficulties with the concept version of materialism about self-consciousness, these difficulties have nothing to do with the concept version of the circularity argument. Reflection on the peculiarities of self-consciousness, even consciousness of the self '*qua* subject', therefore does nothing to vindicate the Exclusion Thesis.

Three arguments will be considered for the thesis that self-consciousness requires awareness of the self as a physical object. The first of these, which will be discussed in Chapter 2, is the Objectivity Argument. This argument assumes that self-consciousness involves being able to think of at least some of one's perceptions as perceptions of objects in the 'weighty' sense, that is, particular items that are capable of being perceived and of existing unperceived. The central claim of the Objectivity Argument is that for one's experience to meet this 'objectivity condition', one must be aware of oneself as a physical object. The concept version of the Objectivity Argument claims that this is the requirement that one must think of oneself, *qua* subject, as a physical object, whereas the intuition version claims that the required form of awareness is intuitive awareness of the self *qua* subject as a physical object.

One objection to the Objectivity Argument would be that it is not entitled to the assumption that self-conscious experience must meet the

objectivity condition. On a more austere conception of self-consciousness, to be self-conscious is simply for one's consciousness to be 'unified'. For one's consciousness to be unified is for one to be capable of
self-ascribing one's 'representations'. So if there is a connection between
self-consciousness and the objectivity condition, it needs to be argued for
by showing that being able to think of some of one's perceptions as perceptions of objects in the weighty sense is a necessary condition of unity
of consciousness. Chapter 3 will discuss one argument along these lines
suggested by Strawson (in 1966: 97–112). This argument, which will be
described as the *Unity* Argument, can be seen as an argument for accepting the premiss of the Objectivity Argument.

While the Objectivity Argument takes it that the connection between
self-consciousness and the objectivity condition is explanatorily prior to
the connection between self-consciousness and awareness of the self as a
physical object, the *Identity* Argument of Chapter 4 reverses the order of
explanation. For the Identity Argument, the core notion of self-consciousness is one according to which a self-conscious subject must not
only be capable of self-ascribing her representations, as the Unity
Argument insists, but must also be capable of consciousness of her own
numerical identity as the subject of diverse representations. According to
the concept version of the Identity Argument, conceiving of oneself as a
physical object is a necessary condition of self-consciousness because it is
a necessary condition of consciousness of self-identity. According to the
intuition version of the Identity Argument, intuitive awareness of oneself as a physical object is a necessary condition of self-consciousness
because it is a necessary condition of consciousness of self-identity.
Unlike the Objectivity Argument, the Identity Argument regards the
connection between self-consciousness and the objectivity condition as,
if anything, a conclusion rather than a premiss.

Chapter 5 will return once again to the robust response to the
Exclusion Thesis. According to what will be described as a moderate
reply to the robust response, the best that can be done for the Exclusion
Thesis would be something along the following lines: suppose that the
subject that thinks or entertains ideas is a person and that persons are
objects among others in the world. Still, the existence of persons is only,
as it were, a derivative fact about the world. One way of making this point
would be to argue that although persons exist, it would be possible to
give a complete description of reality without claiming that persons exist.
This 'impersonal description thesis' is one element of Derek Parfit's
Reductionist account of persons and personal identity (see Parfit 1987:

Part III). The aim of Chapter 5 will be to undermine the impersonal description thesis. Since the best that can be done for the Exclusion Thesis is not good enough, the moral is that despite its distinguished history, this thesis should be abandoned once and for all.

2

THE OBJECTIVITY ARGUMENT

1. *Introduction*

According to the Objectivity Argument, a self-conscious subject is one whose experience satisfies the *objectivity condition*. For one's experience to satisfy this condition is for one to be in a position to think of it as including perceptions of objects in the 'weighty' sense, that is, particular items which are capable of being perceived and of existing unperceived (Strawson 1966: 88). The central claim of the Objectivity Argument is that awareness of oneself, *qua* subject of experience, as a physical object is a necessary condition of self-conscious experience in this sense.

It might be objected that the Objectivity Argument takes too much for granted by stipulating that a self-conscious subject is one whose experience satisfies the objectivity condition. Can there not be subjects who are self-conscious but whose experience does not satisfy this condition? In reply to this question, it would be worth remarking that the Objectivity Argument's conception of what it is for experience to satisfy the objectivity condition is relatively modest. On a strong reading of the objectivity condition, to say that experience satisfies this condition is to say not just that it is *thought of* or conceptualized as experience of objects in the weighty sense but also that it involves *knowledge* of such objects.[1] The claim that self-conscious experience involves knowledge of objects is stronger than the claim that it simply involves the conception of itself as experience of objects, but for the purposes of the Objectivity Argument no more is required to establish a connection between self-consciousness and awareness of oneself as a physical object than the stipulation that self-conscious experience is experience which satisfies the weaker of these objectivity conditions.

This will not satisfy all those who believe that the Objectivity Argument takes too much for granted at the outset, for it has yet to be explained why self-consciousness even involves being in a position to *con-*

---

[1] This is Strawson's reading of the objectivity condition. See Strawson 1966: 88.

ceptualize one's experience as experience of objects in the weighty sense. This residual anxiety about the Objectivity Argument invites one of two responses. According to a less ambitious response, all explanation comes to an end, and the connection between self-consciousness and the objectivity condition is so fundamental as to exclude the possibility of explanation in terms of anything more basic. So while the Objectivity Argument simply takes it for granted that a self-conscious subject is one whose experience satisfies the weaker objectivity condition, it is no objection to it that it does not attempt to explain something which neither calls for nor permits explanation. According to a more ambitious response, the most basic notion of self-consciousness is one according to which a self-conscious subject is one who is capable of thinking of her experiences *as* her experiences. If there is a connection between self-consciousness and the objectivity condition, that is because being in a position to think of one's experience as including experiences of objects in the weighty sense is a necessary condition of the possibility of the self-ascription of experiences.[2] This line of reasoning represents the core of the Unity Argument, which will be the focus of Chapter 3. For the moment, the question of whether the connection between self-consciousness and the objectivity condition should be seen as a reflection of a deeper connection between self-consciousness and the possibility of self-ascription of experiences may be set aside. For if it turns out that the Objectivity Argument fails to establish that awareness of oneself as a physical object is a necessary condition of one's being in a position to think of one's experience as experience of objects in the weighty sense, then questions about the status of the Objectivity Argument's starting-point will have been deprived of much of their significance in the present context. So the question which needs to be addressed in the present chapter is whether the Objectivity Argument succeeds on its own terms. Consideration of the question of whether its terms are the right ones will be postponed until Chapter 3.

What has been described as the central claim of the Objectivity Argument is in need of clarification on a number of counts. Firstly, an account needs to be given of how the Objectivity Argument conceives of physical objects. It will be assumed here that for the purposes of the Objectivity Argument physical or material objects are spatio-temporally located, shaped, three-dimensional space-occupiers. Such objects occupy space in virtue of their solidity or impenetrability. In Locke's words,

---

[2] Something along these lines is suggested in Strawson 1966: 108.

the solidity of a 'body' consists in the 'utter exclusion of other bodies out of this space which it possesses' (1975: 125). This conception of what makes an object a physical object is not uncontroversial,[3] but it does appear to capture what might be described as the ordinary, unreflective notion of a physical object.[4] Awareness of oneself as a physical object is therefore to be understood as awareness of oneself, *qua* subject of experiences, *as* shaped, located, and solid.

As remarked in Chapter 1, to say that one is aware of oneself as a physical object is not just to say that one is aware of what is *in fact* the subject of one's experiences as a physical object. The sense in which, according to the Objectivity Argument, self-consciousness requires awareness of oneself as a physical object is that it requires awareness of oneself *qua* subject of experiences as shaped, located, and solid. To bring out the significance of this formulation, consider the possibility that the subject of one's experiences is a certain human animal with which one is identical. Even if one is aware of this human animal as a physical object, this does not count as awareness of oneself as a physical object in the sense that matters unless one is also aware of this animal as the subject of one's experiences. This is the force of the requirement that self-consciousness is bound up with a sense of oneself *qua* subject of experience as a physical object. The question of what is involved in being aware of something *qua* subject of experience will be addressed at some length later on in this chapter. For ease of exposition, however, the qualification '*qua* subject of experience' will be dropped in the initial account of the Objectivity Argument.

It was suggested in the last chapter that there is more than one way of understanding what is involved in 'awareness' of something as a physical object. One possibility is that to be aware of something as a physical object is simply to conceive of it as such. On this reading, the thesis on which the Objectivity Argument turns is this:

(C1) For one to be in a position to think of or conceptualize one's perceptions as perceptions of objects in the weighty sense, one must conceive of oneself as a physical object.

It will be assumed in what follows that conceiving of oneself as a physical object is simply believing that the subject of one's experiences is a physical object. On a different interpretation, to be aware of oneself as a physical

---

[3] For example, Peacocke questions Locke's claim that solidity is a metaphysically necessary condition of matter. See Peacocke 1993: 170–1.

[4] See Joske 1967 for a good account of this notion.

object is to *experience* oneself as such, to be immediately and sensibly aware of oneself as a physical object. Kant describes as 'intuitive' those modes of knowledge which are in immediate relation to objects and through which objects are given to us. So another way of formulating the central claim of the Objectivity Argument would be this:

> (C2) For one to be in a position to conceptualize one's perceptions as perceptions of objects in the weighty sense, one must be intuitively aware of oneself as a physical object.

(C1) is the 'concept version' of the Objectivity Argument while (C2) is its 'intuition version'. Together, they amount to a defence of what was described in Chapter 1 as a materialist conception of self-consciousness. It remains to be seen what (C2) amounts to, but, as a first approximation, the point of distinguishing (C1) and (C2) is that there appears to be a distinction between *believing* that something is a physical object and *experiencing* it as a physical object. That there is such a distinction is no more surprising than the idea that there is a difference between, for example, experiencing the lines in the arrow illusion as being of unequal lengths and believing that they are of unequal lengths.[5] If there is, in general, a distinction between experiencing or being intuitively aware of something as thus and so and conceiving of it as thus and so, then this is not a distinction which the Objectivity Argument can afford to ignore.

While an account has yet to be given of what it would be to be intuitively aware of oneself as a physical object, it would be worth emphasizing at this stage that in drawing a distinction between these two versions of the Objectivity Argument one does not thereby commit oneself to the idea that intuitive awareness of oneself as a physical object is a form of awareness which is 'non-conceptual' or 'pre-conceptual'. To say that intuitive awareness of oneself as a physical object does not require the belief that one is a physical object is one thing; to say that intuitive awareness of oneself as a physical object is 'non-conceptual' might well be another, although the final verdict on this question will of course depend on what is meant by 'non-conceptual' in this context.[6] In any event, if there is a case for regarding intuitive self-awareness as 'non-conceptual', it has yet to be made.

---

[5] It is in this sense that perceptual content is, in Evans's terminology, 'belief-independent' (Evans 1982: 122–4).

[6] See McDowell 1994: 60–3 for an important discussion of the question of whether, in denying that perceptual content is wholly or partly non-conceptual, one is also committed to denying that it is belief-independent.

What would it be for one to be 'in a position' to conceptualize one's experience as including perceptions of objects in the weighty sense? At this point, more needs to be said about the notion of an object in the weighty sense. The characterization given at the outset was that objects in this sense are capable of being perceived and of existing unperceived; in Hume's terminology, objects in the weighty sense are capable of *continued* existence, that is, existence 'even when they are not present to the senses' (Hume 1978: 188). Another way of characterizing objects in the weighty sense would be to describe them as capable of what Hume calls *distinct* existence, that is, existence distinct from the subject and its perceptions. Hume claimed that the notions of continued and distinct existence stand in a relation of mutual entailment (p. 188), but this gives rise to the following difficulty: unlike Hume, supporters of the Objectivity Argument need to keep open the possibility that subjects of experience are themselves capable of being perceived, either by themselves or others, and of existing when they are not present either to their own senses or to anyone else's. Yet, even if subjects are capable of continued existence, it does not follow that they are capable of distinct existence, understood as existence distinct from themselves.[7]

In view of this complication, it will be assumed here that when the Objectivity Argument refers to our ability to think of our experience as including perceptions of objects in the weighty sense, this is to be understood as the claim that we are in a position to think of our experience as including perceptions of objects that enjoy both continued *and* distinct existence. As has already been remarked, the Objectivity Argument assumes that objects in this sense must be physical objects. Something will be said in defence of this assumption later on in this chapter, but even those who are not convinced that objects in the weighty sense must be physical objects will surely have to concede that we do in fact think of our experience as including perceptions of objects in this sense. So the main concern of the Objectivity Argument is with the necessary conditions of our being in a position to think of our experience as experience of physical objects.

To be in a position to think of one's experience as including perceptions of distinct physical objects, one must of course have the ability or the conceptual resources to understand the idea that one's perceptions include perceptions of objects in this sense. One way of mounting a

---

[7] Perhaps Hume can be defended against this line of attack by taking 'distinct' to mean 'distinct from being known by me'. This suggestion, which I owe to Michael Ayers, will not be pursued here.

defence of (C1) would therefore be to argue that one must conceive of oneself, *qua* subject of experience, as a physical object if one is to have the resources to grasp the idea that one's experience includes perceptions of objects in the weighty sense. This claim represents the core of the concept version of the Objectivity Argument.

It may be worth pausing for a moment to consider whether an argument along these lines deserves to be regarded as a 'transcendental' argument. This question is worth asking because of the doubts that have frequently been expressed about the viability of such arguments. On one interpretation, transcendental arguments are attempts to demonstrate that the truth of some proposition which is the target of sceptical attack is a necessary condition of the truth of some other proposition which the sceptic does not or cannot doubt. Transcendental arguments in this sense are 'truth-directed' (Peacocke 1989: 4). A familiar objection to truth-directed transcendental arguments is that they are far too ambitious to stand a serious chance of succeeding. According to this objection, the most that a transcendental argument can hope to achieve is to show that *belief* in the truth of a proposition concerning which sceptical doubts have been expressed is a necessary condition of our possession of a conceptual capacity which is not itself in question.[8] Transcendental arguments in this sense are 'belief-directed'.

More will be said in Chapter 4 about a possible objection in principle to belief-directed transcendental arguments, but the important point to notice at present is the concept version of the Objectivity Argument is, in effect, a belief-directed transcendental argument. The major difference between the concept version of the Objectivity Argument and more familiar belief-directed transcendental arguments is that the former is not concerned with the necessary conditions of something which the sceptic seems compelled to accept. At any rate, even if it is true that self-conscious subjects must be capable of thinking of their experience as including perceptions of distinct physical objects, it is not the business of the Objectivity Argument, as distinct from the Unity Argument, to establish this truth.

What, then, of the intuition version of the Objectivity Argument? It has already been conceded that it is by no means obvious what it would *be* to be intuitively aware of oneself, *qua* subject, as a physical object, but it would still be worth attempting to give a preliminary indication of how an argument for (C2) might go. One possibility is this: suppose that (C1)

---

[8] This point is associated with Barry Stroud. See Stroud 1982.

turns out to be defensible more or less as it stands, and that one is also persuaded of the truth of something like Kant's principle that concepts without intuitions are empty.[9] What this principle amounts to is a difficult question, but the thought in the present context would be that one's conception of oneself as a physical object must be, as Kant puts it, '*made sensible*' (A240) by intuitive awareness of oneself as a physical object. In other words, if the concept version of the Objectivity Argument succeeds in demonstrating that one must conceive of oneself as a physical object, then one must also be intuitively aware of oneself as such, on pain of one's self-conception lacking the kind of 'concreteness' demanded by Kant's principle.[10] This might be described as an *indirect* argument for (C2), since it presupposes the correctness of (C1).

To the extent that there are doubts about the concept version of the Objectivity Argument, these doubts also threaten the indirect defence of (C2). It is, however, not necessary to assume that the only way of arguing for (C2) is to assume the correctness of (C1). To see how a more direct argument for (C2) might go, consider once again the question of what is involved in being 'in a position' to think of one's experience as experience of a world of physical objects. The focus of the discussion so far has been on what is required for one to be able to understand the idea that one's experience is of such a world. On the face of it, however, being 'in a position' to think of one's experience in these terms is not just a matter of one's having the appropriate conceptual resources; one's experience must also be so structured as to permit or warrant conceptualization as experience of a world of physical objects.

What is it for one's experience to permit or warrant conceptualization as experience of such a world? According to what might be described as a *direct* argument for (C2), for experience to permit conceptualization in these terms, it must at least present itself as including perceptions of distinct physical objects. The point of (C2) is that for one's experience to present itself as experience of objects with shape, solidity, and location, one must be intuitively aware of oneself, *qua* subject of experience, as shaped, located, and solid. And to be intuitively aware of oneself as shaped, located, and solid just is to be intuitively aware of oneself as a physical object. To put it another way, it makes no sense to suppose that a subject who is incapable of spatial perception would be 'in a position' to

---

[9] Kant's claim, to be more precise, is that 'thoughts without content are empty, intuitions without concepts are blind . . . The understanding can intuit nothing, the senses can think nothing. Only through their union can knowledge arise' (A51/B75–6).

[10] See the closely related line of thought in Evans 1982: 265–6.

conceive of her experience as experience of physical objects, and spatial perception is bound up with a sense of oneself, *qua* perceiver, as a physical object among physical objects.[11]

2. The Concept Version of the Objectivity Argument

A roundabout but nevertheless illuminating way of working up to a defence of (C1) would be to examine Kant's account in his Transcendental Deduction of the Categories of what it is for 'representations' to relate to an 'object'. Kant's claim is that the 'unity of consciousness' constitutes 'the form of all knowledge of objects' (A129). For diverse representations to be united in one consciousness is for their subject to be (a) capable of attaching an 'I think' to them, and (b) capable of consciousness of his or her own identity as the subject of these representations. So when Kant claims that the unity of consciousness 'constitutes the relation of representations to an object' (B137), the suggestion seems to be that it is both necessary and sufficient for a series of representations to have objective bearing that their subject be capable of self-ascribing them and of grasping the numerical identity of that to which they are ascribed.[12]

It is not immediately obvious how this bears on (C1). In the first place, it is doubtful whether 'objects' in the context of the Transcendental Deduction are physical objects. As has frequently been pointed out, Kant's conception of an 'object' in the Deduction is far more formal than this; an object is, as Kant himself puts it, simply 'that in the concept of which the manifold of a given intuition is *united*' (B137). Secondly, there is no suggestion that the unity of consciousness, which is also 'formal', involves the conception of oneself as a physical object. Nevertheless, there is still something right about the idea that the relation of representations to an 'object' involves some form of unity of consciousness, even if 'object' is taken to mean 'physical object'. The concept version of the Objectivity Argument can be seen as an attempt to spell out exactly what is right about it.

The first step of the concept version of the Objectivity Argument,

[11] It is in this sense that, as Ayers remarks, 'our experience of *ourselves* as being a material object among others permeates our sensory experience of things in general' (1991: ii. 285).

[12] For a more detailed account of Kant's argument, see Cassam 1987.

then, is this: in order to think of one's experience as including perceptions of objects in the weighty sense, one must be capable of self-ascribing one's perceptions and of grasping the identity of that to which these perceptions are ascribed. Since the possibility of ascribing diverse representations to what is, and is represented as being, a numerically identical subject, is the core of what Kant calls unity of consciousness, it would not be inappropriate to describe this step as the claim that satisfaction of the objectivity condition requires unity of consciousness; in short, *objectivity requires unity* (ORU). The second step of the concept version of the Objectivity Argument is the claim that the 'I' to which one ascribes one's perceptions must be represented not only as numerically identical through the diversity of experience, but also as a physical object if one's representations are to be thought of as relating to physical objects. This may be referred to as the *physical object requirement*.

This account of the concept version of the Objectivity Argument raises two major questions, one about each of its steps: firstly, *why* does objectivity require unity of consciousness? In other words, what is the connection between the thought that one's experience includes perceptions of objects in the weighty sense, and the possibility of ascribing perceptions to oneself, conscious of the numerical identity of their subject? Secondly, even if it is plausible that objectivity requires unity of consciousness, why must the subject to whom the diverse perceptions are ascribed be conceived of as a physical object?

In connection with the first of these questions, it follows from the definition of 'object in the weighty sense' that to regard one's perceptions as perceptions of objects in this sense is to regard them as perceptions of what can exist unperceived. In addition, one must be able to make sense of the idea that different perceptions are perceptions of one and the same object. Perceptions are transient, and we could not count a single transient perception as a perception of a non-transient object unless, as Strawson puts it, 'we were prepared or ready to count some different perceptions as perceptions of one and the same enduring and distinct object' (1974a: 52). So an answer to the first question must show that unity of consciousness is a necessary condition for one to be in a position to regard diverse perceptions as perceptions of one and the same enduring and distinct object.

Consider, in this connection, the notion of existence unperceived. It is plausible that in order to get a grip on the idea of perception of what can also exist unperceived, one must think of perception as having certain spatio-temporal enabling conditions, such that in order to perceive something one must be appropriately located—both spatially and tempo-rally—with respect to it. The way in which this conception of the enabling conditions of perception provides for the possibility of existence unper-ceived is this: it enables one to account for the fact that a perceivable object is not actually perceived by appealing to the possibility that the spatio-temporal enabling conditions of perception are not met with respect to it.[13]

Consider, next, what is involved in the thought that diverse percep-tions are perceptions of a single enduring object. What thoughts of this form require is a capacity to apply the distinction between successively perceiving one and the same object and successively perceiving qualita-tively indistinguishable but numerically distinct objects. For example, suppose that there are distinct perceptions (P1 and P2) which are to be conceptualized as successive perceptions of a single enduring object O1. Given that the world may contain another object O2 which is qualitative-ly indistinguishable from O1, on what basis are P1 and P2 to be thought of as successive perceptions of O1 rather than of O2, or perceptions first of O1 and then of O2? Not surprisingly, the theory of perception appealed to in connection with the notion of existence unperceived also holds the key to answering this question. Suppose that P2 is a current perception and that P1 is a remembered past perception. One's own past perceptions are the only ones which one can correctly be said to remem-ber, and one can only perceive things with respect to which one is appro-priately located. So a remembered perception P1 can be conceptualized as a perception of O1 rather than its duplicate O2 just if one's route through the world was such that at the time of P1's occurrence, one was appropriately located with respect to O1 rather than O2. For example, if a replica of London's Marble Arch were built in Dallas, one could assure oneself that the Marble Arch that one remembers seeing was the one in London by appealing to the fact that one has been in London before but never in Dallas.

This argument relies upon a conception of the enabling conditions of perception and memory which has been well described by Shoemaker:

The spatio-temporal region which is 'rememberable' by a given person can be charted by specifying the intervals of past time during which the person was con-scious, and by specifying the person's spatial location, and indicating what por-tions of his environment he was in a position to witness, at each moment during those intervals. If someone reports that he remembers an event of a certain kind,

---

[13] This line of thought is due to Evans 1980: 88–90.

we know that unless his memory is mistaken an event of that kind occurred within the spatio-temporal region rememberable by him, and in principle we can chart this region by tracing his history back to its beginning (1984b: 28).

The suggestion, then, is that successive perceptions can properly be regarded as perceptions of the very same thing precisely because of the possibility of ascribing them to a numerically identical subject whose route through the world anchors them to a single object. Equally, for perceptions to belong to a unified consciousness in Kant's sense just is for their subject to be capable of self-ascribing them and grasping her own identity as their subject. The present point is that if one were not prepared to ascribe diverse perceptions to oneself or represent them as belonging to the very same subject, it would no longer be possible to make sense of the identity of the objects of diverse perceptual experiences. For if one were unwilling to ascribe P_1 to oneself, one's own location at the time of its occurrence would simply drop out of consideration as irrelevant. So objectivity requires unity of consciousness in Kant's sense.

This account of the first step of the concept version of the Objectivity Argument needs to be qualified in one important respect, for just as one might argue from where one is to what one is perceiving, so one might also infer one's location from what one takes oneself to be perceiving. There is an element of circularity here, but this circularity is neither objectionable in itself, nor such as to undermine the idea of a connection between consciousness of object-identity and potential consciousness of the identity of the subject. To bring this out, suppose that as one looks at London's Marble Arch, one seems to remember an earlier perception, P_1, as of a Marble-Arch-type monument. Was P_1 a perception of the very same monument as the monument of which the current perception (call it P_4) is a perception? This is not a question which needs to be answered on the basis of P_1 and P_4 alone, for one might also appeal to the intervening perceptions P_2 and P_3. Suppose that P_2 was as of Hyde Park Corner and P_3 as of Park Lane, and that no more than a few minutes elapsed between P_1 and P_4. Given the knowledge that in London, Marble Arch, Hyde Park Corner, and Park Lane are spatially adjacent places, one will have grounds for regarding P_1 and P_4 as perceptions of the very same monument, as long as P_1, P_2, P_3, and P_4 are all regarded as one's own perceptions. If one were to regard P_1 as a perception of Marble Arch's Texan duplicate, P_1, P_2, P_3, and P_4 would no longer be explainable by reference to the idea of their subject having travelled

through adjacent places in London.[14] Assuming that the duplicate's sur-
roundings do not include anything like Park Lane and Hyde Park Corner,
regarding P1 as a perception of a Texan monument would require the
assumption that one has travelled several thousand miles in the space of
a few minutes without realizing it. The point is not that this could not
have happened, but that it is an assumption of our theory of self-location
that such things do not generally happen.

In Peacocke's terminology, these considerations may be characterized
as constituting *intertemporal restrictions* on self-location. There are two
related points here. The first is that one's location is determined on the
basis of *sequences* of perceptions, where these sequences are regarded as
relating to spatially *adjacent* places; as Peacocke puts it, 'The spatial
scheme constrains the possible sequences of experiences it explains to
those corresponding to *paths* through the space' (1979: 33). The second
related restriction concerns the speed of one's movement. To quote
Peacocke once again, 'It could be argued that it is *a priori* that there is
some restriction . . . on which places are accessible to the experiencer at a
given time interval after he has been at a given place . . . if it were not so,
the experiencer could not have empirical reasons for believing he is at
one rather than another of two qualitatively similar places' (p. 33). These
intertemporal restrictions, together with some geographical knowledge,
enable one to answer questions about one's past and present location
simultaneously. The best explanation of the perceptions P1, P2, P3, and
P4 would be that they relate to adjacent places in London, and this in
turn provides one with a reason—if one were needed—for regarding P1
and P4 as perceptions of the very same London monument rather than
as perceptions of a monument in Dallas followed by one of a monument
in London, or, for that matter, as perceptions of the very same Texan
monument.

The idea that there are intertemporal restrictions on self-location
helps to reinforce the claim that objectivity requires unity, since the
application of these restrictions presupposes that the successive perceptions to which they apply are all ascribed or ascribable to a single, numerically identical self. Without being unified by means of their actual or

---

[14] As Evans remarks, 'self-location cannot in general be a momentary thing. For . . . self-
location depends crucially upon the axiom that the subject moves continuously through
space; and that axiom can be brought to bear upon particular questions of location only if
the subject has the capacity to retain information about his previous perceptions, and to use
that information in making judgements about his past, and thereby his present, position'
(1982: 243).

potential ascription to a single subject, diverse perceptions would be independent units, and no one perception would have any bearing upon any other. For example, the fact that P2 was a perception as of Hyde Park Corner only contributes to the conceptualization of P1 as a perception of *London's* Marble Arch if P1 and P2 are represented as belonging to the same subject. Without this assumption, the appeal to how far a *single* subject could have travelled within a short space of time would be quite ineffective, for the subject S1 of P1 might indeed have been located in Dallas and the subject S2 of P2 located in London as long as it is not assumed that S1 and S2 are numerically identical. This is at least one sense in which, as Kant puts it, 'we are conscious *a priori* of the complete identity of the self in respect of all representations which can ever belong to our knowledge, as being a necessary condition of the possibility of all representations' (A116).

At first glance, the second step of the argument, the physical object requirement, seems straightforward. The argument for the first step proceeded on the assumption that the subject of one's self-ascriptions must be conceived of as spatially located. Henceforth, this will be referred to as the *self-location requirement*. The second step is simply this: for one to conceive of oneself as spatially located in the sense required for one to think of one's experience as subject to spatio-temporal enabling conditions, one must also think of oneself as a physical object.

Some will regard this defence of the physical object requirement as far too quick. Since it makes sense to suppose that something can be spatially located without being a physical object, further work needs to be done to justify the transition from the self-location requirement to the physical object requirement. This point will be discussed below, in Section 4. First, there is another objection to consider to the thesis that objectivity requires unity.

3. *Quasi-Memory*

Those who are familiar with attempts to define or explain personal identity in terms of memory-involving psychological continuity might be tempted to criticize the first step of the concept version of the Objectivity Argument by appealing to the notion of 'quasi-memory'. Derek Parfit proposes the following definition of the concept of 'quasi-memory', or, for short, 'q-memory', in the context of his neo-Humean account of personal identity:

I have an accurate quasi-memory of a past experience if

(1) I seem to remember having an experience
(2) *someone* did have this experience

and

(3) my apparent memory is causally dependent, in the right kind of way, on that past experience.

On this definition, ordinary memories are a sub-class of quasi-memories. They are quasi-memories of our own past experiences. (1987: 220)

It is supposed to be compatible with this proposal that apparent memories come to us in the first-person mode of presentation; they present themselves as concerning the rememberer's *own* past experiences. However, the belief that they are about own experiences is, in principle, 'separable'.

Suppose that two subjects A and B visit London. A regularly visits London but it is B's first visit. Neither has ever been to Dallas. Suppose also that prior to their visit, B has had some of A's memory traces copied in her brain. As B sees Marble Arch, she apparently remembers a past perception as of Marble Arch; it seems to her that she has seen this monument before. What should B make of her apparent memory? She could dismiss it as a case of *déjà vu* rather than a genuine memory, but if she knows of the memory-trace copying, would it not be more sensible for her to conclude that she must be q-remembering one of A's experiences? Moreover, if B knows that A has been to London before but never to Dallas, would B not also be entitled to regard the q-remembered perception as a past perception of the monument which she is currently perceiving rather than its Texan duplicate? If all of this is correct, then here we have a case in which B can conceptualize a pair of perceptions as perceptions of the same thing without thinking of them as belonging to the same subject. Although B is entitled to think of both perceptions as perceptions of *London's* Marble Arch, she should ascribe the apparently remembered perception of this monument to A rather than herself, even if the apparent memory comes to her in the first-person mode of presentation. Hence, consciousness of self-identity is not a necessary condition of the ability to anchor diverse perceptions to one and the same object.

A striking feature of this counter-example is its reliance upon B's possession of background information both about the memory-trace transfer and about A's past location. Without this background information, it would simply be a shot in the dark for B to suppose that she is q-remembering someone else's past experience of this very monument. This is a reflection of a more general feature of the epistemology of q-memory, namely, that for q-memories to give one knowledge of someone's past one must know roughly how they were caused (see Parfit 1987: 221). Does this reliance upon extraneous information matter in the present context? It might matter if, without independent information concerning A's past location—that is, information that is extraneous to the content of B's apparent memory—B would have no grounds at all for taking the apparently remembered past perception to have been a past perception of London's Marble Arch. For it is surely difficult to believe that something as fundamental as the capacity to reidentify objects could, *in general*, depend upon one's possession of such extraneous information.

The claim that the counter-example requires the assumption that B has *independent* information concerning A's past location is, however, open to dispute. Suppose that B seems to remember not just a past perception of a Marble-Arch-type monument, but a coherent sequence of perceptions, including perceptions as of Park Lane and Hyde Park Corner. Would B not be entitled to take it that these past perceptions were of places in London, and hence that the perception as of Marble Arch was of the London monument rather than its Texan duplicate? Moreover, B need not think of them as her own past perceptions. She could reason that given the order and content of the apparently remembered perceptions, their subject, whoever she or he was, must have been located in London at the relevant time. This is just the kind of reasoning that B engages in when she is dealing with what she takes to be her own past perceptions, so why should she not be entitled to engage in parallel reasoning to fix the location of the subject of past perceptions when she does not believe that she was their subject? The intertemporal restrictions are still applicable *within* the series of past perceptions, whether or not B is prepared to ascribe them to herself. B need not first settle the question of whether their subject, presumably A, was in London and then anchor the past perceptions to London's Marble Arch rather than the duplicate. Since the apparently remembered perceptions themselves give B grounds for supposing their subject to have been in London, it is not the case that B requires independent knowledge of A's past location in order to infer that the past perceptions were of the very same monument as the one which she is currently perceiving.

This reply brings out the importance of not overestimating the extent to which the counter-example turns on the attribution to B of information extraneous to the content of the apparently remembered perceptions themselves, but it is unlikely to trouble those who are committed to the thesis that objectivity requires unity. For even if B does not require independent knowledge of A's past location, it remains true that unless B knew of the memory-trace copying, it would be a shot in the dark for B to suppose that she is q-remembering rather than just imagining past experiences of the currently perceived monument. The question remains whether the counter-example's reliance upon B's possession of extraneous information in this sense in any way diminishes its force.

One way of seeing that the force of the counter-example is significantly diminished by this point would be consider how someone who does not generally take it that her apparent memories concern her own past is supposed to be to able to establish propositions about their causal origin. For example, B might be said to know about the memory-trace copying because she can remember having arranged for it or can remember being told about it by A or someone else. Suppose, however, that B initially regards it as an open question whether these apparent memories of being told about the copying operation are actually memories of *her* being told about an operation performed on *her* or q-memories of someone else's experience of being told about an operation performed on 'her'. B might be able to settle this question on the basis of circumstantial evidence, or by investigating the causal origin of the apparent memory of being told about the operation, but the attempt to establish the causal origin of *this* apparent memory is itself bound to rely, at some point, upon further apparent memories. If it were always in question whether one's apparent memories constitute access to one's own past, such investigations could never get off the ground. The only way of blocking the regress is to concede that q-memories can only yield inferential knowledge of the past because ordinary memory is a source of non-inferential knowledge of the past (cf. Evans 1982: 235–48).

This reply to the q-memory objection might appear to be based on quite general epistemological considerations rather than on the concept version of the Objectivity Argument, but there is little to be said for drawing a sharp distinction between considerations which are internal to the Objectivity Argument and more general epistemological considerations. For it would only make sense to suppose that B is in any position to so much as understand the idea of an investigation of the causal origin of her apparent memories if she is already assumed to have the conception of her experience as experience of a stable, causally ordered world in which she herself is embedded. Since the Objectivity Argument is an account of the necessary conditions for one to be able to think of one's experience in such terms, it is unacceptable for objections to that argument to rely on counter-examples in which someone's possession of the relevant conception is simply taken for granted. This reply helps to bring out the full force of the earlier suggestion that something as fundamental as the capacity to reidentify objects cannot plausibly be regarded as being based upon one's possession of extraneous information concerning the causal origin of one's apparent memories. The underlying point is, as Wiggins observes, that the epistemological role of experiential remembering is to 'help to provide us with a starting-point for any further inquiry about how things are in the world. This need not be a philosophically indubitable or infallible starting-point . . . What it must be is a place I can start out from without making an inference from something else' (1992: 348). Unless experiential memory played this role, one could not begin to make sense of the idea that one's experience is experience of an objective world. And, for experiential memory to help sustain the idea of experience of the objective, one must in general be entitled and prepared to ascribe apparently remembered past perceptions to oneself, without first having to *establish* on the basis of anything more fundamental that one was indeed their subject. If this is correct, then the q-memory objection does little to undermine the fundamental insight of the first step of the concept version of the Objectivity Argument.

4. *Geometrical Self-Location*

The second step of the concept version of the Objectivity Argument is simply the transition from the self-location requirement to the physical object requirement. In other words, for one to regard oneself as located in the world in the sense required to sustain the idea that one's experience is subject to spatio-temporal enabling conditions, one must also regard oneself, *qua* subject of experience, as a physical object. Earlier, it was objected that this argument is too quick. One way of bringing out the fact that there is more work to be done would be to ask why it would not be sufficient for one to be able to think of one's experience as subject to spatial enabling conditions that one regards oneself as *spatially located* even if one does not conceive of the subject of one's perceptions as *shaped and solid*. As Strawson puts it:

It is not entirely clear to me that the following concept is, *in the context of the present considerations alone*, incoherent: the concept, namely, of a located but incorporeal centre of consciousness, tracing a subjective experiential route through an objective world (consciously conceived as such), conscious of the possibility of other such routes through that world and hence capable of self-ascription of its own experience of it. (1995: 417)

The considerations referred to here are those employed by the concept version of the Objectivity Argument. The suggestion is not that the concept of a located but incorporeal centre of consciousness is ultimately coherent but rather that its incoherence cannot be demonstrated simply by reflecting on what is involved in one's being able to think of one's experience as experience of an objective world.

What would it be to conceive of oneself as located but incorporeal? If one does not regard the subject of one's perceptions as a physical object, how is one supposed to be able to sustain the idea of its location in the world? One influential response to these questions has been to claim that one can regard the subject of one's perceptions as located in the world simply as a point of view on the world, where the location of this point of view is in turn defined by reference to the egocentric spatial content of its experience.[15] To describe the spatial content of experience as egocentric is to draw attention to the fact that the objects of perception are perceived as standing in various spatial relations *to the perceiver*.[16] Ordinarily, when the subject is thought of as a physical object among physical objects, it is natural to suppose that whether it sees something as above or below, to the left or to the right, will be a function of its location and orientation. In contrast, when the subject is thought of as located in the world simply as a point of view on it, the natural order of explanation is reversed. In the words of Jay Rosenberg,

Rather than reconstructing the experienced perspectival spatial relationships among the contents of awareness from the geometry and topology of lines-of-sight, *given* the *position* of the subject of awareness, we can instead think of *locating* the subject as *situated* within a three-dimensional 'experiential' space, itself *constituted* by projecting line-of-sight 'inward' in accordance with the perspectival spatial relationships experienced as obtaining among items within it. (1986: 110)

To conceive of oneself as located in the world simply as a point of view defined by the egocentric spatial content of one's experience is to conceive of oneself as located in the world only 'geometrically' (McDowell 1994: 104). So the question raised by the Objectivity Argument's physical object requirement is this: why would it not be sufficient for one to be

---

[15] Something along these lines is suggested in Penelhum 1970: 25.
[16] This way of characterizing the spatial content of perceptual experience is due to Evans 1982: 153–4.

able to think of one's experience as subject to spatial enabling conditions that one conceives of oneself as located in the world only geometrically?

Before going any further, it would be worth emphasizing that to say that one is aware of oneself as located in the world *only* geometrically is to deny that this form of self-awareness involves the idea that the subject of one's perceptions is shaped and solid. So those who claim that, in thinking of oneself as located at a point of view defined by one's experience, one is thereby committed to thinking of oneself as a *bodily* subject of consciousness, are simply mistaken.[17] This is not to say that when a subject conceives of itself as located in the world geometrically it cannot, in McDowell's words, 'register a special role played by a particular body in determining the course of its experience' (1994: 103). But registering this special role does not amount to one's conceiving of oneself *qua* subject as 'a bodily element in objective reality . . . a bodily presence in the world' (ibid.). Indeed, if this were not so, then the appeal to the notion of geometrical self-location would do nothing to explain how a self-conscious subject is supposed to be able to conceive of itself as located but *incorporeal*. It would also be worth remarking at this stage, that talk of the subject as geometrically located but incorporeal does not amount to a form of Cartesian dualism. The Cartesian thinking self is supposed to be something substantial, whereas the geometrical self is supposed to be purely 'formal'; it is 'in' the world solely in virtue of the fact that it has a point of view on it, not as a peculiar kind of substance. To the extent that the present objection to the second step of the concept version of the Objectivity Argument involves some form of dualism, it is not a dualism of two substances.

How much of a threat does the notion of merely geometrical self-location pose to the Objectivity Argument? One way of defending the Objectivity Argument's transition from the self-location requirement to the physical object requirement against this line of attack would be this: for one to be in a position to think of one's experience as experience of objects in the weighty sense, it is not enough simply that one has *some* conception of self-location. It is also essential that one has the conception of one's location as a genuine causal constraint on what one can perceive. The problem with the notion of merely geometrical self-location is that it does not provide for this. If this is correct, then one consequence might be that a subject who conceives of itself as only geometrically located cannot have an adequate grasp of the distinction between per-

---

[17] Someone who claims this is Richard Aquila. See Aquila 1979: 277–8.

ception and illusion. Yet it is an essential part of the idea that one's experience is experience of an objective world that one has a proper grasp of this distinction.

Why should the notion of merely geometrical self-location be unable to accommodate a distinction between perception and illusion? The point is that in order to grasp this distinction, one must understand that there might be occasions on which, even though one seems to be perceiving some object O, one cannot actually be perceiving O because one is not appropriately located with respect to it. If it seems to one that one is perceiving O, then, leaving aside cases of assisted perception, it will normally seem to one that one is in the vicinity of O. This might be described as one's *presented* location. To say that one is not actually appropriately located with respect to O in such a case is therefore to be committed to a distinction between one's actual and presented location. This is a distinction for which the notion of geometrical self-location makes no provision since, *ex hypothesi*, one's geometrical location is defined by reference to the point of view presented by one's experience. The underlying point, therefore, is this: for one's location to constitute a genuine causal constraint on one's perceptual experience, it must be logically independent of where the experience presents one as being, but one's actual geometrical location just is one's presented location. If the fact that one seems to see O a few feet away entails that the point of view with which one is identical is in the vicinity of O, there no longer seems to be any room for the idea that one's experience is non-veridical precisely because one is not where one is presented to oneself as being.

The suggestion, then, is that in order to get a grip on the distinction between perception and illusion, one must conceive of oneself as having an *objective* spatial location, that is, one which cannot be defined in purely experiential terms. To conceive of oneself as located in the world only geometrically is not yet to conceive of oneself as objectively located; in contrast, to regard oneself as a physical object is to regard oneself as objectively located, since it certainly makes sense to suppose that the physical object that is the subject of one's perceptions is not where those perceptions present it as being. This is not to say that it is in general illegitimate to infer one's location from what one takes oneself to be perceiving, or that regarding oneself as having an objective spatial location involves the thought that one's actual and presented locations regularly come apart. The point is simply to insist that if the subject's location is to serve as a proper constraint on its experience then there must be a distinction at least in principle between its actual and presented location.

   This might prompt the thought that this distinction, together with the related distinction between perception and illusion, can be provided for by reference to considerations of coherence. Even if one regards oneself as located in the world only geometrically, the location presented by a given experience can still be dismissed as non-veridical on the grounds that it does not cohere in the right way with the overall course of one's experience. The question this raises is whether the notion of coherence can be understood without reference to the idea of the subject as a bodily presence in the world. One reason for giving a negative answer to this question would be this: there is nothing wrong with the idea that considerations of coherence do significant work in anchoring the distinction between perception and illusion, but the notion of coherence is not, as it were, purely qualitative. For example, the reason that a series of perceptions as of adjacent places in London followed immediately by a perception as of the Golden Gate Bridge does not constitute a coherent sequence is that the subject is conceived of as tracing a continuous path through space and as only being able to move at restricted speeds. As long as the subject is regarded as a bodily presence in the world, such intertemporal restrictions can be viewed as restrictions on the movement through the world of its body. In contrast, the idea that there are such restrictions on the 'movements' of geometrical points of view is difficult to understand. To the extent that the notion of merely geometrical self-location fails to sustain the application to oneself of the intertemporal restrictions, it fails to sustain an adequate notion of coherence. Without a proper distinction between what does and what does not constitute a coherent route through the world, there cannot be a proper distinction between perception and illusion.

   These considerations have considerable force in bringing out the extent to which the notion of coherence is enriched by reference to the notion of the subject's bodily presence in the world, but it cannot be claimed that they constitute a vindication of the transition from the self-location requirement to the physical object requirement. There are two points to be made in this connection. The first is that just as it is experience which tells us which ways our bodies can and cannot move through space, so there appears to be no reason in principle why it should not be possible to develop an empirically based theory about the restrictions on one's movements through the world as a merely geometrical point of view. The second point is that if, as has already been conceded, someone who regards herself as geometrically located can still register the special role played by a particular body in determining the course of her experience, there is no reason why she should not regard the intertemporal restrictions as a reflection of the restrictions on the progress through the world of the body which has this special role. To think of a particular body in this way is, in a sense, to think of oneself as embodied, and as long as one thinks of oneself as *em*bodied, the idea that there are restrictions on which places are accessible to one at a given time interval after one has been at a given place presents no special difficulties. On the other hand, to regard the subject of one's experiences as embodied in this sense is not yet to regard it as a physical object.

The position, then, is this: the objection to the second step of the concept half of the Objectivity Argument was that it does not follow from the fact that one must conceive of oneself as spatially located that one must regard oneself as a physical object. One way of thinking of oneself as located but incorporeal would be to regard oneself as located in the world merely geometrically, and all attempts to demonstrate that this conception of self-location cannot sustain the idea that one's experience is experience of an objective world have so far proved inconclusive. There is, however, one last attempt to justify the transition from the self-location requirement to the physical object requirement which it would be worth considering. The emphasis so far has been on the idea that in order to be in a position to think of one's experience as experience of an objective world one must think of one's perceptual experience as subject to spatio-temporal enabling conditions, and so must regard oneself as spatio-temporally located. It is important to recognize, however, that while the idea that perception is subject to such conditions may be necessary for the idea of experience of the objective, it is not sufficient. For it is possible to accept that in order to perceive some object or phenomenon one must be appropriately located with respect to it without accepting that the object or phenomenon continues to exist when nobody is in the right place to perceive it. What is required to capture the full force of the notion of existence unperceived is the idea that when the enabling conditions of perception are met, one perceives something which is there anyway. It is extremely plausible that in order to make sense of this idea, one must think of at least some of the locations at which perceivers might or might not be present as occupied by possessors of Lockean primary qualities, such as shape and solidity. In other words, one must think of at least some such locations as populated by abiding space-occupiers.[18] This helps to bring out the point of the assumption made above that objects in

---

[18] This line of argument is developed in Evans 1980.

the weighty sense are *physical* objects, since it is the possession by an object of primary qualities which *makes* it a physical object. So another way of defending the second step of the concept version of the Objectivity Argument would be to argue that for one to be able to think of objects of perception as not only located but also as possessors of solid shape, one must think of the subject of one's perceptions as not only located but also as shaped and solid.

How might such an argument go? One plausible and influential suggestion is that the primary qualities of physical objects are, in a certain sense, theoretical. To say this is not to deny that primary qualities can be sensed. The point is rather, as Evans puts it, 'to highlight an analogy between the way our grasp of them rests upon implicit knowledge of a set of interconnected principles in which they are employed, and the way our understanding of such a property as electric charge rests upon explicit knowledge of a set of propositions more familiarly regarded as a theory' (1980: 95–6). Suppose that the interconnected principles required for an understanding of the primary qualities of physical objects are characterized as amounting to a 'primitive mechanics' (p. 95). The suggestion might then be made that grasp of such a mechanics requires the conception of *oneself* as an object with primary qualities and so as something whose presence in the world is not merely geometrical.

It is difficult to believe, however, that reflection on what is involved in grasp of a primitive mechanics can carry so much weight. It may well be true that among the concepts which figure in the mechanics are ones which can only be properly grasped by someone who is capable of spatial perception. For example, it is plausible that mastery of certain elementary shape concepts requires an ability to perceive shapes (cf. Evans 1985: 367). According to the intuition version of the Objectivity Argument, spatial perception is bound up with a sense of oneself, *qua* perceiver, as a physical object. So there is certainly something to be said for the idea that grasp of the primitive mechanics requires a sense of oneself as a possessor of primary qualities. However, this is not enough to justify the concept version of the Objectivity Argument, for even if it is true that spatial perception is bound up with intuitive awareness of oneself as a physical object, it does not follow that it requires the conception of oneself as a physical object. For someone who is keen to deny that self-consciousness requires the conception of oneself *qua* subject as a physical object will claim that the intuition version of the Objectivity Argument only shows that spatial perception embodies an illusion about the true nature of the perceiving subject. However unattractive this claim might be on other grounds, it is hard to believe that the problem with it is that someone who argues in this way would be in no position to make sense of the primitive mechanics. If this is correct, then it remains to be shown that in order to think of one's experience as including perceptions of physical objects one must conceive of the subject of one's perceptions as a physical object.

On the assumption that the concept version of the Objectivity Argument is intended as a belief-directed transcendental argument, the moral of this discussion is that the argument is unsuccessful. The central claim of the Objectivity Argument is that a certain belief or self-conception is a strictly necessary condition for one to be in a position to think of one's experience as experience of a world of physical objects, but this claim does not appear to be correct. So, as with many other belief-directed transcendental arguments, the concept version of the Objectivity Argument exaggerates the tightness of the link between a given conceptual capacity and a given belief. On the other hand, to say that the Objectivity Argument exaggerates the tightness of this link is not to say that there is no such link. For what has emerged from the preceding discussion is the extent to which *our* understanding of the enabling conditions of perception and the intertemporal restrictions on self-location draw upon the conception of ourselves as physical objects. In this sense, the Objectivity Argument is perfectly right to insist that this self-conception is of fundamental importance in providing us with the resources to think of our experience as experience of an objective world. The fact that this conception of experience might still be available to someone who regards herself as present in the world only geometrically does not make it any less plausible to claim that the concept version of the Objectivity Argument provides an accurate account of the closeness of the connection *for us* between a certain belief and a certain conceptual capacity. On the assumption that the exploration of unobvious connections between major structural features of our thinking about the world is the central task of metaphysics,[19] this is a significant achievement.

5. *The Intuition Version of the Objectivity Argument*

Earlier, a distinction was drawn between direct and indirect versions of the intuition half of the Objectivity Argument. The present concern is

---

[19] This conception of metaphysics is mainly associated with Strawson. See his account of 'descriptive metaphysics' in the Preface to Strawson 1959, and in ch. 1 of Strawson 1985.

with the direct argument for (C2). The argument is this: for one to be 'in a position' to think of one's experience as experience of physical objects, it is not enough that one has the appropriate conceptual resources; it must also be the case that one's experience permits or warrants conceptualization in these terms. To say that it warrants conceptualization in these terms is to say that it presents itself as experience of a world of objects with, among other things, shape, location, and solidity. For one's experience to present itself as experience of such objects, one must be intuitively aware of oneself, *qua* subject of experience, as shaped, located, and solid.[20] To be intuitively aware of oneself *qua* subject as shaped, located and solid is to be intuitively aware of oneself as a physical object. So intuitive awareness of oneself as a physical object is, as (C2) claims, a necessary condition for one to be in a position to think of one's experience as including perceptions of physical objects that are distinct from oneself.

One way of bringing out the force of this argument for (C2) would be to reflect on what is involved in the perception of solidity and location. Solidity can be either seen or felt, and an extremely important aspect of the perception of solidity by touch is the way in which it is bound up with a sense of the solidity of the perceiver. Solidity is typically felt as an impediment to one's movements,[21] and to experience a solid object as an 'obstructive something' (O'Shaughnessy 1989: 41) is at the same time to be sensibly or intuitively aware of that which is obstructed—the *subject* of tactile perception—as something solid.

Next take the case of location. It has already been remarked that the spatial content of perception is egocentric. As Husserl puts it, 'all spatial being necessarily appears in such a way that it appears either nearer or farther, above or below, right or left' (1989: 166). The important point is that in egocentric spatial perception the objects of perception are experienced as standing in such spatial relations *to the perceiver*; in Husserl's words, 'the "far" is far from me, from my Body' (ibid.). The 'Body' (*der Leib*) is the 'animated flesh of an animal or human being', a bodily *subject*; in contrast, a mere 'body' (*der Körper*) is simply 'inanimate physical matter'.[22] Egocentric spatial perception can be therefore be described as

---

[20] As O'Shaughnessy puts it, 'the intuitional given-ness of the world to one is dependent upon one's sometime veridically seeming to oneself to be a determinately shaped, determinately sized, determinately hard-or-soft something' (1980: i. 244).

[21] This aspect of the perception of solidity by touch has been emphasized by a number of writers, including Locke (1975: I. iv. 1–4), Joske (1967: 18), O'Shaughnessy (1989: 41), and Martin (1993: 213).

[22] Translators' Introduction to Husserl 1989: xiv.

self-locating; in experiencing objects as spatially related to one, one literally experiences the bodily self as located in the perceived world.

What is it for the content of perception to be egocentric? Does egocentric spatial perception depend upon the subject's possession of a concept of 'self' or can the egocentric content of perception be fully explained simply by reflecting on the connections between perception and action? Important as these questions are, they will not be pursued here, although it is difficult to believe that the connection with action does not have an important part to play in the explanation of the spatial content of perception.[23] The important point for present purposes is that the intuition version of the Objectivity Argument simply takes it as a *datum* that perceptual awareness of physical objects is bound up with a sense of such objects as standing in various spatial relations to a located subject. Whether it is right to do so is a question which will be addressed shortly.

When the notion of egocentric spatial perception was first introduced into the present discussion, the point of its introduction was to try to make something of the notion of merely geometrical self-location. In contrast, one of the merits of Husserl's discussion of these matters is that it insists that egocentric spatial perception involves a sense of oneself as a *bodily* presence in the world. For it is one's Body that is at the point of origin of egocentric space, and in relation to which other bodies are experienced as being to the left or right, above or below. To quote Husserl once again, the Body 'has, for its particular Ego, the unique distinction of bearing in itself the *zero point* of all these orientations. One of its spatial points, even if not an actually seen one, is always characterized in the mode of the ultimate central here . . . it is thus that all things of the surrounding world possess an orientation to the Body' (1989: 166). The Body which is the zero point or point of origin of egocentric spatial perception is the same as the Body whose solidity manifests itself in the perception of the solidity of other bodies by touch. So when a realistic account is given of what is actually involved in egocentric spatial perception, the suggestion that reflection on this notion provides any support for the idea of merely geometrical self-location seems far-fetched. For one's experience to be so structured as to warrant conceptualization as experience of physical objects, one must be capable of spatial perception, and it is a striking feature of spatial perception that it carries with it a sense of oneself as a physical object among physical objects.

[23] See the discussion of this issue in Brewer 1992.

How convincing is the intuition version of the Objectivity Argument? What will not be disputed here are its initial stages, the insistence that for one's experience to satisfy the objectivity condition it must present itself as experience of physical objects, and the claim that this requires a capacity for spatial perception. A more problematic aspect of the argument for (C2) is the suggestion that perception of spatial properties requires intuitive awareness of oneself as a physical object. The first objection to this claim is that the earlier defence of it was guilty of confusing two quite separate points. Consider, to begin with, the question of what is involved in the tactile perception of solidity. It may be true that, as O'Shaughnessy puts it, 'the space and solidity of our bodies provides the access to the space and solidity of other bodies' (1989: 38), but this only shows that the perception of solidity by touch is bound up with a sense of the solidity of one's *body*. Since this is not at all the same thing as awareness of the solidity of the *self*, the argument does not achieve what it sets out to achieve.

There is a parallel objection to the Husserlian account of perceptual self-location. If, as Husserl claims, the Body is the 'zero point' of egocentric spatial perception, this only goes to show that in this form of perception one is aware of the location of one's Body in the world. Once again, the objection is that this is not at all the same thing as intuitive awareness of the self as located in the world, given Husserl's account of the relationship between 'Body' and 'Ego'. So what the intuition version of the Objectivity Argument takes as a *datum* is no such thing. The distinction between *der Leib* and *der Körper* fails to disarm this objection because the fact that Husserl effectively characterizes the Body as something *possessed* by a particular Ego implies that Body and Ego are not the same thing. In that case, must there not be a gap between having a sense of a particular Body as an object among others in the world and having a sense of the Ego which possesses it as an object among others in the world? The objection, then, is that talk of the role of bodily awareness in spatial perception does not amount to an adequate gloss on the idea of intuitive awareness of oneself *qua* Ego as a physical object. This will be referred to as the Inadequacy Objection to (C2).

Suppose that the Inadequacy Objection can be met. According to what might be called the Dispensability Objection, the problem with (C2) is not that there can be no such thing as intuitive awareness of oneself as a physical object. The problem is, rather, that this form of awareness is not *necessary* for one's experience to present itself as experience of physical objects. For example, it might be claimed that even someone who lacks the forms of bodily awareness required for tactile perception can still see the surrounding world as a world of physical objects (cf. Aquila 1979: 277). Even if such a subject must still have a sense of her own location in the world, she need not be intuitively aware of herself as located in the world as a physical object among physical objects; it is enough that the subject is aware of herself as located only geometrically. So the question is whether spatial perception is compatible with 'body blindness'.

One response to the Inadequacy Objection would be this: the objection is that there is a gap between awareness of the location and solidity of one's body and awareness of the location and solidity of oneself, but there is no such gap if body (or 'Body') and self (or 'Ego') are identical. So the Inadequacy Objection rests on the unargued assumption that body and self are distinct. If a given body B is the subject of one's perceptions, then awareness of the shape, solidity, and location of B is awareness of what is *in fact* the subject as a physical object.

There are at least two difficulties with this response to the Inadequacy Objection. The first is that even non-dualists who accept that subjects of experience must have corporeal characteristics might be reluctant to accept the identification of subjects and their bodies. Secondly, and more importantly, even if body (or 'Body') and self (or 'Ego') are identical, this does not mean that awareness of the body (or 'Body') as a physical object is, in the relevant sense, awareness of the self or Ego as a physical object. This goes back to the point made at the outset that the sense in which, according to the Objectivity Argument, self-consciousness requires awareness of oneself as a physical object is that it requires awareness of oneself *qua* subject as shaped, located, and solid. From the fact that Body and self are identical, it would not follow that one is aware of the Body with which one is identical as the subject of one's perceptions. If one is not aware of a given body or Body as the subject of one's perceptions, then one is not aware of oneself *qua* subject as a physical object.

This line of argument raises a question which is of fundamental importance in the present context, namely, how is the phrase 'awareness of the self *qua* subject' to be understood. To put it another way, what would it be for one to be intuitively aware of *anything* as the subject of one's perceptions? This question will be the focus of the next section. Assuming that a satisfactory account can be given of the notion of awareness of oneself *qua* subject, then a further question is this: are these conditions such that the forms of bodily awareness involved in spatial perception qualify as intuitive self-awareness in the relevant sense?

Suppose, next, that this question can be answered in the affirmative. Another objection to the above argument for (C2) would then be this: the conditions on awareness of something *qua* subject and awareness of something 'as an object' are such that if one is aware of something *qua* subject, then one cannot *also* be aware of it 'as an object'. This Schopenhauerian objection is the Incompatibility Objection to (C2). Something like this objection underpins Sartre's remark about the body that 'either it is a thing among other things, or it is that by which things are revealed to me. But it cannot be both at the same time' (1989: 304). In order to assess this objection, more needs to be said about what it would be to be aware of something 'as an object'.

The next three parts will address the Inadequacy and Incompatibility Objections to the intuition version of the Objectivity Argument. The remaining sections will be concerned with the Dispensability Objection and with the indirect argument for (C2). It will turn out that (C2) has at least as much force as (C1) and, indeed, that the argument for it is somewhat more robust than the concept version of the Objectivity Argument.

6. *Awareness of the Self* 'Qua Subject'

One of the insights yielded by the notion of geometrical self-location is that the intuitive notion of awareness of something *qua* subject is that of awareness of it as one's point of view on the world. To say that one is aware of something as one's point of view on the world is to say that it is experienced as being at the point of origin of egocentric space. If this is correct, then the forms of bodily awareness involved in spatial perception qualify as awareness of oneself *qua* subject because 'the living body [Body] . . . functions as the absolute point about which spatial relations are experienced as orientated' (Bell 1990: 210). Because the Body is the 'zero point' of egocentric spatial perception, intuitive awareness of its shape, solidity, and location is awareness of the shape, solidity, and location of oneself *qua* subject. So the intuition version of the Objectivity Argument is not, as the Inadequacy Objection claims, guilty of confusing two quite separate points.

One source of resistance to the suggestion that the forms of bodily awareness involved in spatial perception are awareness of the self *qua* subject is the thought that a 'mere' body cannot *present* itself as the subject of one's perceptions. There is an interesting parallel between this thought and one way of explaining what the problem of other minds is supposed to be. For as McDowell remarks, one of the factors which underlies scepticism about other minds is the 'displacing of the concept of the *human being* from its focal position in an account of our experience of our fellows' and the substitution of a 'philosophically generated concept of a *human body*', conceived of as a merely material object (McDowell 1982: 469). The sceptic then finds it utterly mysterious that mere bodies can turn out to be 'points of occupancy for psychological properties as well' (ibid.), but that is because the concept of a 'mere' body is already an *abstraction* from the concept of a human being. Since there is nothing paradoxical about the idea that human beings are, and can be perceived as being, points of occupancy for psychological properties, the first response to the sceptic about other 'minds' should be to 'restore the concept of a human being to its proper place' (McDowell 1982: 470) and point out the extent to which the sceptic's problem is generated by the initial abstraction.[24]

The Inadequacy Objection rests on a similar misunderstanding of the concept of bodily self-awareness. There would undoubtedly be something odd about the suggestion that one's *body* presents itself as the subject of perception, but that is because the claim that the body is the zero point of spatial perception is already a philosophically generated abstraction from the more accurate claim that it is the Body or bodily self that is the apparent subject of spatial perception. The important point in this connection is not the stipulation that Body and Ego are identical but rather that, as Ayers puts it, the bodily self is involved in spatial perception 'neither simply as the postulated subject of experience, nor simply as an ever-present object of experience, but as the *presented* subject of experience and action' (1991: ii. 286). The point of this formulation is to emphasize that the physical entity that is the zero point of spatial perception presents itself as being a point of occupancy for psychological properties. For example, the physical entity that is at the point of origin of egocentric space is also one in which sensations such as pain present themselves as located; in this sense, it presents itself as 'a bearer of sensations' (Husserl 1989: 168). So just as scepticism about other minds rests in part on a failure to grasp the full force of the distinction between the concept of a human being and that of a merely material object, so the Inadequacy Objection rests on a parallel failure to grasp the full force of the concept of the presented subject of spatial perception.

The position, then, is not that one has, as it were, to build up to the

---

[24] Cf. the discussion of the Abstraction Argument in Chapter 1.

idea that egocentric spatial perception is self-locating by first reflecting
on the way in which perception places the perceiver's body in the world
and then postulating a relation of identity between subject (or 'Ego') and
body. Rather, perception places the subject's body in the world because,
in the first instance, it locates the (bodily) *self* in the world. Reference to
its bearing on the location of the self is essential if justice is to be done to
the content of egocentric spatial perception. Because the subject whose
location in the world is given in the content of egocentric spatial perception is presented as being a physical object among physical objects, it is
always possible to abstract the notion of the subject's body from that of
the bodily subject. Having performed this abstraction, it can begin to
look as though there must be a gap between intuitive awareness of the
location and solidity of the body and intuitive awareness of the location
and solidity of the self. This is to forget, however, that the impression of
a gap is simply a product of the employment an artificial, philosophically
generated concept of body in specifying egocentric content of experience.

It would be worth emphasizing that this response to the Inadequacy
Objection cuts right across the debate between materialism and dualism.
The issue is not whether the subject is a physical thing but whether it is
experienced as a physical thing. The claim that the bodily self is the presented subject of experience would be compatible with maintaining that
the subject is in fact non-physical. It might therefore be useful to distinguish between what might be called three 'grades' of 'apparent presence'
in the world. The first grade involves intuitive awareness of oneself as
present in the world only geometrically, as something bodiless. The second grade involves awareness of oneself as a point of view which 'has' a
body which plays a special role in determining the course of one's experience, but it does not involve awareness of oneself *qua* subject as a bodily presence. The third grade of presence involves intuitive awareness of
oneself *qua* subject as a bodily presence in the world. In these terms, the
proposed reponse to the Inadequacy Objection is that egocentric spatial
perception involves the third grade of apparent presence in the world,
since one is aware of that about which spatial relations are experienced as
orientated *as* a bodily subject, not just as a bodiless point of view. So the
claim that one is intuitively aware of oneself *qua* subject as a physical
object is the claim that one is intuitively aware of the *presented bodily subject* of one's perceptions as shaped, located, and solid.

Is this response to the Inadequacy Objection adequate? One objection
to it would be to argue that the proposed gloss on the notion of aware-

ness of oneself '*qua* subject' is too weak; there is more to something's being the presented subject of experience than its being the zero point of egocentric spatial perception and something in which sensations present themselves as located. There are also questions about the claim that the bodily self is the zero point of spatial perception, for the contents of different forms of spatial perception might need to be specified in terms of different points of origin. In the case of visual perception, for example, it might be held that the objects of perception, including other visible parts of one's own body, are experienced as standing in various spatial relations to the head. In contrast, the point of origin of certain of some forms of tactile perception might be the hand.[25] This helps to bring out the peculiarity of the claim that the presented subject of perception is that about which spatial relations are experienced as orientated, for it would surely be paradoxical to describe an individual body-part such as one's hand as the presented subject of tactile perception, even if it is a body-part in which some sensations present themselves as located.

This objection is not committed to denying that there is anything to the idea that awareness of oneself *qua* subject is or involves awareness of oneself *qua* point of view on the world. The objection is rather that reference to the role of bodily self-awareness in spatial perception does not succeed in capturing the relevant notion of 'point of view'. For apart from the fact that talk of the Body or bodily self as the zero point of spatial perception ignores important differences between the various senses, it is also important to acknowledge that one's Body can itself become an object of awareness. When one is aware of something in this way, it is something *on* which one has a point of view. In contrast, the intuitive notion of awareness of something *qua* subject is awareness of it as the focal point of one's point of view on the world. Since nothing which can become, as it were, the object of a given point of view can also present itself as its focal point, bodily self-awareness cannot be awareness of oneself *qua* subject. This point is closely related to what was described earlier as the Incompatibility Objection to (C2) and it leads inevitably to the conclusion that nothing which one is aware of as an object among others in the world can be the presented subject of experience; the self *qua* point of view shrinks to an extensionless point that is in the world only geometrically.

The question raised by this objection is this: if intuitive awareness of

---

[25] Thus Peacocke writes that 'in giving the content of tactile experience, we would sometimes have to use as origin something labelled with the property of being the centre of the palm of a human hand, with axes defined by relation to parts of the hand' (1989: 9).

the bodily self as the zero point of egocentric spatial perception is not sufficient for bodily self-awareness to count as awareness of the self *qua* subject, then what more is required? One possibility is this: there are indeed further conditions which need to be met for a form of awareness to count as awareness of the self *qua* subject, but these conditions are not such that they cannot be met by bodily self-awareness. In other words, the self *qua* subject need not shrink to an extensionless point. What are the further conditions? One extremely influential line of thought in this connection is that awareness of oneself *qua* subject cannot be a form of awareness which requires the identification of a presented object as oneself. This is related to Wittgenstein's distinction between the use of 'I' 'as subject' and its use 'as object' (Wittgenstein 1958: 66–7). In Shoemaker's terminology, the point of this distinction seems to be that statements in which 'I' is used as subject are those which are 'immune to error through misidentification' relative to 'I'. To say that the statement '*a* is F' is immune to error through misidentification relative to '*a*' is to say that the following is not possible: the subject knows some particular thing to be F, but makes the mistake of asserting '*a* is F' because, and only because, she mistakenly thinks that the thing she knows to be F is what '*a*' refers to (see Shoemaker 1994a: 82). The suggestion, then, is that for a form of awareness to count as awareness of the self *qua* subject, it must be a form of awareness on the basis of which it is possible to make first-person statements that are, in this sense, immune to error through misidentification.

With the notion of immunity to error through misidentification in place, it is possible to see the full force of the Inadequacy and Incompatibility Objections. The first of these can be reformulated as follows: for awareness of something as the zero point about which spatial relations are experienced as orientated to count as awareness of oneself *qua* subject, it would need to be a form of awareness on the basis of which it is possible to make first-person statements in which 'I' is used as 'subject'. First-person statements in which 'I' is used 'as subject' must be immune to error through misidentification relative to 'I'. Perceptually based ascriptions of location to one's bodily self are not immune to error through misidentification in this sense. Therefore, intuitive awareness of one's own location in egocentric spatial perception cannot be awareness of the location of the bodily self *qua* subject.

As for the Incompatibility Objection, this may now be stated as follows: awareness of something 'as an object' is, in its most basic sense, a form of perceptual awareness. Perceived objects are, as Shoemaker puts it, 'candidates for several sorts of perceptually based identification' (1994b: 126), sortal identification, particular identification, and, in the case of continuants, re-identification. Identification 'necessarily goes together with the possibility of misidentification' (Shoemaker 1994a: 87), so awareness of something as an object cannot be the basis of statements that are immune to error through misidentification. This explains why there is a conflict between the idea that one is aware of the bodily self *qua* subject and the idea that one is aware of it as an object among others in the world. If one is aware of it as an object among others in the world, then it must be possible for one to misidentify it, but if this is possible, then, by definition, one's awareness of it is not awareness of it *qua* subject.

One response to this argument would be to dispute the assertion that awareness of oneself *qua* subject has anything to do with the immunity to error through misidentification of certain first-person statements. A more plausible response, to be developed below, would be to accept the proposed gloss of the notion of awareness *qua* subject, but to argue that the forms of bodily self-awareness involved in spatial perception meet the immunity condition.

7. *Immunity to Error through Misidentification*

Why should it be supposed that intuitive awareness of one's spatial location cannot be the basis of first-person statements that are immune to error through misidentification relative to 'I'? Consider the following example: suppose that a subject S has a perceptual experience as of seeing Marble Arch directly ahead of her in the middle distance. The point of the claim that egocentric spatial perception is self-locating comes out in the present case when it is remarked that in being aware of Marble Arch as being directly ahead of *her* in the middle distance, S is at the same time, and in virtue of such awareness, also aware of *herself* as being located in the vicinity of Marble Arch. Thus, she would ordinarily take herself as entitled to assert in such circumstances something along the following lines: 'I am in front of Marble Arch.' But now consider the following possibility: suppose that unknown to S, she is hooked up to someone else's body (call it body B) in such a way that she is registering visual information about *its* environment. So when B is facing Marble Arch, it seems to S as if *she* is facing Marble Arch. If, in such circumstances, S were to judge 'I am facing Marble Arch', her judgement will be mistaken in the following way: although it will be expressive of knowledge that *someone* is facing Marble Arch, it will be mistaken because, and only because, the person known by S to be facing Marble Arch is not herself. In other words, this would be a case of error through misidentification relative to 'I'. Since perceptually based self-ascriptions of location are open to this kind of error, the awareness upon which they are based is not awareness of the self *qua* subject.

A similar point can be made with respect to proprioceptive awareness of the disposition of one's limbs or body. The intuition version of the Objectivity Argument claims that tactile perception provides us with a sense of our own solidity, and the significance of proprioception in this connection is that tactile perception requires proprioception.[26] Suppose, for example, that S is aware of her right arm as moving forward in relation to her own body until it meets an obstruction which prevents it from going any further despite the fact that it is not yet fully outstretched. It would be natural to describe this as a case in which S is aware of something solid at the point of obstruction, and is thereby also aware of her own solidity, or, at any rate, the solidity of her arm. The important point here is that this awareness of solidity depends upon S's proprioceptive awareness of the position and movement of her arm in relation to the rest of her. Once again, however, it is possible to envisage a case in which, unknown to her, S is hooked up to B in such a way that she is registering proprioceptive information from B rather than her own body.[27] If she were to judge 'My arm is moving', then although her judgement would be expressive of knowledge that *someone's* arm is moving, it would be mistaken because, and only because, the person whose arm she knows to be moving is not herself. So, as with intuitive awareness of self-location, intuitive awareness of the solidity of the bodily self fails to count as intuitive awareness of the solidity of the self *qua* subject.

How convincing are these examples? To take the case of self-location, for S's judgement 'I am facing Marble Arch' to be subject to error through *misidentification*, it must be the case that it is at least expressive of knowledge that someone is facing Marble Arch. Evans rightly objects that this condition is not satisfied in the example. Since 'it is not sufficient for knowledge that a true belief be causally dependent on the facts which render it true' (Evans 1982: 245), it would not be correct to regard

---

[26] See O'Shaughnessy (1994: 207–10) for a defence of the claim that tactile perception requires proprioception.

[27] An example along these lines is set out in Armstrong 1984: 113.

S's judgement as expressive of *knowledge* that anyone is facing Marble Arch. Similarly, if S is, without realizing it, registering proprioceptive information from someone else's body and so does not know that *her* arm is moving, then she 'does not know *anything* on this basis' (Evans 1982: 221). So while such examples show the possibility of a certain kind of mistake, it is one which 'cannot be regarded as a mistake of identification' (p. 188). If the mistakes in these examples are not mistakes of identification, then they do nothing to show that the first-person statements in question are *not* immune to error through misidentification. And if they do not show this, then they also fail to establish that the forms of bodily self-awareness upon which the statements are based are not awareness of the self *qua* subject.

This powerful epistemological argument against one particular attempt to demonstrate that the statements in question are not immune to error through misidentification may be supplemented by the following metaphysical considerations: suppose that proprioceptively-based self-ascriptions of limb-position or movement are referred to as 'L-ascriptions'. Then one possibility that is worth considering is that L-ascriptions are immune to error through misidentification relative to 'I' because of the correctness of what might be described as an *idealist* account of body-ownership. Consider the following analogy: if one asks what makes a pain one's own, then one answer would be that what makes a pain one's own pain is simply the fact that one is aware of it in the appropriate way. This is idealism about pain-ownership. Suppose, next, that it is asked what makes a particular limb or body one's own. A parallel answer would be that one's own body just is the one that one is aware of in the appropriate way, that is, 'from the inside'. If this is so, then it would be no more possible for one to be mistaken in thinking that the body one is aware of from the inside is one's own that for one to be mistaken in thinking that the pain one feels is one's own pain. Hence, L-ascriptions are immune to error through misidentification.

One example of idealism about body-ownership is Locke's account of what makes a limb a part of one, that is, a part of one's thinking conscious self. In the context of a discussion of how personal identity is compatible with a change of substance, he writes:

That this is so, we have some kind of evidence in our very bodies, all whose particles, whilst vitally united to this same thinking conscious self, so that we *feel* when they are touched, and are affected by, and are conscious of good or harm that happens to them, are a part of our *selves* i.e. of our thinking conscious *self*. Thus the limbs of his body are to everyone a part of himself; he sympathizes and is

concerned for them. Cut off an hand, and thereby separate it from that consciousness we had of its heat, cold, and other affections; and it is then no longer a
part of *himself*, any more than the remotest part of matter. (1975: 336–7)

In other words, (a) to experience a limb as a part of one is to feel when it
is touched, to be conscious of its temperature properties and other 'affections', and to have sympathy and concern for it, and (b) to experience a
limb as a part of one is necessary and sufficient for it to be a part of one.

This argument is difficult to assess without seeing how the reference
to 'other affections' in (a) is explained, but there seem to be grave difficulties with (b) as it stands. On the one hand, for a bodily part to be a
part of one, it cannot be necessary that one is conscious of it, since one
has many bodily parts of which one is not normally conscious at all.[28] As
for the sufficiency component of (b), it might be wondered in the light of
the examples given above why it should not be possible for one's brain to
be connected to someone else's arm in such a way that one is conscious of
heat or cold in it, feels when it is touched, and so is concerned for it.
Clearly, the idealist is committed to rejecting this description of the case.
The fact that one is conscious of it in these ways would mean that it is
one's own arm. The question, however, is whether this is anything more
than an arbitrary stipulation.

One idealist response to the charge of arbitrariness would be to enrich
(a). An important ingredient of bodily awareness which Locke does not
mention is proprioceptive awareness. It also seems to be a part of normal
bodily awareness that individual limbs or body-parts are experienced as
parts of an integrated totality. This might be described as the *unity* condition on bodily awareness. This condition explains why the earlier worry
about different points of origin for different forms of spatial perception
cannot be pressed too hard, because, when all is said and done, the various points of origin are all parts of what is, and is experienced as being,
an integrated bodily totality. Suppose, then, that to experience a limb as a
part of one is to have feeling in it, to be concerned for it, to be proprio-
ceptively aware of its position and movement in space, and to experience
it as part of an integrated bodily totality. A limb or body-part which
meets all of these conditions is, in O'Shaughnessy's terminology, *immediately present* to one (O'Shaughnessy 1980: i. 145). Locke's conditions

---

[28] A Lockean reply to this objection would be to draw a distinction between questions of
animal identity and questions of personal identity; thus, insensitive internal organs and
limbs without feeling would be a part of the 'man' or animal in which one is 'realized', but
not of the person that one is. See Snowdon 1990 and Ayers 1991: ii. 283–4 for an account of
some of the paradoxes generated by Locke's man/person distinction.

may now be revised as follows: (a*) to experience a limb or body-part as a part of one is for it to be immediately present to one, and (b*) the immediate presence to one of a limb or body-part is necessary and sufficient for it to *be* a part of one.

Despite this enriching of the idealist's account, the necessity component of (b*) remains problematic, for many parts of one's body are not immediately present to one. What of the sufficiency component? Suppose that the immediate presence to one of a limb is sufficient for it to be one's own. If an arm is immediately present to one and one judges 'My arm is moving' on the basis of its immediate presence, then one's judgement cannot be mistaken because the immediately present arm is not one's own; *ex hypothesi*, its immediate presence to one makes it a part of one. So the L-ascription would come out as immune to error through misidentification. The earlier objection to the idea that L-ascriptions are immune to error through misidentification can now be restated as follows: L-ascriptions cannot be immune to this kind of error because it is logically possible that the immediately present limb actually belongs, say, to one's twin on the other side of the room, and that it is immediately present to one simply because one's brain is registering information from it. Suppose that such examples are described, somewhat question-beggingly, as *alien limb* examples. If they are coherent, then is it not the case that they not only show that idealism is unacceptable but also that the awareness upon which L-ascriptions are based cannot therefore be awareness of oneself *qua* subject?

As before, the idealist's response to the alien limb examples might be to deny that they are cases in which someone else's limbs are immediately present to one; if they are immediately present to one, then they are one's own limbs. The reason that this response is unacceptable is that it fails to respect the intuition that a limb with which one is not materially united cannot be a part of one.[29] While the notion of material unity is not straightforward, this can be seen as at least a preliminary gloss on the earlier suggestion that the idealist's response to such cases amounts to a piece of arbitrary stipulation. Whatever else needs to be said about the notion of material unity, it is surely plausible that one cannot be materially united with a spatially distant limb, one with which one is not locally conjoined.[30] It is because the alien limb examples violate the material

---

[29] See Ayers 1991: ii. 229–38 for an account of the notion of material unity.

[30] Ayers rightly draws a distinction between material unity and local conjunction in 1991: ii. 232.

unity condition that they cannot properly be described in the manner recommended by the idealist.

This suggests the following *realist* alternative to idealism: for a limb or body-part to be a part of one, it is necessary and sufficient that one is materially united with it. On this view, there is still an important sense in which it is the bodily self rather than individual body-parts which is the presented subject of perception. For different forms of spatial perception are integrated with each other precisely because their different 'local' points of origin are materially united. Even if it is true, for example, that the objects of visual perception are, in the first instance, perceived as standing in various spatial relations to one's head, this form of awareness only has the significance and content which it has because the head is one part of the materially united whole which constitutes the bodily self. It is this materially united whole which is, as it were, the *ultimate* presented subject of perception.

The key question about realism in the present context is this: on the assumption that the alien limb examples are ones in which the material unity condition is violated, what becomes of the issue of whether L-ascriptions are immune to error through misidentification? It might appear that the realist is committed to denying such immunity to L-ascriptions, but such an impression would be mistaken. The idealist takes it for granted that the alien limb examples are ones in which a limb with which one is not materially united is nevertheless immediately present to one, and this leads to the wholly implausible suggestion that immediate presence is more important for limb-ownership than material unity. The realist's alternative response is to claim that the examples are ones in which the immediate presence condition is violated, and that this is so precisely because the material unity condition is violated. In other words, if one is not materially united with a limb, then it can only be seemingly immediately present to one.[31] In contrast, actual immediate presence requires material unity. And if an L-ascription is based upon an arm's merely seeming presence to one rather than its actual immediate presence to one, then, just as Evans argues, it cannot be expressive of knowledge that someone's arm is moving, for knowledge cannot be grounded in an illusion. So whatever else is wrong with the L-ascription, it is not guilty of an error of identification.

---

[31] Cassam (1995a) fails to attach sufficient weight to this point and so comes to the mistaken conclusion that L-ascriptions are only '*de facto*' immune to error through misidentification.

How well does realism fare with the question of whether perceptually based self-ascriptions of location are immune to error through misidentification relative to 'I'? It might be objected that realism lacks the resources to deal with this question. For what is now at stake is the location of the bodily self 'as a whole' rather than the disposition or movement of an individual body-part. It is one thing to say that an individual body-part 'belongs' to S if and only if she is materially united with it, but the idealist will claim that this can only mean that it belongs to her if and only if it is materially united with her body. In that case, is the realist not now faced with the question of what makes a given body S's body? If the only way that one can be materially united with something is for one's body to be materially united with it, then realism is surely in trouble, for S's body cannot belong to her in virtue of being materially united with itself.

The correct response to this objection to realism would be to argue that the idealist's question 'What makes a given body *my* body?' is simply illegitimate, for there is no independent 'I' whose ownership of a particular body can be in question. As Wittgenstein puts it, 'There is a criterion for "this is my nose": the nose would be possessed by the body to which it is attached. There is a temptation to say that there is a soul to which one's body belongs and that my body is the one that belongs to me' (1979: 24). This is clearly a temptation to which the realist should refuse to succumb once it is understood that the 'me' can only properly be conceived of as a *bodily* 'me'. So in the case in which S is in receipt of visual and other sensory information from B, it would be a mistake to claim that B's seeming immediate presence to S somehow makes it the case that B is really S's body. As before, the correct response is to point out that S's judgement 'I am in front of Marble Arch' is mistaken but that the mistake is not one of misidentification. This is simply a case in which S is the victim of an illusion about her own location, and an illusion about S's location cannot be the basis of a legitimate claim to knowledge of B's location.

The position that has been reached is this: the question which was raised above was whether the forms of bodily self-awareness involved in spatial perception are awareness of the self *qua* subject. The initial response to this question was to argue that they are awareness of the (bodily) self *qua* subject, at least to the extent that awareness of something *qua* subject is awareness of it *qua* bearer of sensations and as that about which spatial relations are experienced as orientated. It was then objected that awareness of the self *qua* subject requires more than this; it must also be a form of awareness on the basis of which it is possible to make first-person statements that are immune to error through misidentification relative to 'I'. It has now emerged that the forms of bodily self-awareness involved in spatial perception meet this condition as well. What now needs to be considered is the objection that the very considerations which establish that a given form of awareness is awareness of the self *qua* subject also establish that it cannnot be awareness of the self as an object among others. This Incompatibility Objection will be the focus of the next section.

8. *The Incompatibility Objection*

The Shoemakerian version of the Incompatibility Objection outlined above argues that: (i) awareness of something as an object is a form of perceptual awareness;[32] (ii) perceived objects are candidates for several sorts of identification; (iii) identification always carries with it the possibility of misidentification; (iv) so if one is aware of something as an object among others in the world, then it must be possible for one to misidentify it; (v) if one's awareness of something is such as to leave open the possibility of misidentification, then this awareness cannot be awareness of it *qua* subject; (vi) so bodily self-awareness cannot be awareness of oneself *qua* subject *and* awareness of oneself as an object among others in the world.

The most obvious objection to this argument is that it conflicts with what it seems plausible to say about demonstrative identification. Perceptually based demonstrative judgements such as 'This is red' are not based on an identification of the object of judgement, and are immune to error though misidentification relative to the demonstrative pronoun.[33] Yet the perceptual awareness upon which the judgement 'This is red' is based might still be awareness of something 'as an object', as long as one is aware of that to which the use of 'this' refers *as* a persisting, bounded, three-dimensional space-occupier that is perceptibly distinct from other individuals in its environment. So it is not true *in general* that there is any incompatibility between the idea that a form of awareness is awareness of

---

[32] This stipulation explains Shoemaker's remark that 'the reason one is not presented to oneself "as an object" in self-awareness is that self-awareness is not perceptual awareness' (1984a: 105).

[33] As Shoemaker himself observes, 'normally it is not the case that I say "This is red" because I find that something is red and identify that thing as "this"' (1994b: 130).

something 'as an object' and the idea that it is such as to yield judgements that are immune to error through misidentification.

If this objection is sound, then step (iv) of the argument for the Incompatibility Objection is problematic. Since (iii) is relatively uncontroversial, it would seem that the problem with the argument for (iv) must be with (i) or (ii). While (i) seems somewhat arbitrary, this cannot be an issue in the present context since the awareness on which the judgement 'This is red' is based is certainly perceptual. That leaves (ii). On the face of it, the claim that perceived objects are candidates for several sorts of identification would be difficult to dispute. But from the fact that perceived objects are candidates for identification, it does not follow that demonstrative judgements must actually be based on an identification. As long as a demonstrative judgement is not based on an identification, it can be true both that it is immune to error through misidentification and that it is based on perceptual awareness of that to which the demonstrative term refers 'as an object'. It might be wondered, by the same token, why it cannot be true both that perceptually-based self-ascriptions of location are not based on an identification of a presented object as oneself and that one is aware of the subject whose location is given in the content of egocentric spatial perception 'as an object'.

It might be objected that this response to the Incompatibility Objection overlooks an important difference between first-person and demonstrative thought. For while past-tense demonstrative judgements rest on an observationally based re-identification of the object referred to, past-tense, memory-based first-person judgements do not, as Shoemaker puts it, 'involve identifications of oneself that are grounded on observed similarities between selves observed at different times, or on a perceptual tracking of a self over a time' (1994b: 131). The question, then, is whether the argument for (C2) can respect this 'no tracking' requirement on self-consciousness. The Incompatibility Objection may now be re stated in the form of the following dilemma: either the forms of bodily self-awareness involved in spatial perception depend upon an ability to keep track of one's body or 'bodily self', in which case they are not awareness of oneself *qua* subject, or they do not involve an ability to keep track in this sense, in which case they are not awareness of oneself 'as an object'. It follows that the notion of immunity to error through misidentification no longer holds the key to the Incompatibility Objection, since past-tense demonstrative judgements can still be immune to error through misidentification despite the dependence of such judgements on

an ability to keep track. The proposal is rather that the concept of awareness of oneself *qua* subject should be characterized directly by reference
to the 'no tracking' requirement, while awareness of something 'as an
object' is to be defined as involving the exercise of an ability to keep track
of it. The thesis that nothing can be apprehended both 'as an object' and
qua subject is then a straightforward consequence of these definitions.

As far as the relationship between the intuition version of the
Objectivity Argument and the 'no tracking' requirement is concerned,
there is no reason to suppose that the former cannot respect the latter.
When a subject is disposed to judge 'I am in front of Marble Arch' and a
few moments later is disposed to judge 'I was in front of Marble Arch',
there is no question of the transition from the former to the latter disposition needing to draw upon an observationally based re-identification of
the subject or an ability to keep track of the subject.[34] To this extent, the
awareness upon which these judgements are based qualifies as awareness
of the self *qua* subject. So if the argument for (C2) is to escape the dilemma which forms the basis of the Incompatibility Objection, it is the latter's conception of awareness of something 'as an object' which it needs
to challenge.

The claim that awareness of something 'as an object' has to do with an
ability to keep track of it is not implausible. So if one is to insist that bodily self-awareness is awareness of oneself 'as an object' *despite* the fact
that it does not depend upon an ability to keep track of the self, care
needs to be taken to give a proper account of the *point* of describing such
awareness as object-awareness. At this stage it would be worth remarking
that while reference to the connection with keeping track captures one
element of the intuitive conception of awareness of something 'as an
object', it is not the only or even the central element. For 'objects' are, in
the first instance, physical objects, that is, shaped, located, and solid
three-dimensional space-occupiers. So the most basic form of awareness
of something 'as an object' is awareness of it as a *physical* object. If it is
the case that for something to be a physical object is for it to be shaped,
located, and solid, then it would seem to follow that to be aware of something *as* shaped, located, and solid just *is* to be aware of it as a physical
object. It is usually the case that awareness of something as a physical
object in this sense also involves the exercise of an ability to keep track of
it, but to insist that it always involves this ability is to beg the question
against the idea of intuitive awareness of the self *qua* subject as a physical

---

[34] This aspect of I-thinking is emphasized in Evans 1982: 237.

object. For, as has already been remarked, spatial perception is bound up with a sense of the perceiver as shaped, located, and solid. Thus, there is a perfectly respectable and, indeed, fundamental sense in which it can be said to constitute intuitive awareness of the perceiver as a physical object. Yet this is also a case in which what it is overwhelmingly plausible to describe as awareness of the perceiver as a physical object does not involve the exercise of an ability to keep track of the perceiver from moment to moment. So it is still a candidate for awareness of the perceiver *qua* subject.

It would also be worth adding that intuitive awareness of a physical object as shaped, located, and solid typically also involves awareness of it as persisting and as distinct from other objects in its environment. In being aware of the shape and location of a physical object, one is at the same time aware of the boundary between it and other objects of the same or different types; the boundary is, in this sense, an experienced boundary. Similarly, it is a striking feature of bodily self-awareness that in providing one with a sense of one's own shape and location, it also provides one with a sense of one's own spatial boundaries. Intuitive awareness of the shape and location of the presented bodily subject of perception is, like other forms of object-awareness, awareness of it as sharply delineated from other objects in the environment. This point will assume considerable importance in the context of the Identity Argument, but for present purposes its significance consists in the fact that it provides further grounds for insisting that there is a perfectly legitimate and straightforward sense in which bodily self-awareness is awareness of oneself as a physical object.[35]

It might be useful, in the light of this discussion, to draw a distinction between two senses in which one might be aware of something as a physical object, a broad and a narrow sense. In the broad sense, to be aware of something as a physical object is simply to be aware of it as a persisting and bounded space-occupier, as shaped, located, and solid. In the narrow sense, to be aware of something as a physical object is to be aware of it as shaped, located, and solid and for one's awareness to involve the exercise of an ability to keep track of the object. The Incompatibility Objection adopts the narrow interpretation of object-awareness and claims that awareness of something as a physical object in this sense is incompatible with awareness of it *qua* subject, given the 'no tracking' requirement on awareness *qua* subject. In contrast, the Objectivity Argument

---

[35] For a different argument for roughly the same conclusion, see Martin 1993.

must be understood as claiming that what is required for satisfaction of
the objectivity condition is intuitive awareness of oneself *qua* subject as a
physical object in the broad sense. So the Incompatibility Objection
misses the point unless the narrow sense is the only legitimate or interesting sense of object-awareness. The moral of the present discussion is
that such a stipulation would be unjustified.

To be intuitively aware of oneself *qua* subject as a physical object in
the broad sense is, of course, not to be intuitively aware of the bodily self
as a 'mere' physical object, one which is not a point of occupancy for psychological properties. It would therefore be appropriate to characterize
this form of self-awareness as, in Merleau-Ponty's terminology, awareness of oneself as a 'subject-object' (1989: 95). The concept of a 'subject-object' is entirely at odds with a form of dualism which has had a
profound influence on much theorizing about the nature of self-consciousness, namely, a dualism of subject and object. The central thesis of
this form of dualism is that the categories of 'subject' and 'object' are
mutually exclusive. As was remarked in Chapter 1, even those who have
emphasized the importance of bodily awareness for self-consciousness
have not been immune to the influence of the dualism of subject and
object. Thus, for Sartre, 'my body as it is for me does not appear *to me* in
the midst of the world', for it cannot both be 'a thing among other things'
and 'that by which things are revealed to me' (1989: 304). This seems to
be no more than a special case of the dualism of subject and object. Even
Merleau-Ponty's own distinction between the 'phenomenal body' and
the 'objective body' seems to represent a failure to register the full force
of the notion of a subject-object.[36] To all such arguments, the response
of the intuition version of the Objectivity Argument is to insist that there
is a perfectly good sense in which the presented subject of perception
appears to itself 'in the midst of the world'. Since the bodily self appears
to itself and to others as being something to which both perceptions and
corporeal characteristics can properly be ascribed, another way of saying
what is said by describing it as a 'subject-object' would be to describe it
as a 'person' in Strawson's sense.[37]

---

[36] It is not entirely clear, however, whether the distinction between 'objective' and 'phenomenal' body is supposed to be a distinction between different entities or between different views of the same entity. The latter interpretation is suggested by Merleau-Ponty (1989:
106 n. 1). For further discussion of this question, see Baldwin 1988: 38–43.

[37] For Strawson, 'the concept of a person is the concept of a type of entity such that
both predicates ascribing states of consciousness *and* predicates ascribing corporeal characteristics, a physical situation etc. are equally applicable to a single individual of that single
type' (1959: 101–2).

This might prompt the objection that there is more to the Incompatibility Objection than the combining of a demanding conception of awareness *qua* subject with an implausibly restrictive account of object-awareness. For while it may well be plausible that in spatial perception one has a sense of oneself *qua* 'empirical' or bodily self as a physical object among others in the world, it does not follow that spatial perception is bound up with a sense of what might be called one's 'core-self' (Ayers 1991: ii. 287) or 'transcendental Ego' as a physical object among others in the world. Since it is the apparent presence in the world of the core-self that has struck many as most deeply puzzling, it might seem that the recent remarks fail to get to the heart of the matter. So instead of a blanket dualism of subject and object, the present suggestion is that the intuition version of the Objectivity Argument leaves open a more subtle dualism of object and *core* subject.

To the extent that the present line of attack is prepared to grant that satisfaction of the objectivity condition requires a sense of oneself *qua* empirical self as a physical object among others in the world, it already makes an important concession to the Objectivity Argument. Nevertheless, *if* there is a distinction between bodily self and core-self, then a failure to demonstrate that satisfaction of the objectivity condition requires the apparent presence in the world of one's core-self might appear to amount to a significant weakness in the Objectivity Argument. To see why such an impression would be mistaken, more needs to be said about the alleged distinction between bodily self and core-self.

9. Core-Self and Bodily Self

There are many different ways of understanding the distinction between core-self and empirical self, but a common theme is that the former is to be understood as the subject of thought rather than perception or sensation. Consider, in the light of this distinction, the intuition version of the Objectivity Argument. It might be true that egocentric spatial perception carries with it a sense of oneself *qua* subject of perception as located in the world, but it does not follow that egocentric spatial perception requires a sense of oneself *qua* subject of thought as located in the world. Similarly, it is one thing to show that the presented subject of tactile perception must itself be experienced as shaped and solid, but the idea that one is aware of the subject of one's thoughts as shaped and solid is an entirely different matter. Thus, it is the subject *qua* thinker or core-self which cannnot be grasped 'as an object' and whose status as an object among others in the world is deeply problematic. From this perspective all the talk of the role of bodily awareness in spatial perception is beside the point, for thinking, unlike perceiving, lacks spatial content, and consciousness of thinking has nothing to do with consciousness of one's body. In other words, the bodily self might be the presented subject of sensation and perception but not of thought.

One objection to this line of argument is that it is difficult to reconcile with the ways in which thought and perception interpenetrate. Consider the case of perceptual-demonstrative thoughts. When a subject judges, say, that 'That monument is ugly' in connection with a currently perceived monument, the object perceived is the object thought about. In this sense, the judgement spans and, as it were, unifies thought and perception; the thought to which the judgement gives expression is both based upon and made available by the perceptual experience. This unity of thought and perception in demonstrative thoughts surely casts doubt on the idea that the bodily self can be the presented subject of the perceptual experience of the monument without also being the presented subject of the perceptual-demonstrative thought. Although the fact that the *object* of a demonstrative thought is the object of the perceptual experience upon which the thought is based is not conclusive proof that the presented *subject* of the thought is, and presents itself as being, the same as the presented subject of perception, it surely makes it unattractive to suppose that consciousness of oneself *qua* thinker can be detached from consciousness of oneself *qua* perceiver. The moral is that if one can be intuitively aware of the presented subject of the experience as located in the world, then there is no good reason to deny that one can also be aware of the presented subject of demonstrative thought as located in the world.

It might be objected that these remarks overlook an important distinction between 'pure' and 'impure' thoughts, in something like Kant's sense.[38] Thoughts or representations are 'pure' if and only if they are not sensation- or perception-involving, so demonstrative thoughts are 'impure'. Even if the bodily self is the presented subject of impure thoughts, it is not the presented subject of pure thoughts, or of the activity of thinking such thoughts. The worry about finding a place in the world for the core-self can now be reinterpreted as a worry about how

---

[38] A pure representation in Kant's sense is one in which 'there is nothing that belongs to sensation' (A20/B34).

the subject of pure thought can be, and present itself as being, an object among others in the world. For Descartes, the solution to this problem was to claim that the core-self, the subject of purely intellectual thought, is an object of an extremely peculiar sort, an immaterial substance. The subject of thought involving sense-perception or sensory imagination is simply this object thinking in a way which involves the body. For Kant, the 'I or he or it (the thing) which thinks' is the transcendental subject, which, unlike the Cartesian thinking substance, is not part of the empirical world at all. Thus, from either a Cartesian or Kantian perspective, reference to the perception-involvingness of demonstrative thoughts is simply beside the point.

There are several objections to this argument. The first would be to call into question the idea that any thoughts are 'pure' in the sense required by it.[39] If all thought is sensation- or perception-involving, then the question of how the subject of pure thought can be a piece of the world does not arise. Secondly, even if some thoughts are 'pure', the perception-involvingness of demonstrative thoughts cannot be dismissed as an irrelevance in the context of (C2). For the intuition version of the Objectivity Argument is concerned with the conditions for *thinking* of one's experience as experience of physical objects. So it would be natural to take (C2) as requiring both that one is intuitively aware of oneself *qua* subject of perception as a physical object, and that one is intuitively aware of oneself as a physical object *qua* subject of those very thoughts in which individual perceptions are conceptualized as perceptions of physical objects. These thoughts will typically include perceptual-demonstrative thoughts, so if it is correct that one is aware of oneself *qua* subject of perceptual-demonstrative thoughts as located in the world, then one is aware of oneself as located in the world *qua* thinker of those thoughts which matter most in the present context.

To dispute this argument, one would need to argue that the ability to think of one's experience as experience of an objective world does not require an ability to think perceptual-demonstrative thoughts, but the prospects for an argument along these lines are not good. Someone who can think of her experience as experience of an objective world must be capable of thinking about one particular sector of the world rather than another. Since the identification of particulars in purely general terms is vulnerable to what Strawson calls 'the possibility of massive reduplication' (1959: 20), the targeting in thought of a particular sector of the universe

[39] This is the position taken in Ayers 1991: ii. 286.

depends upon the thinker's capacity for identifying particulars demon-stratively. The object of a demonstrative thought must be one which the thinker can sensibly discriminate, so awareness of the subject of sensa-tion as a bodily presence in the world is also awareness of this bodily presence as the subject of demonstrative thought.

A striking feature of the attempt to show that there is no such thing as awareness of oneself *qua* subject of pure thought as an object among oth-ers in the world is its reliance on the Abstraction Argument which was criticized in Chapter 1. For in ordinary self-awareness, one is aware of one's thoughts, sensations, and perceptions as belonging to one and the same self. Indeed, such awareness is an important element of the 'unity of consciousness'. So when one speaks of the core-self as the subject of, say, 'pure' thought, one is abstracting one aspect of one's mental life from its normal context, a context in which it is integrated with various other aspects, including sensation and perception. Having performed this abstraction, it can then seem puzzling how awareness of oneself *qua* core-self could have anything to do with a sense of oneself as a bodily pres-ence in the world. As has been repeatedly argued here, the source of the puzzle is the initial abstraction, and the solution is to refuse to allow talk of the core-self to take on life of its own (cf. McDowell 1994: 103). Once it is remembered that the talk of core-self is simply shorthand for a part-icular aspect of the life or functioning of the empirical or bodily self, there is no longer any mystery about its place in the world. To put it bluntly, either the core-self is a *mere* abstraction, in which case it is hard-ly suprising that it is difficult to think of it as an object among others in the world, or it is something substantial. But there is only one substantial entity which the core-self can be, namely, the bodily self which presents itself as being both the subject of thought, sensation, and perception, and a physical object among physical objects.

10. *The Dispensability Objection*

It might be helpful at this point to summarize the current state of play. The Inadequacy Objection to (C2) claims that satisfaction of the objec-tivity condition requires, at best, intuitive awareness of one's body as a physical object, and that this is not at all the same thing as satisfaction of the objectivity condition requiring intuitive awareness of the subject as a physical object. In reply, it was argued that the forms of spatial percep-tion required for satisfaction of the objectivity condition involve aware-

ness of the bodily self as the subject of perception. For a form of awareness to count as awareness of something *qua* subject is for it to be (i)
awareness of it as one's point of view on the world, (ii) awareness of it as
a bearer of sensations, and (iii) awareness on the basis of which it is possible to make first-person statements that are immune to error through
misidentification relative to 'I'. On the face of it, the bodily self-awareness required for spatial perception satisfies each of these conditions.
This is the force of the claim that the bodily self or living Body is the
presented subject of perception. Given the links between thought and
perception, it is also plausible that the bodily self is the presented subject
of thought. Since spatial perception involves intuitive awareness of the
presented bodily subject of thought and perception as shaped, located,
and solid, it can also be said to involve intuitive awareness of oneself *qua*
subject as a physical object.

One response to this argument would be to claim that the proposed
conditions on awareness of something *qua* subject are necessary but not
sufficient. So the fact that bodily self-awareness satisfies all of them is
not enough to show that it is awareness of oneself *qua* subject. This
objection is difficult to assess without an account of what the further conditions are supposed to be, but it is certainly not obvious that the three
conditions do not capture all there is to the intuitive notion of awareness
of oneself *qua* subject. There must be a strong suspicion that the imposition of further conditions is motivated, at least in part, by a prior commitment to the thesis that one cannot be aware of anything, *qua* subject,
that one is also aware of as an object among others in the world. Given a
prior commitment to this thesis, it will always be tempting to exclude
apparent counter-examples by strengthening the conditions on object-
awareness or awareness of oneself *qua* subject until the desired result has
been secured. But unless the further conditions can be shown to be
grounded in an *independently* plausible conception of what these forms of
awareness require, their imposition will do little to persuade those who
do not already believe the conclusion of the argument. While the possibility that there are independently plausible further conditions cannot be
ruled out, it would be unwise for opponents of (C2) to expect too much
from this line of thought.

It would therefore be more fruitful for opponents of the intuition version of the Objectivity Argument to pursue a somewhat different line of
attack. Instead of challenging the intelligibility of the claim that bodily
self-awareness is intuitive awareness of oneself *qua* subject as a physical
object, opponents of (C2) would be better advised to argue that intuitive

awareness of oneself *qua* subject as a physical object is not a strictly necessary condition of the forms of spatial perception required for satisfaction of the Objectivity Condition. This is the Dispensability Objection
to the intuition version of the Objectivity Argument.

Consider, to begin with, the claim that the content of spatial perception is egocentric, and that in experiencing objects as standing in various
spatial relations to one, one is at the same time aware of oneself as located in the world. This claim formed part of the argument for (C2), but it
might be wondered why the spatial content of perception must be egocentric for it to present itself as experience of an objective spatial world.
Why would it not be enough, for example, that the perceiver experiences
things as being, say, to the left or to the right without experiencing them
as being to *her* left or to *her* right? In Campbell's terminology, this
amounts to the suggestion that the spatial information acquired through
vision might be 'monadic' rather than 'relational'; it need not employ the
first person (Campbell 1994: 119). To describe the content of spatial perception as monadic is, among other things, to be committed to denying
that it shows anything about the perceiver's location in the world. Yet
this is compatible with the supposition that the world is perceived as a
spatial world.

It is not entirely clear what the claim that visual information need not
'employ' the first person amounts to, if it is accepted that a significant
part of the point of attributing egocentric spatial content to perception is
to explain the connections between perception and action. Monadic visual
information is supposed to be usable as a guide to action, yet if a subject
reaches out in the appropriate direction for an object which is perceived
as being 'to the right', then is this not already enough to justify the claim
that the subject sees the object as being to *her* right? It may well be true
that vision can be used as a guide to action by creatures who, as Campbell
puts it, are incapable of 'using the first person to articulate the knowledge provided by vision' (1994: 120), but the fact that a creature lacks the
conceptual resources to articulate its perceptions in first-person terms
does not mean that they do not in fact represent things as standing in
various spatial relations to *it*.

Even if these considerations are held to be inconclusive, there is a
much more straightforward reason for insisting that satisfaction of the
objectivity condition requires intuitive awareness of oneself *qua* subject
as located in the perceived world. It will be recalled that the starting-
point for the intuition version of the Objectivity Argument was the suggestion that for one to be 'in a position' to think of one's experience as

experience of physical objects, it must be so structured as to *warrant* conceptualization in these terms. According to the concept version of the Objectivity Argument, to think of one's experience as experience of an objective spatial world is, at least in part, to think of it as subject to spatial enabling conditions. Thus, for one's experience to be so structured as to warrant conceptualization as experience of an objective world of physical objects, it must present itself as had from a located point of view. In other words, there must be something in the content of experience itself which makes it appropriate to regard it as subject to spatial enabling conditions, and what makes it appropriate is precisely the fact that its content is egocentric and so provides one with a concrete sense of self-location. So egocentric spatial perception is, just as (C2) implies, indispensable if one is to be 'in a position' to think of one's experience as experience of an objective, spatial world.

This argument will not convince those who are not already convinced by the concept version of the Objectivity Argument's defence of the self-location requirement. Even if the argument that has just been given is corrrect, however, there is another, more obvious objection to the intuition version of the Objectivity Argument. Just as, in the context of the concept version, it was argued that a subject can conceive of herself as located in the world without conceiving of herself as shaped or solid, so it might now be argued in the context of (C2) that one can be intuitively aware of oneself as located in the world without being intuitively aware of oneself as shaped or solid. Just as conceiving of oneself as located but not shaped or solid is conceiving of oneself as located in the world only geometrically rather than as a bodily presence, so being intuitively aware of oneself as located but not shaped or solid is being intuitively aware of oneself as located in the world only geometrically rather than as a bodily presence. As long as the egocentric spatial content of one's perceptions provides one with a concrete sense that one is located in the world, it will remain appropriate to regard one's experience as subject to spatial enabling conditions. But if one is not intuitively aware of oneself as shaped or solid, one cannot be said to be intuitively aware of oneself as a physical object.

This defence of the Dispensability Objection raises an obvious question about the perception of solidity. It was argued earlier that the perception of solidity by touch requires bodily awareness. In particular, it requires a sense of oneself, *qua* bodily subject of tactile perception, as solid. If one is intuitively aware of oneself *qua* bodily subject of tactile perception as solid, then one is not aware of oneself as located in the world only geometrically. So it might seem that for one's experience to present itself as experience of a world of solid physical objects, one must be intuitively aware of oneself as just such an object. The difficulty with this argument is that solidity can be seen as well as felt, and it is not obvious that the *visual* perception of solidity requires a sense of oneself as a solid bodily presence in the world. If the perception of solidity by sight does not require bodily self-awareness, then someone who is intuitively aware of herself as located in the world only geometrically could presumably still *see* the world as a world of physical objects even if she is not intuitively aware of herself as a physical object.

What would it be for one to see the world as a world of physical objects even if one lacks a sense of oneself *qua* subject of experience as a bodily presence in the world? Consider the following example from a paper by Richard Aquila:

> Suppose, for example, that I awake, face-up, on an operating table (of which I have no awareness) and have experienced a loss of any memories which serve to determine who I am. Suppose, farther, that I am in no way aware of my body as an object. (I experience no bodily sensations, or at least none which I am able to identify in connection with some particular body I perceive, and I perceive no body at all which I would identify as my own). It is compatible with this supposition that I perceive my surroundings and regard what I see as a real world and no mere object of hallucination or fantasy . . . My awareness of a personal identity is provided by my very awareness of the *world* presented to me. I identify myself by identifying myself with a particular point of view *on* that world. (1979: 277)

Since the subject in this example has no bodily awareness, she has no sense of touch. Since she has no sense of touch, she has no tactile sense of the solidity of objects in the world and no sense of her own solidity *qua* subject of perception. If she lacks intuitive awareness of her own solidity, then she is not intuitively aware of herself as a physical object. On the other hand, she can still see objects in the surrounding world as shaped and solid, and as egocentrically located. To the extent that the spatial content of her perception is egocentric, she is intuitively aware of herself as located in the world, but only geometrically. So here is a detailed apparent counter-example to the intuition version of the Objectivity Argument. Aquila's 'body blind' subject is one whose experience warrants conceptualization as experience of a world of physical objects even though she is not intuitively aware of herself, *qua* subject, as a physical object.

In the earlier discussion of egocentric spatial perception, it was claimed to be a great merit of Husserl's account that it represents the Body or bodily self as being at the origin of egocentric space. To quote Husserl again, 'all things of the surrounding world possess an orientation to the Body, just as, accordingly, all expressions of orientation imply this relation' (1989: 166). In a sense, examples such as Aquila's leave Husserl's central insight untouched, for there can be little doubt that egocentric spatial perception is, in normal circumstances, bound up with a sense of one's living Body as the 'ultimate central here'. In the present context, however, the question is not whether Husserl succeeds in capturing what spatial perception is actually like for all or most of us, but whether the connection with bodily self-awareness is a *necessary* connection. The intuition version of the Objectivity Argument is committed to the view that bodily awareness is strictly necessary for spatial perception, and this is the claim which Aquila's example calls into question. Thus, reflection on the possibility of body blindness is an especially vivid way of bringing out the force of the Dispensability Objection.[40]

The simplest reply to this version of the Dispensability Objection would be to argue that the alleged counter-example to (C2) only shows that one's bodily presence in the world is not, as McDowell puts it, 'always borne in on one in self-awareness' (1994: 104). The aim of the example is to demonstrate that only the first grade of apparent presence in the world is required for satisfaction of the objectivity condition, but it makes no sense to suppose that the experience of someone who has *never* had a sense of herself as a bodily presence in the world could present itself as experience of a world of physical objects. So the example is either incoherent or relatively insignificant. It is incoherent if it is supposed to be one in which the subject has always been body blind, and it is relatively insignificant in the context of (C2) if it assumes a history of normal bodily awareness in which the subject has, until now, always been intuitively aware of herself as a physical object among physical objects.

Why should it be supposed that someone who has never been intuitively aware of herself as a bodily presence in the world could not see the world as a world of physical objects? According to what might be called the Concept Acquisition Argument, in order to see the world as a world of physical objects one must have the *concept* of a physical object. To have the concept of a physical object is, among other things, to be able to think of perceived objects as solid, and the concept of solidity can only

---

[40] There is a moving and fascinating account of an actual case of (partial) body blindness in Cole 1991.

be acquired by tactile contact with other solid objects. So someone who has always been body blind could not have acquired the conceptual resources necessary for her to be able to see objects as physical objects.

On the face of it, there is very little to be said for this argument. In the first place, it is based upon a conceptualist view of perception, and it would be surprising if the crux of the intuition version of the Objectivity Argument turned out to be the thesis that perceptual content is conceptual. Secondly, and more importantly, the Concept Acquisition Argument is, like all acquisition arguments, vulnerable to the reply that the concept under consideration might be innate or, less radically, that the proposed route is only one among a range of possible routes to the acquisition of the concept of a physical object. If the possibility that someone without a sense of touch could have acquired the concept of a physical object in some other way cannot be ruled out with any confidence, then the Concept Acquisition Argument is, to say the least, inconclusive.

A variation on the Concept Acquisition Argument is the Acquired Ability Argument, which is suggested by the views of Berkeley and Kant on the nature of spatial perception. In an interesting passage in his *Anthropology from a Pragmatic Point of View*, Kant seems to suggest that a sense of touch is required for the perception of shape (1974: 33–4). Since tactile perception requires bodily awareness, Kant concludes in his *Opus Postumum* that spatial perception must be mediated by 'tactile awareness of one's own body, as to its three dimensions' (1993: 94). As Gary Hatfield points out, Kant's *Anthropology* account of shape-perception expresses a commitment to the Berkeleyan thesis that 'the construction of three-dimensional percepts in vision is an acquired ability' (Hatfield 1990: 105). For Berkeley, distance is not immediately perceived by sight, and the acquisition of the ability to see objects in depth depends upon one's possession of a sense of touch (Berkeley 1975: 21). Thus, Kant's claim that sense of touch is required for the perception of shape is the claim that a sense of touch is required for the perception of *solid* shape.

This account of spatial perception suggests the following response to the possibility of body blindness on behalf of (C2): if the experiences of the body blind subject are to present themselves as experiences of physical objects, she must have the ability to see objects as possessors of solid shape. The acquisition of this ability depends upon one's possession of a sense of touch and therefore upon one's having once had a sense of the solidity of the bodily subject of tactile perception. So if the body blind subject is assumed *never* to have had a sense of touch, then it makes no sense to suppose that she has the ability to see objects as physical objects.

Unlike the Concept Acquisition Argument, this argument does not assume that in order to see something as a physical object one must have the *concept* of a physical object; all it requires is the thesis that the body blind subject must have acquired the *ability* to see objects in depth, together with the claim that she could not have acquired this ability without her bodily presence in the world having been borne in on her at some point in her life.

While the Acquired Ability Argument is an improvement on the Concept Acquisition Argument, it faces a very similar objection. In the first place, it is certainly not obvious that the ability to see objects in three dimensions is acquired rather than an innate.[41] Secondly, even if it is in fact an acquired ability, there seems no reason in principle why it could not be innate. As long as this possibility cannot be excluded, there is no incoherence in the supposition that someone who has never been intuitively aware of herself as a bodily presence in the world might have the (innate) ability to see the world as a world of physical objects. This will come as no surprise to those who recognized at the outset that reflection on what is involved in the acquisition of a given concept or ability was never likely to provide one with the right kind of basis for a transcendental argument, for questions about acquisition are, unlike the questions with which transcendental arguments are concerned, largely empirical questions.

A third response to the problem of body blindness would be to point to an epistemological difficulty which faces the body blind subject. The problem is this: it makes sense to suppose the 'objects' which she sees are not physical objects but perfect holograms of physical objects. These holograms may be visually indistinguishable from physical objects, and their behaviour may mimic the behaviour of physical objects. For example, they appear to change shape or to repel others when they come into 'contact'.[42] In Joske's terminology, such 'objects' are not impenetrable but 'apenetrable' (Joske 1967: 19). As long as the body blind subject does not come into bodily contact with the objects which she sees, she can never be certain that they are impenetrable and not just apenetrable. This explains the importance of tactile and bodily awareness; it is required for *knowledge* that the perceived world is a world of impenetrable physical objects. This might be described as the Knowledge Argument for (C2).[43]

[41] See Carruthers 1992: 91–4 for further discussion of this issue.

[42] This example is due to Peacocke 1993: 174.

[43] The Knowledge Argument is suggested by the discussion in Joske 1967: 19–20, but Joske tends to confuse this argument with the Concept Acquisition Argument.

Even if the Knowledge Argument succeeds in identifying an episte-mological difficulty for the body blind subject, the significance of this difficulty in the context of (C2) is far from obvious. The fact that a sub-ject is unable to determine whether the objects she sees are impenetrable or merely apenetrable does not mean that she does not see them as solid physical objects. As far as the intuition version of the Objectivity Argument is concerned, the question is not whether the body blind sub-ject can know whether she is in perceptual contact with physical objects, but whether her perceptions can present themselves as perceptions of physical objects. Since these are quite separate questions, the Knowledge Argument is simply irrelevant.

While none of the three responses to the possibility of body blindness given so far has been convincing, there is undoubtedly something right about the suggestion that appealing to this possibility is not enough to vindicate the Dispensability Objection to (C2). An argument which attempts to combine the most promising aspects of the Concept Acquisition, Acquired Ability, and Knowledge Arguments is the follow-ing Content Argument: the starting-point for this argument is the prin-ciple that if a subject's experience is said to have a given representational content, there must be, as Peacocke puts it, 'an account which distin-guishes what is involved in the state's having that content rather than any other' (1989: 3). The significance of this 'Discrimination Principle' in the context of (C2) may be brought out by examining the suggestion that the body blind subject's visual experience is capable of representing objects as located in particular directions from her. According to the Discrimination Principle, it must be possible to give an account of what it is for her visual experience to have this spatial content.

It has already been remarked that a major part of the point of saying that someone sees something as being to her left rather than to her right is to explain why, if she desires the object, she would reach out in one particular direction rather than another. This suggests the following explanation of the connection between spatial perception and intuitive awareness of oneself as a physical object: to be capable of egocentric spa-tial perception, one must be capable of physical action. To be capable of physical action, one must be intuitively aware of how one's body is dis-posed in space; in other words, one must have a 'body-image'.[44] Finally,

---

[44] As O'Shaughnessy puts it, 'if an animal's body is to be actively employable then that animal must be such that at any point in time it incorporates a veridical body-image' (1980: i. 240). The short-term body-image is how one's body seems to one at a certain instant. To delineate the long-term body-image 'is to characterize the relatively unchanging body-

to be intuitively aware of how one's body is disposed in space is to be intuitively aware of oneself as a bodily presence in the world. According to this argument, examples such as Aquila's simply bring out the fact that egocentric spatial perception is compatible with a loss of short-term body-image, which is how one's body seems to one at a certain instant. But even in such cases, the long-term body–image persists, that is, a stable picture of one's own physical dimensions (cf. O'Shaughnessy 1980: i. 244).

In connection with the claim that the body blind subject can see things as solid or impenetrable, the Content Argument claims that the crucial question is not whether the subject can tell whether what she sees is impenetrable and not just apenetrable. Rather, what is needed is an account of why it is corrrect to say that her visual experiences represent objects in her environment as impenetrable rather than as merely apenetrable. Without such an account, we will not be entitled to say that her experience presents itself as experience of *physical* objects. What might such an account look like? Here one might appeal to the idea that someone who sees objects in her environment as impenetrable will be *surprised* if they offer no resistance to her own body when she comes into 'contact' with them (cf. Peacocke 1993: 174). In contrast, someone who sees things as apenetrable will not expect them to display any resistance to touch. This account of why it is correct to say that a subject sees objects as solid assumes that she is not completely lacking in a sense of her own embodiment. Thus, to imagine a subject who has *never* had a sense of herself as a bodily presence in the world is to imagine one whose perceptions cannot be said to be *as of* physical objects.

How convincing are these arguments? In connection with the first argument, it would be natural to object that the connections between egocentric spatial perception and action are surely not so tight as to exclude the possibility of someone paralysed from birth seeing things as being in specific directions from her. So while it may be plausible that the ability to act in the world requires possession of a body-image, it does not follow that someone born body blind would be incapable of egocentric visual perception. As for the account of the representation of solidity, consider the following possibility: suppose the permanently body blind subject has a theoretical grasp of the distinction between impenetrability and apenetrability. Even though she is not intuitively aware of

image without which the embodied self cannot be given to itself as determinately disposed in space' (p. 243).

herself as a physical object, she might still conceive of herself and the objects which she sees as impenetrable physical objects. So what makes it correct to say that she sees objects as impenetrable is simply the fact that this is how she herself finds it natural to describe her experience. If it is objected that a body blind subject could not have acquired a theoretical grasp of the distinction between impenetrability and apenetrability, then we are back with the Concept Acquisition Argument, which has already been shown to be inconclusive.

There are several things to be said about this response to the Content Argument. The first is that even if the permanently body blind subject believes that what she sees are physical objects—perhaps because she has been told that this is so—it does not follow that this belief is grounded in her experience of the world. As far as the Content Argument is concerned, the challenge is to give an account of what makes it the case that a subject sees objects in her environment as physical objects, and the fact that the subject describes her perceptions as perceptions of solid objects is surely not what it is for her perceptions to represent solid objects. The question is whether the subject's perceptions are so structured as to warrant conceptualization as perceptions of physical objects, and what warrants their conceptualization in these terms cannot be the fact that this is how the subject actually conceptualizes them.

Nevertheless, it would not be right simply to dismiss the intuition that the experiences of someone paralysed from birth and who has never been intuitively aware of herself as bodily presence in the world might still present themselves as experiences of physical objects. Moreover, there is no need for the Content Argument to be so dismissive. The natural way of accommodating such examples would be to point out that we think of them as involving disabled human beings or higher animals, and are prepared to attribute egocentric spatial content to their experiences because members of their kind typically have the ability to perceive the world as a world of physical objects and are typically aware of themselves as bodily presences in the world. To put it another way, even radical cases of body blindness are only intelligible as cases in which, say, an individual human subject has visual experiences of the same kind as other more fortunate human subjects.[45] This is in line with the requirements of the Content Argument, because when pressed to give an account of what makes it the case that the experiences of unimpaired human subjects present themselves as experiences of physical objects, the answer must draw upon pre-

---

[45] This is similar to Peacocke's proposal in 1989: 14.

cisely those connections between perception, action, and bodily aware-ness which were exploited by the original Content Argument.

What are the consequences of this modified Content Argument for the Dispensability Objection to (C2)? If this objection is understood as denying that for a given subject S to be 'in a position' to think of her experience as including perceptions of physical objects, S must be intu-itively aware of herself as a physical object, then it is not without justifi-cation. To this extent, the direct argument for (C2), like the argument for (C1), is not an unqualified success. On the other hand, just as the concept version of the Objectivity Argument succeeded in establishing a some-what looser but still important connection between a certain conceptual capacity and a certain belief, so the intuition version succeeds in estab-lishing a somewhat looser but still important connection between the conceptual capacity in question and intuitive awareness of the subject as a physical object. The Dispensability Objection leaves the fundamental insight of (C2) untouched because the possibility that a subject who is not intuitively aware of herself as a physical object might still be able to think of her experience as experience of a world of physical objects is only intelligible on the assumption that there are other subjects who *are* presented to themselves as physical objects. The fundamental insight is that satisfaction of the objectivity condition cannot in general be detached from apparent bodily presence in the world, and the fact that limited sense can be made of isolated cases of extreme body blindness is, on this reading of (C2), neither here nor there.

This might prompt the thought that there is a much more obvious objection to (C2) which does not need to draw upon the possibility of body blindness. Earlier, a distinction was drawn between three grades of apparent presence in the world, and the point of the body blindness example was to try to argue that satisfaction of the objectivity condition only requires the first grade of apparent presence in the world. Suppose that this version of the Dispensability Objection is deemed to be a fail-ure, for the reasons that have just been given. The more obvious objec-tion is that satisfaction of the objectivity condition only requires the second rather than the third grade of apparent presence in the world. The second grade involves intuitive awareness of oneself *qua* subject as 'having' a body but not intuitive awareness of oneself *qua* subject as a physical object. As long as one is aware of oneself as, in this sense, an *em*bodied subject, one can have a body-image, perceive objects in the world as standing in various spatial relations to one's body, and experi-ence the resistance which other solid objects offer to one's solid body.

But none of this amounts to intuitive awareness of oneself as a physical object in the sense that matters for (C2); it does not amount to the third grade of apparent presence in the world.

This Cartesian-sounding objection is less threatening than it appears at first sight. For while it is possible to understand how someone might believe that she 'has' a body without believing that the subject of her thoughts and perceptions is a physical object, it is not easy to understand what it would be to experience oneself as embodied in the Cartesian sense without also experiencing oneself *qua* subject as a physical object. As Descartes recognized, the distinction between the second and third grades of apparent presence is a distinction drawn at the level of thought or reflection rather than one that is simply given at the level of intuitive self-awareness. To be intuitively aware of oneself as embodied is not to be aware of oneself as 'in' one's body like a pilot is in a ship; it is to be aware of oneself as nothing less than a bodily *subject*. So the second grade of apparent presence in the world is not a stable halfway house between the first and third grade. If egocentric spatial perception requires a sense of one's embodiment, then it requires what was described above as the third grade of apparent presence in the world.

Before drawing this chapter to a close, there is one more question to address. Earlier, a distinction was drawn between direct and indirect versions of the intuition half of the Objectivity Argument. The recent discussion has been of the direct version, and it would strengthen the case for (C2) if the indirect version can also be shown to be plausible. It will be recalled that the indirect version assumes the correctness of (C1). The argument is then that if being in a position to think of one's experience as experience of physical objects requires the conception of oneself as a physical object, then, given the Kantian principle that concepts without intuitions are empty, it also requires intuitive awareness of oneself as a physical object. This need not be understood as amounting to the demand that one must at all times be intuitively aware of oneself as a physical object. Rather, it is the demand that for one's conception of oneself as a physical object to be a substantive conception, one must sometimes be presented to oneself as, in O'Shaughnessy's words, 'a determinately shaped, determinately sized, determinately hard-or-soft something' (1980: i. 244).

This argument will not persuade those who do not accept the concept version of the Objectivity Argument, but the central questions in the present context concern the use made by the indirect argument of principle that concepts without intuitions are empty. In the first place, it might be wondered precisely what it means to say that a conception of oneself as a physical object would lack substance in the absence of the appropriate intuitive backing. Secondly, the claim that a given thought would lack 'substance' in certain circumstances is presumably not the claim that the thought would be unavailable in those circumstances. In that case, why should the fact that a subject's conception of herself as a physical object is not a substantive conception matter from the perspective of (C1)? After all, (C1) simply demands a certain self-conception; it says nothing about the need for this self-conception to be intuitively grounded.

In connection with the first of these questions, it is difficult to explain the idea that concepts without intuitions are empty in terms of anything more basic, but there does appear to be something right about the idea that someone who has never been intuitively aware of herself as a physical object would have, at best, a seriously impoverished conception of herself as a physical object. A temporarily body blind subject may have a fully-fledged conception of herself as a physical object among physical objects, but this does not affect the main point of the indirect argument. As for the second question, it matters whether one's conception of oneself as a physical object is a substantive conception as long as it matters whether one's conception of one's experience as experience of an objective world is a substantive conception. It is not as if, having been persuaded of the correctness of (C1), one can reasonably ask whether the self-conception demanded by (C1) needs to be substantive. If the concept version of the Objectivity Argument has any force at all, it is because it brings out the extent to which being able to make proper sense of the idea that one's experience is of a world of physical objects involves being able to make proper sense of the idea that the subject of one's experience is a physical object. To be able to make 'proper sense' of the latter idea is not something different from having a 'substantive' conception of oneself as a corporeal object among corporeal objects. So if (C1) and the Kantian principle are both correct, then (C2) must also be correct.

11. *Conclusion*

The Objectivity Argument is a transcendental argument for materialism about self-consciousness; its concept version is a belief-directed transcendental argument and its intuition version is an intuition-directed transcendental argument. It has emerged that the connections established by the two versions of the Objectivity Argument are not as tight as might have been hoped for at the outset, for it is possible to make some sense of the possibility that a subject's experience might satisfy the objectivity condition even if she does not conceive of herself as a physical object or is not, at least for a time, intuitively aware of herself as a physical object. On the other hand, it has also emerged that our ability to think of our experiences as including perceptions of physical objects draws in many fundamental respects upon the conception of ourselves as physical objects and cannot be completely detached from intuitive awareness of ourselves as physical objects. To the extent that the Objectivity Argument establishes and explains these connections, it achieves as much as it is reasonable to expect from arguments of this form.

There is, however, one major issue on which the Objectivity Argument casts no light. It takes it for granted that self-conscious experience is experience which satisfies the objectivity condition but makes no attempt to explain why this should be so. As remarked at the outset, this may create the impression that the Objectivity Argument does not take certain forms of scepticism about the external world as seriously as they deserve to be taken. One response to this worry would be to argue that a self-conscious subject must be able to think of her experience as experience of a world of physical objects in order to satisfy a deeper requirement on self-consciousness which even a determined sceptic must accept. This deeper requirement is the requirement of unity of consciousness. Whereas the concept version of the Objectivity Argument claimed that objectivity requires unity of consciousness, the present suggestion is that it is also true that unity of consciousness requires satisfaction of the objectivity condition. In short, unity requires objectivity (URO). If this claim is defensible, the Objectivity Argument begs no questions against scepticism since even the most determined sceptic cannot coherently deny that self-consciousness requires unity of consciousness. The thesis that unity of consciousness requires objectivity is the central claim of the Unity Argument, to which the discussion must now turn.

3

THE UNITY ARGUMENT

1. *Unity and Objectivity*

The Objectivity Argument for materialism about self-consciousness
assumes that self-conscious experience must be such as to satisfy the
'objectivity condition'. For experience to satisfy this condition is for its
subject to be in a position to think of it as including perceptions of
objects in the weighty sense, that is, particular items which are capable of
being perceived and of existing unperceived. In Chapter 2, there was a
brief discussion of the suggestion that the Objectivity Argument is guilty
of taking too much for granted at the outset by assuming a connection
between self-consciousness and the objectivity condition. The aim of the
present chapter is to examine versions of what was described as the more
ambitious response to this suggestion. This response agrees that the connection between self-consciousness and satisfaction of the objectivity
condition is something which needs to be argued for and not just
assumed. It claims that the most basic notion of self-consciousness is one
according to which a self-conscious subject must at least be capable of
self-ascribing her experiences, and argues that there is a connection
between self-consciousness and the objectivity condition because being
in a position to think of one's experience as experience of 'weighty'
objects is a necessary condition of self-consciousness in the most basic
sense. This thesis forms the core of the Unity Argument.

   The two versions of the Unity Argument which will be the focus of
the present chapter are both due to Strawson (see Strawson 1966:
97–112). He claims that 'the condition under which diverse representations may be said to be united in a single consciousness is precisely the
condition, whatever that may be, under which a subject of experiences
may ascribe different experiences to himself, conscious of the identity of
that to which these different experiences, at different times, belong' (pp.
95–6). The central claim of the Unity Argument is that 'unity of diverse
experiences in a single consciousness requires experience of objects' (p.
98). In brief, unity requires objectivity (URO). Whether or not the Unity

Argument is, as Strawson suggests, Kant's argument in the Transcendental Deduction of the Categories, its importance is such as to make it worthy of detailed consideration in its own right.

Strawson's objectivity condition is stronger than the Objectivity Argument's objectivity condition. To say that unity of consciousness requires experience of objects is to say that it requires *knowledge* of objects in the weighty sense, not just the conception of experience as experience of 'weighty' objects. On the other hand, being in a position to conceive of one's experience as experience of an objective world is a necessary condition of experiential knowledge of such a world. So if unity requires objectivity in Strawson's sense, then it also requires objectivity in the Objectivity Argument's sense. Suppose, next, that the Objectivity Argument achieves what it sets out to achieve. The result of combining it with the Unity Argument would be a complex argument for the thesis that unity of consciousness requires awareness of oneself as a physical object.

The thesis that self-consciousness requires unity of consciousness in Strawson's sense is not uncontroversial. It might be objected, for example, that certain non-human animals are self-conscious despite the fact that they are incapable of self-ascribing their 'representations'. To begin with, however, it is simply to be taken as a premiss that self-consciousness requires unity of consciousness. Despite this element of stipulation, it remains plausible that the assumption that self-consciousness involves being able to self-ascribe representations is more austere than the assumption that it involves being able to think of representations as representations of independent objects. If the Unity Argument can derive the fundamental premiss of the Objectivity Argument from nothing more than the thought of what is required for the self-ascription of experiences, this would be a remarkable achievement.

An immediate complication is that Strawson proposes two different versions of the Unity Argument. One version turns on the notion of personal self-consciousness (PSC). Self-consciousness in this sense involves the fulfilment of the 'full conditions for ordinary empirical self-ascription of experiences' (1966: 107). These conditions are said to include 'the existence of the subject as an intuitable object in the world' (p. 106). Since, by Strawson's lights, it is also the case that 'the full conditions involve the objectivity-condition' (ibid.), this suggests that the Unity Argument is an argument from personal self-consciousness to objectivity. To put it succinctly, self-consciousness requires unity of consciousness; unity of consciousness requires the ability to self-ascribe experiences,

and the satisfaction of the full conditions of the possibility of self-ascription of experiences, which is constitutive of personal self-consciousness,
requires experience of objects. This argument, which will be referred to
as the PSC version of the Unity Argument will be discussed later in this
chapter and in Chapter 4. The other version of the Unity Argument
turns on the notion of *transcendental* self-consciousness (TSC). This version will be the focus of the next section.

2. *Transcendental Self-Consciousness*

According to the TSC version of the Unity Argument, what underlies
the objectivity condition is 'something less than, though entailed by the
full conditions of the possibility of empirical self-ascription of experiences' (Strawson 1966: 107). This 'lesser thing' (Strawson 1995: 416) is
transcendental self-consciousness or the necessary self-reflexiveness of
experience:

What is meant by the necessary self-reflexiveness of a possible experience in general could otherwise be expressed by saying that experience must be such as to
provide room for the thought of experience itself. It provides room, on the one
hand, for 'Thus and so is how things objectively are' and, on the other, for 'This
is how things are experienced as being'; and it provides room for the second
thought *because* it provides room for the first. (Strawson 1966: 107)

Strawson's suggestion is that transcendental self-consciousness is the
essential core of personal self-consciousness. The fulfilment of the objectivity condition is not sufficient on its own to provide for the empirical
self-ascription of experiences, and so is not introduced *as* making personal self-consciousness possible. On the other hand, it *is* introduced as
making possible a form of consciousness which is necessary but not sufficient for personal self-consciousness.

   There are two crucial steps in the TSC version of the Unity Argument. The first is the derivation of the notion of transcendental self-consciousness from that of personal self-consciousness. The second consists
of the transition from the requirement of transcendental self-consciousness to the objectivity condition. These steps are explained as follows:

For 'This is how things are (have been) experienced *by me* as being' [PSC] presupposes 'This is how things are (have been) *experienced* as being' [TSC]; and the
latter in turn presupposes a distinction, though not (usually) an opposition

between 'This is how things are experienced as being' and 'Thus and so is how things are'. (Strawson 1966: 108)

The first step of this argument will not be in question for the moment, but the second step is very much open to dispute. Surprisingly little is said in defence of this transition. At one point, Strawson suggests that all experience involves the recognition of particular items as falling under concepts, that is, a 'component of recognition' (p. 100) which is distinct from the item recognized. The necessity of providing room in experience for the thought of experience itself is claimed to be identical with the necessity of saving the recognitional component in an experience from 'absorption' (p. 110) into the item recognized, but this does not explain why the self-reflexiveness of experience requires experience of objects in the 'weighty' sense.

The most natural way of reading the argument would be to see it as claiming that the ability to think of experience *as* experience requires possession of the concept of 'experience', and that this in turn requires one to have the conception of objects or states of affairs which are capable of being experienced and of existing unexperienced. Even this much is not obvious, but in any case it does not appear to follow from the fact that one has this conception that one's experience must actually be of objects in the weighty sense or even that one must believe that it is experience of such objects. There are, in fact, at least three senses in which 'objectivity' might be thought to be a necessary condition of transcendental self-consciousness. The strongest objectivity requirement, and the one which the argument purports to establish, states that self-reflexive experience must actually be of independent objects. A more modest requirement is that self-reflexive experience must be believed by its subject to be experience of objects in the weighty sense. Finally, the weakest objectivity requirement merely states that self-reflexive experience must at least be such that its subject is, as Evans puts it, 'able to understand the hypothesis, even if, in fact, he never believes it to be the case, that the phenomena of which he has experience should occur unperceived' (1980: 88). In other words, the idea of experience of objects in the weighty sense must at least be one which the subject finds *intelligible*. On the face of it, it is this last requirement which is supported by the most natural reading of the TSC version of the Unity Argument.

If the TSC version of the Unity Argument is only able to establish the weakest objectivity requirement, what would be the significance of this? Given that Strawson's argument is intended as an anti-sceptical argument, it would have to be concluded that it fails of its purpose.[1] For the purposes of refuting scepticism about the external world, nothing short of a successful argument for the strongest objectivity requirement will do. On the other hand, if the aim of the Unity Argument is to provide a foundation for the fundamental premiss of the Objectivity Argument, then the picture is rather different. It was remarked in Chapter 2 that being 'in a position' to think of one's experience as experience of objects involves two things. Firstly, one must have the conceptual resources to make sense of the idea of experience of objects which are capable of existence unperceived. Secondly, one's experience must *present* itself as experience of objects in this sense. The first of these conditions is equivalent to the weakest objectivity requirement. To the extent, therefore, that the TSC version of the Unity Argument establishes that satisfaction of the weakest objectivity requirement is a necessary condition of transcendental self-consciousness, it provides direct support for at least one element of the Objectivity Argument's initial conception of self-conscious experience. In this context, the failure of the Unity Argument as an anti-sceptical argument is of relatively little importance.

It might be wondered, however, whether the TSC version of the Unity Argument succeeds even as a defence of the weakest objectivity requirement. One question, which will be discussed in due course, is whether it is plausible that self-conscious experience must be such as to provide room for the thought of experience itself. The immediate question is this: granted that self-conscious experience must be self-reflexive, why is grasp of the idea of experience of objects in the weighty sense a necessary condition of being able to think of experience as experience? It might be tempting to respond to this question as follows: our perceptual experience is thoroughly 'permeated' with concepts of experience-independent objects, in the sense that the employment of such concepts is indispensable for the purposes of giving a veridical characterization of the representational content of experience.[2] Since experience presents itself as experience of independent objects, it follows that in order to think of one's experience as experience one must grasp precisely those concepts with which it is, in this sense, 'permeated'.

There is nothing wrong with this argument if one is prepared to accept the assumption that the experience which is to be thought of as

---

[1] As Strawson concedes in 1995: 416.
[2] This point is developed in Strawson 1988: 94–9.

experience presents itself as experience of independent objects. The difficulty is that it is not clear that this is an assumption to which the Unity
Argument is entitled. To the extent that the point of this argument is to
provide a basis for the fundamental premiss of the Objectivity Argument,
what is needed is a defence of the weak objectivity condition on self-
reflexiveness which does not presuppose that our perceptual experience
is permeated with concepts of objects in the weighty sense. This may be
brought out by examining what Strawson calls 'the hypothesis of a purely sense-datum experience' (1966: 100). This is the hypothesis of a subject or 'consciousness' whose experience is and presents itself as being of
'a succession of items such that there was no distinction to be drawn
between the order and arrangement of the objects (and of their particular features and characteristics) and the order and arrangement of the
subject's experiences of awareness of them' (pp. 98–9). The 'objects' of a
purely sense-datum experience are 'subjective objects',[3] objects which
cannot exist unperceived. The suggestion is not that our experience is
actually a purely sense-datum experience, only that a possible experience
might have this limited character.

The relevance of Strawson's hypothesis is this: *ex hypothesi*, a purely
sense-datum experience would not present itself as being experience of
objects in the weighty sense. It is also plausible that the subject of a purely sense-datum experience would not be able to understand the notion
that the phenomena of which she has experience should occur unperceived. It follows that Strawson's sense-datum subject does not satisfy
the weak objectivity requirement. So the question which now arises is
whether it would still be possible for such a subject to think of her experience as experience. Unless it can be shown that this would not be possible, the TSC version of the Unity Argument has failed to establish that
transcendental self-consciousness is subject to the weak objectivity
requirement.

One reason for thinking that it would be possible in principle for a
purely sense-datum experience to provide room for the thought of experience itself is this: on the assumption that a purely sense-datum experience is, and presents itself as being, experience of subjective rather than
'weighty' or 'objective' objects, its subject can still be transcendentally
self-conscious as long as she grasps those concepts of subjective objects
with which *her* experience is 'permeated'. Since the subjective 'objects'

---

[3] This way of putting things is taken from Allison 1983: 261–2.

of a purely sense-datum experience include, in Strawson's words, 'red, round patches, brown oblongs, flashes, whistles, tickling sensation, smells' (1966: 99), these are the 'objects', concepts of which must be exercised by the sense-datum subject in thinking of her experience as experience.

What is it to be able to think of subjective 'objects' of experience as subjective objects? On one view, grasp of concepts of subjective objects is wholly independent of grasp of the concept of experience of objects in the weighty sense. This may be referred to as the *independence thesis*. If this thesis is correct, there is no incoherence in the idea of the subject of a purely sense-datum experience being able to think of his experience as experience of subjective objects, such as flashes, whistles, and so on, despite the fact that he does not meet the weak objectivity requirement. On the face of it, such a subject would still be transcendentally self-conscious, so transcendental self-consciousness is not subject to the weak objectivity requirement.

Support for the independence thesis is provided by Hume's discussion of the origins of the belief in the continued and distinct existence of objects. Hume's starting-point is the familiar empiricist assumption that the immediate objects of perceptual awareness are subjective objects. He thought that there is little room for argument over the claim that nothing is ever really present to the mind but its perceptions or impressions. He also held that the contents of the mind are, as it were, ontologically transparent. This is the thesis that 'since all notions and sensations of the mind are known to us by consciousness, they must necessarily appear in every particular what they are and be what they appear. Everything that enters the mind being in reality a perception, 'tis impossible that anything should to *feeling* appear different' (1978: 190). In other words, not only is it the case that everything that enters the mind is in fact a perception, it is also being claimed that the perceptions which enter the mind present themselves as perceptions, as 'internal' existences. As Hume puts it in a discussion of internal and external impressions, 'whatever other differences we observe among them, they appear all of them, in their true colours, as impressions or perceptions' (p. 190). This suggests the following way of explaining the failure of the Unity Argument for the weak objectivity condition: if the subjective objects of experience are, as Hume asserts, transparently subjective, then, just as the independence thesis suggests, there is no reason to suppose that the ability to think of experience as experience of subjective objects depends upon an ability to grasp

the idea of experience of objective objects. Once again, the moral appears
to be that transcendental self-consciousness is not subject to the weak
objectivity requirement.

A quick response to this 'sense-datum objection' would be to argue
that the hypothesis of a purely sense-datum experience cannot pose a
threat to the Unity Argument, since this hypothesis is thoroughly confused. It assumes that there is a parallel between experience as of objects
in the weighty sense and experience as of subjective 'objects', but this
assumption is based upon what has been called the 'sense-datum fallacy'.
This is the fallacy of assuming that when, say, a subject seems to see
something red, there is a red 'seeming' or sense-datum with which she is
'acquainted'. The core of the fallacy consists in the treatment of this
'seeming' as an entity in its own right. This is the so-called 'act-object'
conception of sensory experience.[4] With this conception in place, it can
then seem that there is a genuine question about what is involved in
thinking of the subjective objects of experience as the subjective 'entities' that they are. The problem with all of this, however, is that talk of a
subject perceiving a red sense-datum is simply a different way of saying
that the subject is 'sensing redly'; it tells us *how* the subject is sensing'
(Chisholm 1994: 103). So-called 'seemings' are, as it were, simply the
'accusatives' of statements of this form; strictly speaking, they are not
'objects' in their own right, not even 'subjective objects'. So talk of experience being permeated by concepts of 'subjective objects' is simply incoherent.

This is familiar territory, and Strawson himself appears to have something like the quick response in mind in his own repeated characteriza-
tions of the 'objects' of a purely sense-datum experience as 'accusatives'.[5]
On the other hand, the quick response to the sense-datum hypothesis is
not one which he ultimately presses. This is hardly surprising, since the
Unity Argument is a transcendental argument which does not simply
reiterate familiar points from the philosophy of perception. The suggestion seems to be that the Unity Argument is prepared to take on the
sense-datum hypothesis on its own terms and show that it is still unable
to account for the possibility of self-consciousness. Thus, in order to
uncover the distinctive contribution of the TSC version of the Unity
Argument, it will be necessary to make the following simplifying assumption: the sense-datum hypothesis is within its rights to describe a purely

---

[4] See Shoemaker 1994b for a discussion of this conception of experience in relation to
Hume's account of introspection.

[5] See, for example, Strawson 1966: 98.

sense-datum experience as experience of 'subjective objects' which are, so to speak, entities in their own right. The simplifying assumption, in other words, is that the 'act-object' conception of sensory experience is correct. Later it will emerge that the dropping of this assumption threatens not only the sense-datum hypothesis but also Strawson's own notion of transcendental self-consciousness. To begin with, however, the question is whether the TSC version of the Unity Argument can resist the sense-datum objection without resorting straight away to the quick response.

The most promising line of defence for the Unity Argument would be this: suppose that the act-object conception of sensation is correct and that the subject of a purely sense-datum experience does indeed stand in some form of acquaintance relation with 'subjective objects'. The TSC version of the Unity Argument still goes through because it makes no sense to suppose that someone would be able to grasp concepts of the so-called subjective 'objects' of experience without also having the resources to understand what it would be to experience objects in the weighty sense. This may be referred to as the Unity Argument's *dependence thesis*. If this thesis is correct, and the pure sense-datum experiencer is thought of as one who simply has no conception of experience of 'objective' objects, objects in the weighty sense, then it follows that he cannot think of his experience as experience of 'subjective' objects either. In that case, it is difficult to see how his experience can be said to provide room for the thought of experience itself.

In defence of the dependence thesis, it might be observed that it is a familiar point that if one is to think of one's perceptions as perceptions of objective objects, one must think of one's perceptual experience as subject to enabling conditions. As Evans remarks, 'the idea of existence unperceived, or rather, the idea of existence now perceived, now unperceived, is not an idea that can stand on its own, without any surrounding theory' (1980: 88). In contrast, it is often supposed that the idea of experience of subjective objects requires little or no theoretical support. Following Hume, the assumption seems to be that if one's experience were of the pure sense-datum variety, the ontological transparency of 'seemings' or Humean 'perceptions' would mean that one would be able to think of one's experience *as* experience of such subjective objects without any surrounding theory. This is the assumption which the dependence thesis calls into question. According to this thesis, the concept of a purely subjective object only makes sense in a limited range of conceptual contexts. In a purely sense-datum experience which does not meet the weakest objectivity condition, the appropriate theoretical support for the concept of a 'seeming' would be unavailable. Hence, the pure sense-datum subject would lack the conceptual resources to think of experience as experience, even as experience of subjective objects.

What is the conceptual framework required to sustain the concept of a 'seeming'? According to the Unity Argument, the framework must be one in which there is a contrast between 'This is how things seem' and 'Thus and so is how things objectively are'. As Strawson puts it, in a case in which one objective judgement is corrected by another, 'what remains unaltered when the correction is made is the subjective experience, the "seeming"' (1966: 106). This is the force of the dependence thesis. To describe a purely sense-datum experience as one which does not meet the weakest objectivity requirement is, in effect, to describe it as one in which there is no conceptual space for a contrast between 'This is how things seem' and 'This is how things objectively are'. In the absence of a contrast along these lines, there would be no basis for the concept of a seeming, and so no possibility of thinking of experience as experience of subjective objects. The claim, then, is that once it is understood that the concept of a 'seeming' is not one that can stand on its own, reflection on the nature of the theory required to sustain this concept makes it apparent that the hypothesis of a purely sense-datum experience is no threat to the Unity Argument for the weak objectivity requirement.

Since this argument is based upon the simplifying assumption that the act-object conception is correct, it might be wondered what the consequences would be of dropping this assumption. On the face of it, the main consequence would be to make life even easier for the Unity Argument. Suppose that no reference is made either to the possibility that experience *might* present itself as experience of subjective objects or to the idea that it *does* present itself as, by and large, experience of objects in the weighty sense. The fact remains that self-conscious experience must still be self-reflexive. In other words, a transcendentally self-conscious subject must still be capable of grasping thoughts of the form 'This is how things are *experienced* as being', and so must have the concept of 'experience'. Just as the concept of a subjective object is not one which can stand on its own, so the concept of 'experience' cannot stand on its own. Just as the contrast required for grasp of the concept of a subjective object is that between 'This is how things seem' and 'This is how things objectively are', so a modified dependence thesis suggests that the contrast required for grasp of the thought 'This is how things are *experienced* as being' is one between 'This is how things are *experienced* as being' and 'Thus and so is how things objectively are'. Since someone who understands this contrast is, in effect, someone who meets the weak objectivity requirement, this vindicates the claim that transcendental self-consciousness is subject to this requirement.

There are two major objections to this argument to consider. The first is to its reading of the self-reflexiveness requirement on self-conscious-ness. The second is to the dependence thesis, in either its original or modified form. Consider, once again, the hypothesis of a purely sense-datum experience, on the assumption that its act-object conception of sensation is correct. It might be objected that even if the 'objects' of such an experience are in fact subjective objects, it is not clear why the subject of a pure sense-datum subject needs to grasp the *concept* of a 'subjective object' in order to count as self-conscious. Suppose, next, that the sim-plifying assumption is given up. It might still be objected that the claim that a self-conscious subject must have the concept of 'experience' in her conceptual repertoire is no more plausible than that she must have the concept of a 'seeming' in her repertoire. In Harrison's terminology, some-one who lacks such concepts 'would not be able to do the philosophy of his own situation' (1970: 219), but this does not appear to be the same thing as the subject not being 'self-conscious'.

This important objection invites the following reply: the Unity Argument stipulates that a self-conscious subject must be capable of grasping self-ascriptive judgements of the form 'This is how things are *experienced* by me as being'. Since the concept of 'experience' figures explicitly in judgements of this form, it follows straightforwardly that the concept of 'experience' must be grasped by a subject who is to count as self-conscious. So if having the concept of 'experience' in one's reper-toire is being able to 'do the philosophy of her own situation', then being able to do this is indeed a necessary condition of self-consciousness. It is, of course, a further question what grasp of the concept of 'experience' involves; in particular, it is a further question whether it would follow, from the thought that the objects of a purely sense-datum experience are 'seemings', that thinking of a purely sense-datum experience as experi-ence would require a grasp of the concept of a 'seeming'. The important point, however, is that like Kant's argument in the Transcendental Deduction of the Categories, the Unity Argument rejects a blanket dis-tinction between the perspective of self-consciousness itself and that of the philosopher of self-consciousness.[6] The same point emerges in con-nection with the suggestion that a pure sense-datum experiencer need

---

[6] This aspect of Kant's argument is emphasized in Henrich 1989: 253.

not be in a position to employ the concept of a 'subject of experience'. By Harrison's lights, this is another example of a concept which need only be employed in doing the philosophy of one's own situation. Once again, the Unity Argument will object that someone who lacks this concept will not be in a position to grasp judgements of the form 'This is how things are experienced by me as being', and so cannot be self-conscious in the sense demanded by the Unity Argument.

To a certain extent, this defence of the self-reflexiveness requirement does not really advance matters. It stipulates that a self-conscious subject must be capable of self-ascribing representations in the form of judgements which employ the concepts of 'experience' and 'subject of experience', but is this not precisely what is in dispute? In order to make any progress with this issue, more needs to be said about the basis of the Unity Argument's self-ascription requirement on self-consciousness. So far it has been presented as a matter of stipulation that self-conscious experience involves being able to self-ascribe representations, but this does not do justice to Strawson's own account of the self-ascription requirement. His position is that the ultimate foundation of this requirement is the Kantian idea that experience, properly so called, requires both particular intuitions and general concepts. It remains to be seen what this amounts to, but perhaps it will become clearer *why* self-consciousness involves being able to think thoughts of the form 'This is how things are experienced by me as being' once this deeper foundation has been explained.

Kant's idea is, in Strawson's words, that 'there can be no experience at all which does not involve the recognition of particular items *as* being of such and such a general kind' (Strawson 1966: 100). The recognition of particular items as being of such and such a general kind is only possible 'because of the *possibility* of referring different experiences to one identical subject of them all' (p. 101). This suggests the following thesis in support of the Unity Argument's reading of the self-reflexiveness requirement: a self-conscious subject must employ concepts such as that of 'experience' in self-ascribing representations because the employment of such concepts is a necessary condition of the bringing of one's experiences under concepts. In other words, self-conscious experience must be self-reflexive in the specific sense demanded by the Unity Argument because there is no such thing as unconceptualizable *experience*, and only experience which is self-reflexive in this sense can be brought under concepts.

This line of argument might prompt the objection that it is one thing to say that all experience involves the recognition of particular items as falling under concepts, but it is not clear what this has to do with the possibility of *self-ascribing* experiences. In particular, it has yet to be explained why the conceptualization of experience requires the employment of concepts such as that of 'experience' or 'subject of experience'. As Harrison remarks in connection with the question of whether a pure sense-datum subject would be capable of bringing his experiences under concepts:

> All that is necessary for this is that the experiencer should be able to distinguish qualitatively between his experiences. He must, that is, be able to use judgements which contain general (or descriptive) parts and particular (or referential) parts . . . He must be able to use, that is, concepts such as 'redness' or 'loudness', but it is not necessary that he should be able to use concepts such as 'subject of experience' . . . For we would be perfectly satisfied if such an experiencer could describe his experiences, even if he were perfectly incapable of classifying them as 'experiences' or saying that they were 'his'. (1970: 219–20)

To summarize: it may be true that the experiences of a pure sense-datum subject must be conceptualized or conceptualizable, but the conceptualization of experiences need not involve the exercise of concepts such as that of an 'experience'. So it does not follow from the Kantian duality of intuitions and concepts that experience must be such as to provide room for the thought of experience itself. Even if, as the dependence thesis implies, a purely sense-datum experience would leave no room for this thought, it would still be *experience*.

Defenders of the TSC version of the Unity Argument might be tempted to dismiss this objection on the grounds that it fails to explain in what sense someone who cannot even think of experiences as 'his' or 'hers' could still be *self*-conscious. It needs to be recalled, however, that as far as the TSC argument is concerned, what is supposed to be doing the work in the argument for the weak objectivity requirement is reflection on what is involved in thinking of experience as *experience* rather than reflection on what is involved in thinking of experience as one's *own* experience. So the important question in this context remains whether the employment of the concept of 'experience' or of a 'seeming' can be dispensed with in the recognition of particular items as falling under general concepts. The present objection is that this presents no difficulties, and that even the subject of a purely sense-datum experience would be able to refer to a subjective state and judge 'This is F'. Would this not be a case in which the subject has succeeded in 'conceptualizing' a subjective object even if she is incapable of thinking of it, or any other subjective object, *as* a subjective object? The judgement has a descriptive and a referential part but is not 'self-reflexive'.

A telling response to this line of argument would be to point out that it relies upon a wholly inadequate conception of what is involved in demonstrative reference to so-called subjective objects. In order to understand the demonstrative reference in the judgement 'This is F', one must know *which* object the judgement is about.[7] This 'knowing which' requirement applies both in the case in which the demonstrated object is a sensation and the case in which it is a physical object. It might also be held that knowledge of *which* thing a judgement is about presupposes knowledge of the *kind* of thing it is. Suppose that this 'knowing what' requirement is applied to the case described by Harrison. If the subjective state referred to by the sense-datum subject is, say, a pain, then the force of the judgement 'This is F' would have to be something along the lines of 'This pain is F'. To paraphrase Wittgenstein, the emphatic stressing of the word 'this' in the presence of pain does not mean that one has succeeded in latching on to a particular sensation in thought unless one knows the category of the thing referred to (cf. Wittgenstein 1978: § 253). Since pains are subjective states or 'seemings', this means that in order to satisfy the 'knowing what' requirement on demonstrative reference to subjective objects, the subject must be capable of grasping the essentially subjective status of the 'object' referred to. So the concept of a seeming cannot be completely absent from the subject's conceptual repertoire even if the bringing of sensations under concepts does not require its explicit employment.

This argument suggests that Harrison's criticism of the self-reflexiveness condition does not ultimately run very deep. The issue is not whether a self-conscious subject must actually 'describe' experiences as 'experiences' when she brings them under concepts, but whether her judgements must be, as it were, informed by a grasp of their subjective status. If they are not so informed, then there would no longer be any basis for regarding the words 'This is F' as expressive of what Kant called a 'judgement of perception', one in which something is predicated of a subjective object.[8] This is the sense in which experience, understood as

---

[7] This is an application of what Evans calls 'Russell's Principle', according to which 'a subject cannot make a judgement about something unless he knows which object his judgement is about' (Evans 1982: 91).

[8] Kant defines judgements of perception as empirical judgements 'which are only subjectively valid' (1977: 298). They merely express 'a reference of our perception to a subject' rather than a quality of the object.

conforming to the duality of intuitions and concepts, must be such as to provide room for the thought of experience itself. So if, as the dependence thesis claims, the subjective status of, say, a pain, can only be grasped against a background in which it is understood that experiences *might* be of objects in the weighty sense, the important question is whether the latter conception is capable of being grasped by the subject of a purely sense-datum experience. On the assumption that someone whose experience has never presented itself as experience of objective objects would find it impossible to make sense of the idea of experience of such objects, the upshot is that a purely sense-datum 'experience' would not really be experience. This suggests that transcendental self-consciousness requires both that the subject meet the weak objectivity condition and that at least some of her experiences present themselves as experiences of objects which are capable of existence unperceived. In the terminology of Chapter 2, someone who meets both of these closely related conditions is 'in a position' to think of his experience as experience of an objective world. Thus, the TSC version of the Unity Argument leads to the premiss of the Objectivity Argument.

This summary serves to emphasize two important points. The first is the similarity between the TSC version of the Unity Argument and Wittgenstein's 'private language argument'. This similarity is a reflection of the fact that both arguments have a common root in Kant's conception of experience. The second is the importance of establishing the plausibility or otherwise of the dependence thesis. In connection with the second of these points, it is not enough for the TSC version of the Unity Argument to point out that the idea of a subjective object is not one that can stand on its own, in the absence of a surrounding theory. Nor is it enough for it to assert that what is required for grasp of the concept of a 'seeming' is grasp of a contrast between 'This is how things seem' and 'This is how things objectively are'. For it might be argued that one has the concept of a 'seeming' as long as one understands what it would be for a judgement of perception to be mistaken, and that the possibility of error has been provided for as long as one is capable of recognizing patterns in one's experience. Since even a purely sense-datum experience can display complex patterns, the dependence thesis faces the objection that a theory which sustains the idea of a subjective object need not be one which leaves any conceptual space for the notion of experience of objects in the weighty sense.

In order to protect the dependence thesis against this line of attack, more needs to be said about the nature of 'subjective objects', including 'seemings'. Strawson once wrote that states of consciousness or experiences '*owe* their identity as particulars to the person whose states or experiences they are' (1959: 97). Suppose that Strawson is right about this. This suggests the following argument for the dependence thesis: since experiences owe their identity as particulars to the person whose experiences they are, knowledge of the thing referred to in a judgement of perception requires the conception of the subjective object of reference *as* a modification of the person whose experience it is. As Evans puts it:

A subject can gaze inwardly with all the intensity he can muster, and repeat to himself 'this pain', 'this pain', as he concentrates upon his pain, but he will not thereby be able to know which pain is in question unless this provides him with a basis for identifying the pain with a pain conceived of as an element in the objective order—which means a pain conceived of as the pain of this or that person in the objective order. (1982: 253)

In other words, grasp of the concept of 'pain' in the judgement 'This pain is F' requires the conception of the subjective object of reference as 'belonging' to an objective object, a person. Since persons must be conceived of as perceivable and as objects in the weighty sense, the thought that a particular experience belongs to a particular person brings with it the idea that the world in which the experience is an occurrence is also a world which contains objects which are capable of being perceived and of existing unperceived. There is room in experience for the thought of subjective objects of experience because, and only because, there is room in experience for the thought of the objective subjects of experience. This is the sense in which, just as the dependence thesis maintains, the ability to think of subjective objects as subjective objects cannot be detached from an ability to make sense of the possibility that at least some objects of experience are not subjective.

One interesting consequence of this argument is that it calls into question the simplifying assumption that the critic of the Unity Argument is entitled to the act-object conception of sensory experience. To describe subjective objects as essentially 'modifications' of persons is, in effect, to deny that they are 'entities' in their own right. Once it is understood that so-called 'experiences' are in fact experiencings, and that, as Shoemaker puts it, 'an experiencing is something whose existence is "adjectival on" a subject of experience' (1994b: 125), it should also be understood that 'experiences' are singularly ill-suited for being 'the primary non-factual objects of a mode of perception'. Since the act-object conception is committed to regarding 'experiences' as 'non-factual' objects of a form of perceptual or quasi-perceptual acquaintance, recognition of this point amounts to the abandonment of the act-object conception.

It might seem that the TSC version of the Unity Argument ought to welcome these criticisms of the act-object conception, since they diminish the threat posed by the hypothesis of a purely sense-datum experience. On further reflection, however, it appear that they also undermine the very idea of 'transcendental' self-consciousness in Strawson's sense. It has already been remarked that this notion is supposed to be an abstraction from that of personal self-consciousness. To be personally self-conscious is to be capable of thinking of experiences not just as experiences but as one's own experiences. In personal self-consciousness, the subject of one's experiences must be thought of not just as a 'formal' or 'logical' subject but as an object among others in the world (cf. Strawson 1966: 102–3). To suppose that transcendental self-consciousness can be abstracted from personal self-consciousness is therefore to suppose that the thought of experiences as experiences is intelligible independently of the thought that they belong to a subject who is an object among others in the world. This 'independent intelligibility' thesis is, however, precisely what Strawson's own conception of the identity of experiences appears to call into question. If experiences owe their identity as particulars to the person whose states or experiences they are, and persons must be conceived of as elements in the objective order, then it is difficult to see how the 'independent intelligibility' thesis can be correct. If the concept of transcendental self-consciousness cannot ultimately be detached from that of personal self-consciousness, then the TSC version of the Unity Argument is in danger of collapsing into the PSC version.

There is support for this assessment in the most recent argument for the dependence thesis. The key to that argument was the claim that there is room in experience for the thought of subjective objects of experience because there is room in experience for the thought of the objective subjects of experience, but the latter thought is part and parcel of personal self-consciousness. Just as according to the PSC version of the Unity Argument, the fulfilment of the full conditions for the empirical self-ascription of experiences, including the existence of the subject as an object among others in the world, involves the objectivity condition, so in the latest TSC version of the Unity Argument, the dependence thesis emerged as a consequence of a certain conception of the nature of subjects of experience. Yet it has already been remarked that as far as the TSC argument is concerned, what is supposed to be doing the work in the argument for the weak objectivity requirement is reflection on what is involved in thinking of experiences as experiences rather than reflection on what is involved in thinking of experiences belonging to a subject. Thus, the independent viability of the TSC version of the Unity Argument is very much in question.[9]

There are several objections to this suggestion which now need to be considered. The first is that the notion of transcendental self-consciousness is independently intelligible because, as Hume implied, experiences do not owe their identity as particulars to the person whose experiences they are.[10] Whatever the merits or difficulties of this proposal, it is instructive that in attempting to make something of the notion of transcendental self-consciousness one should find oneself tempted by a Humean view of experiences. On the assumption that this view is both indefensible and profoundly unKantian,[11] this would be an excellent illustration of the dangers inherent in any attempt to detach the notion of transcendental self-consciousness from that of personal self-consciousness.

A more subtle argument for the 'independent intelligibility' thesis is this: even if it is true that experiences owe their identity to the person whose experiences they are, it does not follow that the demonstrative identification of an experience in a judgement of perception requires an identification of the person whose experience it is. There are several ways in which this point might be developed. One would be to dispute the claim that demonstrative identification of experiences is subject to a 'knowing which' requirement. Another would be to accept the 'knowing which' requirement while rejecting the 'knowing what' requirement. To know which thing a demonstrative judgement is about is to be able to discriminate it from other things in the world, but it makes perfectly good sense to suppose that a subject is able to delineate an object of reference even if she does not know what sort of thing it is. So the fact that experiences are in fact adjectival upon subjects who are elements in the objective order does not mean that the conceptualization of experiences in

[9] Strawson also expresses doubts about the TSC version of the Unity Argument in 1966: 108.

[10] As Hume puts it, 'since all our perceptions are different from one another, and from everything else in the universe, they are also distinct and separable, and may be consider'd as separately existent, and have no need of anything else to support their existence' (1978: 233).

[11] Kant's opposition to Hume's conception of the ontological status of 'perceptions' comes out in his claim that 'everyone must . . . necessarily regard himself as substance, and thought as [consisting] only [in] accidents of his being, determinations of his state' (A349).

judgements of perception requires the conception of them as modifications of objective subjects or an identification of their subject.

In Chapter 4 it will be argued that as far as demonstrative reference to
physical objects is concerned, there is a great deal to be said for the idea
that knowledge of which object a demonstrative judgement is about is
compatible with one's not knowing what sort of object it is. The reason
for this, however, is that physical objects are, and are generally perceived
as being, 'unitary and discrete wholes' (Ayers 1991: ii. 114). This is what
makes it possible for someone who is in a state of what might be called
'sortal ignorance' (Hirsch 1982: 76) with respect to a physical object to
discriminate it from other things in the world. In contrast, experiences or
states of consciousness are not given individuals with sharply defined
boundaries. This is part of the force of the idea that whereas physical
objects are 'substances', experiences are 'modes' (cf. Ayers 1991: ii.
114–22). Since experiences are not naturally bounded individuals, it is
much more difficult to make sense of the claim that the ability to single
out an experience in thought does not require knowledge of what it is,
than it is to make sense of the idea that the ability to single out a physical
object in thought does not require knowledge of what sort of thing it is.

A better argument for the 'independent intelligibility' thesis would be
this: it does not follow from the fact that experiences owe their identity as
particulars to the person whose experiences they are, that the demonstrative identification of an experience in a judgement of perception requires
an identification of the person whose experience it is. It does not follow
because, as Peacocke remarks, 'it is a substantive issue whether, when a
particular thing or event is thought about, it must be thought about by
thinking about what, metaphysically, individuates it' (1991: 126). Thus, a
thinker can think about a particular experience demonstratively 'in part
because it is his experience, without having an independent identification
of himself' (Peacocke 1991: 129). This proposal promises to cast fresh
light upon the relationship between transcendental and personal self-
consciousness. Suppose that, when a subject conceptualizes one of her
own experiences by means of a judgement of the form 'This is F', knowledge of which experience is at issue does not require an independent
identification of the subject of experience. This might be thought to
amount to the suggestion that it is possible to conceptualize experiences
without thinking of them as one's own experiences. On the face of it, this
is precisely what is required for transcendental self-consciousness to be
detachable from personal self-consciousness.

The difficulty with this proposal is that, as Peacocke himself recognizes, it is only 'in the context of a general ability of the thinker to think of things of the sort in question' that the fact that an experience is one's own makes it possible for one to think about it demonstratively without an independent identification of its subject (Peacocke 1991: 129). So the question which now arises is this: what is it for a thinker to have the 'general ability' to think about experiences? Opponents of the 'independent intelligibility' thesis will now insist, and be right to insist, that possession of this general ability requires an understanding that experiences are adjectival upon objective subjects of experience. Even if, on a particular occasion, it is possible to refer to one's own pain and judge 'This pain is F' without thinking of it as one's own pain, this is not to say that grasp of judgements of this form can in general be detached from an ability to think thoughts of the form 'This is how things are experienced *by me* as being'. So transcendental self-consciousness remains inextricably linked to personal self-consciousness.

In the light of this discussion, supporters of the Unity Argument would be well advised to abandon the attempt to show that the TSC version of the Unity Argument is an independently viable route to the objectivity condition. Neither the thought of subjective objects as subjective objects nor, if one prefers, the thought of experience as experience, is intelligible independently of personal self-consciousness. With or without the act-object conception, the TSC version of the Unity Argument cannot establish the weak objectivity condition without appealing to the full conditions of the self-ascription of experiences. From now on, the argument for the dependence thesis which was inspired by Strawson's account of the identity of experiences will simply be referred to as the PSC argument for the dependence thesis. The question which now arises is not whether this argument helps to make sense of the notion of transcendental self-consciousness—since it manifestly does not—but whether the argument is successful in its own right as an argument for the weak objectivity requirement on self-consciousness.

There are at least two gaps in the PSC argument for the dependence thesis which need to be filled in. So far, it has been assumed not only that must one think of individual experiences as adjectival upon subjects of experience but also that the subjects upon whom experiences are adjectivally dependent must be regarded as objective subjects or objects in the weighty sense. According to the Exclusion Thesis of Chapter 1, the problem with this assumption is that the subject of one's representations cannot be conceived of as an object at all, let alone as an object in the weighty sense. As Kant puts it, it is one thing to say that 'in all our

thought the "I" is the subject, in which thoughts inhere only as determinations' (A349), but this 'I' is 'as little an intuition as it is a concept of
any object; it is the mere form of consciousness' (A382). Although Kant
is concerned in these passages with the subject of thoughts rather than of
experiences or sensations, his argument does suggest that there is work
to be done in order to justify the transition from the idea that experiences
must be regarded as adjectival upon ('determinations of') subjects of
experience to the thesis that the conceptualization of one's experiences
involves the conception of their subject 'as an element in the objective
order' (cf. Evans 1982: 253).

In contrast, Cartesian dualists will have no difficulty accepting that
one must regard the subject of one's thoughts and experiences as a substantial object among others in the world, but they will wonder why this
object must be regarded as an object in the 'weighty' sense. For both
Strawson and Evans, objects in the weighty sense are physical objects,
and the dualist's objection to the PSC argument for the dependence thesis is that it fails to demonstrate that the thought of one's experiences as
modifications of an 'objective' subject must also be the thought of them
as modifications of a subject who is a physical object among physical
objects rather than an immaterial thinking substance among immaterial
thinking substances. Once again, it is clear that there is more work to be
done, since the falsity or incoherence of the dualist's suggestion that the
subject is an immaterial substance needs to be argued for and not just
assumed.

The second gap in the PSC argument for the dependence thesis is
this: even if one must think of subjective objects as modifications of subjects who are physical objects, it is not clear that it follows from this that
self-conscious experience is subject to the weak objectivity requirement.
In particular, it might be objected that the PSC argument turns on an
ambiguity in the idea that one must have the conception of individual
experiences as experiences 'of' objects in the weighty sense. According to
what might be called the 'ownership' reading, for an experience to be 'of'
an object in the weighty sense is for it to belong to an object in this sense.
According to what might be called the 'representational' reading, for an
experience to be 'of' an object in the weighty sense is for it to represent
such an object. What the PSC argument for the dependence thesis establishes is that the bringing of subjective objects under concepts in judgements of perception requires the conception of such objects as belonging
to objective subjects. It does not establish that one must be able to think
of one's experiences as representative of objects in the weighty sense, as

having objective bearing. Yet it is surely the latter claim which the Unity Argument aims to establish.

These are serious objections, and it is not immediately obvious how they should be dealt with. The best bet at this point would therefore be to turn to Strawson's own PSC version of the Unity Argument. Since it has already been established that the TSC version is not independently intelligible, the hope is that an examination of the full conditions of personal self-consciousness will explain both why the subject of self-conscious experience must be conceived of as a physical object and how it is supposed to follow from this that self-consciousness is subject to the weak objectivity requirement.

3. *Personal Self-Consciousness*

The PSC version of the Unity Argument claims that self-consciousness requires unity of consciousness; unity of consciousness requires the ability to self-ascribe experiences, and the satisfaction of the full conditions of the possibility of self-ascription of experiences, which is constitutive of personal self-consciousness, requires experience of objects. The objectivity requirement which this argument purports to establish is not just the weak objectivity requirement but the strong requirement. So the first question which needs to be addressed is whether the argument succeeds by its own lights. Even if Strawson's argument turns out to be too ambitious, it remains to be seen whether it might not provide grounds for accepting either the modest or weak objectivity requirements on self-consciousness.

The key to the PSC version of the Unity Argument is its conception of what is involved in the empirical self-ascription of experiences. The full conditions of empirical self-ascription include the existence of 'empirically applicable criteria of identity for subjects of experience' (Strawson 1966: 102), where an empirically applicable criterion is one which 'must at least relate to an object of experience, an empirical object' (Strawson 1987: 213). For there to be such criteria, each of us must be 'a corporeal object among corporeal objects' (Strawson 1966: 102), since it is only as corporeal objects, objects of what Kant calls 'outer sense' (A22/ B37), that subjects of experience can become objects of experience. Finally, the existence of that to which one ascribes one's experiences as a corporeal object among corporeal objects requires that one's experience include awareness of objects conceived of as capable of existence unperceived. In summary, an adequate explanation of the unity of consciousness 'would involve referring to the full conditions of the possibility of self-ascription of experiences (including the existence of the subject as an intuitable object in the world); and *then* pointing out that the full conditions include the objectivity condition' (Strawson 1966: 106).

It would appear that this argument provides a way of closing both of the gaps detected in the PSC argument for the dependence thesis. It explains, on the one hand, why the subject upon whom one regards one's experiences as adjectival must be conceived as a physical object rather than as an immaterial thinking substance or the mere form of consciousness. The objection to transcendental idealism and Cartesian dualism is that they both, in their different ways, fail to do justice to the fact that a necessary condition of personal self-consciousness is the existence of the subject of one's experiences as a point of application for empirical criteria of personal identity. Neither Cartesian thinking substances nor the formal Kantian 'I' can be objects of empirical awareness, so the thought of oneself as a Cartesian thinking substance or as a formal Kantian 'I' cannot provide for personal self-consciousness. On the other hand, the PSC version of the Unity Argument also explains the link between conceiving of the subject of one's experiences as a physical object and the satisfaction by one's experience of the weak objectivity requirement. If the former conception requires experience of objects conceived as capable of existence unperceived, then it follows straightforwardly that it also requires the ability to think of experiences as having objective bearing.

Those who are committed to a Cartesian or Kantian view of self-consciousness will no doubt object that the PSC version of the Unity Argument carries no weight unless an account is given of the basis of its insistence that personal self-consciousness depends upon the existence of empirical criteria of personal identity. This question will be addressed in the next chapter, but even if one were to grant both the empirical criteria requirement and the claim that satisfaction of this requirement depends upon the existence of the subject as a corporeal object among corporeal objects, there is still a question about the final step of Strawson's argument. The objection to the earlier defence of the dependence thesis was that it turned on a confusion between two senses—an 'ownership' and a 'representational' sense—in which experiences might be 'of' objects in the weighty sense. On the face of it, the PSC version of the Unity Argument is guilty of precisely the same confusion. To say that the full conditions of the possibility of self-ascription of experiences include the existence of the subject as an intuitable object in the world is to make a claim about the nature of the 'owner' of one's experiences. In contrast, to say that the full conditions involve the objectivity condition is to make a claim about the representational content of experiences. The fact that the last step of Strawson's argument is a *non sequitur* may be brought out by reflecting that for experiences to have objective bearing is for them to 'possess a certain unity or interconnectedness among themselves' (Strawson 1966: 89), yet there seems nothing wrong with the idea that experiences which *lack* this unity and interconnectedness are nevertheless modifications of a subject who is in fact a corporeal object among corporeal objects. To dismiss this suggestion on the grounds that 'we seem to add nothing but a form of words to the hypothesis of a succession of disconnected impressions by stipulating that they all *belong* to an identical consciousness' (Strawson 1966: 100) is to invite the reply that even disconnected impressions cannot exist 'unowned'. So talk of the ownership of experiences by a corporeal subject cannot just be a form of words, even if the experiences lack objective bearing.

This line of attack might prompt the following response on behalf of the PSC version of the Unity Argument: if it were simply a question of personal self-consciousness requiring the existence of the subject as a point of application for empirical criteria and therefore as a physical object, then it would certainly be unclear how this is supposed to lead to the objectivity condition. If, on the other hand, personal self-consciousness is understood as requiring not just the existence of that to which one ascribes one's experiences as an object among others in the world, but also the conception of the subject of one's experiences as a point of application for empirical criteria and therefore as a physical object, then the position is more hopeful. In particular, it might be that there is a connection between personal self-consciousness and the weak objectivity condition because conceiving of the subject of one's experiences as a corporeal object requires at least the ability to think of experiences as having objective bearing. More precisely, for one's experiences to be thought of as being the experiences 'of' a weighty object in the ownership sense, it is necessary that one should have the capacity to think of them as experiences 'of' weighty objects in the representational sense, and this is the force of the last step of the PSC argument.

There are at least two difficulties with this response to the *non sequitur* objection, a minor difficulty and a major difficulty. The minor difficulty is this: so far in this chapter, objects in the weighty sense have been defined as objects that are capable of being perceived and of existing unperceived. In Chapter 2, however, reference was made to a stricter notion of objects in the weighty sense. According to the strict definition, objects in this sense must be capable of both continued and distinct existence. If 'distinct' existence means 'distinct from the subject and its perceptions', then it is a contradiction in terms to describe the subject of one's perception as capable of distinct existence, since this would have to mean existence distinct from itself. Strictly speaking, therefore, one cannot regard the subject of one's perceptions as an object in the weighty sense. If it makes no sense to conceive of that to which one ascribes one's perceptions as an object in the weighty sense, then the question of what is required for one to have this conception plainly does not arise.

The reason that this is a minor difficulty is that it turns on a question of terminology. As has already been remarked, the real point of the insistence that one must regard that to which one ascribes one's experiences as an object in the weighty sense or an 'objective' object, is to insist that one must regard the subject of one's experiences as a physical object, and this is certainly not a contradiction in terms. So the real issue is whether the conception of the subject of one's experiences as a physical object requires the ability to think of one's experiences as representative of objects in the weighty sense. This leads on to the major difficulty with the response to the *non sequitur* objection, which is that it might be held that the reason why the conception of the subject as a physical object requires the ability to think of one's experiences as having objective bearing, is no more obvious than why the existence of the subject as a physical object requires this ability. For all that has been said so far, the gap between the last two steps of the PSC version of the Unity Argument is still open.

At this point, there appear to be two ways of proceeding. The first would be to attempt to defend the suggestion that for one's experiences to be thought of as being the experiences 'of' a physical object in the ownership sense, it is necessary that one should have the capacity to think of them as experiences 'of' weighty objects in the representational sense. It might be argued, for example, that one would not be able to think of one's experiences as 'modifications' of a subject who is a physical object unless one has the concept of a 'physical object', and that to have this concept one must have the conceptual resources to think of experiences as representative of physical objects, and so as having objective bearing.

This argument has considerable plausibility, but it will not be explored here because it is unnecessary. It will be recalled that one of the central aims of the Objectivity Argument was to establish a connection between self-consciousness and having the conception of oneself *qua* subject as a physical object. Since the Unity Argument was a response to the objection that the Objectivity Argument takes too much for granted at the outset, the focus of the recent discussion has been the question of whether the Unity Argument succeeds in explaining why self-consciousness involves being able to think of experiences as representative of objects in the weighty sense. Even if the PSC version of the Unity Argument fails on this score, it is important to see why it fails. Suppose that it fails for the following reason: it establishes that unity of consciousness requires the conception of the subject of one's experiences as a physical object, but fails to demonstrate that that grasp of this conception requires an ability to think of experiences as experiences 'of' weighty objects in the representational sense. If this is why the PSC version of the Unity Argument fails, then the one thing which it does establish is precisely what the Objectivity Argument sets out to establish. If conceiving of oneself as a physical object is a necessary condition of personal self-consciousness, then there is simply no need to go via the Objectivity Argument in attempting to establish a connection between self-consciousness and conceiving of oneself as a physical object. This connection can be established much more directly, by reflecting on full conditions of personal self-consciousness. The fact that these conditions do not lead to the weak objectivity requirement would hardly matter if, as is the case here, one's primary concern is to show that self-consciousness requires the conception of oneself as a physical object.

This suggests that it is the thesis that personal self-consciousness requires the conception of oneself as a physical object that really needs explaining, rather than the connection between conceiving of oneself as a physical object and the weak objectivity requirement. How might such an explanation go? It has already emerged that the key to the first half of the PSC version of the Unity Argument is the idea that self-consciousness requires the conception of oneself as a point of application for empirical criteria of personal identity and therefore as a physical object among physical objects. This idea is the core of the Identity Argument for materialism about self-consciousness, which is an attempt to spell out, without appealing to the Objectivity Argument, the sense in which awareness of oneself as a physical object is a necessary condition of self-consciousness. It is therefore to the Identity Argument that the discussion must now turn.

4

THE IDENTITY ARGUMENT

1. *Introduction*

The Identity Argument for materialism about self-consciousness maintains that a self-conscious subject is, at the very least, one who is capable of consciousness of his or her own identity as the subject of different experiences or representations. There is, no doubt, more to the intuitive notion of self-consciousness than this, but the Identity Argument is concerned with what it regards as our core conception of self-consciousness. The central thesis of the Identity Argument is that a necessary condition of consciousness of one's own identity as the subject of different experiences or representations is awareness of oneself as a physical object.

Like the Objectivity Argument, the Identity Argument assumes that physical objects are shaped, located, and solid, and takes awareness of oneself as a physical object to involve awareness of oneself '*qua* subject' as a physical object. Both arguments are therefore arguments for the thesis that self-consciousness requires awareness of oneself *qua* subject as shaped, located, and solid. The difference between the two arguments is that, unlike the Objectivity Argument, the Identity Argument does not assume at the outset that a self-conscious subject is one whose experience satisfies the objectivity condition. Rather, the need for a self-conscious subject to be able to think of her experience as experience of a world of distinct physical objects is, if anything, supposed to be a consequence of the Identity Argument rather than a premiss. Hence, self-conscious experience must satisfy the objectivity condition *because* self-consciousness, understood as involving consciousness of self-identity, requires awareness of oneself as a physical object.

At the end of the last chapter, doubts were expressed about the move from the claim that a self-conscious subject must be aware of herself as a physical object to the claim that such a subject must be able to think of her experience as experience of a world of physical objects that are distinct from herself. In contrast, this chapter will address the prior question of whether the central thesis of the Identity Argument is correct; in

other words, is it true that consciousness of self-identity requires awareness of oneself as a physical object? In Chapter 2, a distinction was drawn
between two senses in which one might be aware of oneself as a physical
object. On one reading, such awareness involves *conceiving* of oneself,
qua subject, as a physical object. On another reading, it is a matter of
being *intuitively* aware of oneself, *qua* subject, as a physical object. So, as
with the Objectivity Argument, there are two different versions of the
Identity Argument to consider. The concept version states that:

> (D1) Consciousness of one's own identity as the subject of different
> representations requires the conception of oneself as a physical
> object.

The intuition version states that:

> (D2) Consciousness of one's own identity as the subject of different
> representations requires intuitive awareness of oneself as a physi-
> cal object.

As remarked in Chapter 2, the distinction between the intuition and concept versions of 'awareness of oneself as a physical object' is the distinction between being *presented* to oneself as a physical object and *believing*
that one is a physical object. It is a further question whether intuitive
awareness of oneself as a physical object should be understood as 'non-
conceptual'.

The discussion in this chapter will proceed as follows: the first three
parts will examine two neo-Kantian arguments for the concept version of
the Identity Argument. Neither argument is unproblematic, and consideration of an objection to the second argument will lead to the formulation of an *intuition* version of the Identity Argument. This argument will
be defended later in this chapter. Finally, Kant's own account of what he
describes as a priori consciousness of 'the complete identity of the self in
respect of all representations which can ever belong to our knowledge'
(A116) will be examined and criticized in the light of the preceding discussion.

2. *The First Concept Version of the Identity Argument*

The first stage of the first concept version of the Identity Argument is
the *self-ascription* requirement. This is the requirement that a self-conscious subject must be capable of thinking of her experiences as *her* expe-

riences, that is, of self-ascribing them. It is not sufficient for satisfaction of the self-ascription requirement that one is capable of self-ascribing experiences individually, without recognizing the identity of that to which the experiences are ascribed; one must also be capable of thinking of the self-ascribed experiences as 'belonging' to one and the same self.

If challenged to justify the self-ascription requirement, the Identity Argument cannot follow the Objectivity Argument in claiming that consciousness of the identity of that to which different experiences are ascribed is a necessary condition of being able to conceptualize some of these experiences as experiences of independent objects. To repeat what was said above, the satisfaction by self-conscious experience of the objectivity condition is not supposed to be a premiss of the Identity Argument. In the context of the Identity Argument, the best that can be said for the self-ascription requirement is that it is a reflection of at least one important element of what might be described as our intuitive notion of self-consciousness. Even if the connection between self-consciousness and consciousness of self-identity is not a necessary connection, the idea that consciousness of self-identity requires the conception of oneself as a physical object is sufficiently interesting in its own right to be worthy of detailed consideration.

The next stage of the first concept version of the Identity Argument is the *empirical criteria* requirement. For a criterion of identity to be 'empirically applicable' is for it to be possible for experience or 'sensible intuition' to present us with an object which satisfies it (cf. Strawson 1966: 162). The empirical criteria requirement states that the self-ascription of experiences by a subject who is conscious of her own identity as their subject must be underpinned by empirically applicable criteria of subject-identity. What is the nature of this 'underpinning'? On the one hand, it is not enough simply that empirically applicable criteria of subject-identity exist, for if the self-ascribing subject has no knowledge of them, they can scarcely be said to 'underpin' her self-ascriptions. On the other hand, the empirical criteria requirement is not the requirement that empirical criteria must actually be employed by the self-ascribing subject to justify her uses of 'I'. For example, when one judges 'I am in pain', one does not first observe that *someone* is in pain and then identify that person as oneself by applying criteria of personal identity. The self-ascription of experiences is, in this sense, 'criterionless' (Strawson 1966: 162).

If the mere existence of criteria of subject-identity is not enough to underpin one's self- ascriptions, and the demand that criteria of identity be employed in ascribing experiences to oneself is too strong, what does the empirical criteria requirement come to? Strawson's suggestive and influential response to this question is to claim that 'I' can be used without criteria of subject-identity and yet refer to a subject because 'even in such a use, the links with those criteria are not in practice severed' (ibid.). To say that links with empirical criteria are not in practice severed is to say, firstly, that the self-ascribing subject must know or understand the appropriate (empirical) criteria of subject-identity, and secondly that the subject must be prepared to 'acknowledge the applicability of those criteria in settling questions as to whether he, the very man who now ascribes to himself this experience, was or was not the person who, say, performed such-and-such an action in the past' (ibid.). Such questions do not normally arise, but if they do arise the self-conscious subject must regard them as answerable by reference to the appropriate empirical criteria.

The next stage of the argument is the *physical object* requirement. The claim which underpins this requirement is that for there to be empirically applicable criteria of subject-identity, each of us must be a physical object among physical objects. This need not amount to the thesis that a person is identical with his or her body. The suggestion is rather that while the criteria for the numerical identity through time of a subject of experiences are not the same as those for bodily identity, they do nevertheless 'involve an essential reference to the human body' (Strawson 1966: 164). Thus, if consciousness of one's own identity as the subject of diverse experiences requires the conception of oneself as a point of application for empirical criteria of subject-identity, it also requires the conception of oneself as a physical object. And if this is correct, then so is (D1).

In Strawson's discussion, (D1) leads to the *objectivity requirement*, according to which it is a necessary condition of one's being able to conceive of oneself as a physical object that one also thinks of some of one's experiences as experiences of physical objects that are distinct from oneself. This claim was discussed in Chapter 3 and is not of primary importance in the context of (D1). In the present context, it is the argument leading up to the physical object requirement that really matters. The most pressing questions raised by this argument appear to be these: firstly, are there good grounds for accepting the empirical criteria requirement? Secondly, how convincing is the transition from this requirement to the physical object requirement? The acceptability or otherwise of the first concept version of the Identity Argument turns on whether it is in a position to provide satisfactory answers to these questions.

One way of bringing out the importance of these questions would be to consider the bearing of the Strawsonian argument on a Cartesian conception of self-consciousness. Suppose that the Cartesian claims to be in a position to respect the links between self-ascriptions of experience and criteria of subject-identity, while endorsing a conception of subject-identity according to which A and B are the same subject if and only if they have the same immaterial soul. Since immaterial souls are not objects of sensible intuition, the Cartesian criterion of identity is not empirically applicable and so violates the empirical criteria requirement. Subjects of experience are only intuitable as objects of outer sense, and to describe something as an object of outer sense is to describe it as spatial object. This is the basis of the physical object requirement, but this anti-Cartesian argument is only as strong as the case for insisting that the criteria of subject-identity needed to underpin the self-ascription of experiences must be such that it is possible for sensible intuition to present us with an object which satisfies them. Hence, the single most important question for the first concept version of the Identity Argument concerns the status of this requirement.

For Strawson, the empirical criteria requirement is based on the 'quite general truth that the ascription of different states or determinations to an identical subject turns on the existence of some means of distinguishing or identifying the subject of such ascriptions as one object among others' (1966: 102). Suppose that this general truth is described as the *discrimination requirement*. The point of the empirical criteria requirement is that for the self-ascribing subject to have some means of distinguishing or discriminating that to which she ascribes her experiences, she must be, and conceive of herself as being, an object of perception or sensible intuition. The discrimination requirement is, in turn, based on a verificationist 'principle of significance', the principle that 'there can be no legitimate, or even meaningful employment of ideas or concepts which does not relate them to empirical or experiential conditions of their application' (Strawson 1966: 16). In other words, there must be empirical means of distinguishing oneself as an object among others if the thought of one's own identity as the subject of different experiences is to so much as make sense. And for there to be such means, one must be a corporeal object among corporeal objects.

The reliance of the first concept version of the Identity Argument upon the principle of significance will come as a serious disappointment to those who regard the form of verificationism to which the principle gives expression as unacceptable. Indeed, even with the principle of significance and the discrimination requirement in the background, there is further work to be done to justify the transition from the empirical criteria to the physical object requirement. Those influenced by Locke's account of personal identity might wonder, for example, why it would not be sufficient for the purposes of the empirical criteria requirement that the identity of the subject should be held to consist in some form of psychological rather than physical continuity. To this, it will presumably be replied that Locke's proposal does not affect the central point of the first concept version of the Identity Argument since persons must be corporeal if Lockean criteria of personal identity are to be empirically applicable (cf. Williams 1973: 11). This only serves to confirm the earlier impression that the demand for empirical applicability holds the key to the argument.

At this point, there seem to be two ways of proceeding. The first would be to attempt to defend the principle of significance and the empirical criteria requirement more or less as they stand. It will be assumed here that the prospects for a convincing defence of the principle of significance are not good, and that the Identity Argument would be deprived of much of its interest and power if it turns out to be an essentially verificationist argument. A potentially more fruitful direction in which to take the discussion would therefore be to consider the possibility that the central insight of the Identity Argument can be detached from Strawson's verificationist framework. The exploration of this possibility is the main aim of what will be referred to as the second concept version of the Identity Argument. This argument claims that the discrimination requirement is not an intrinsically verificationist requirement and that it provides a basis for (D1) which is independent of any commitment to the principle of significance or the empirical criteria requirement as Strawson understands it. This is the proposal to be examined below.

3. *The Second Concept Version of the Identity Argument*

According to what Evans calls 'Russell's Principle', 'a subject cannot make a judgement about something unless he knows which object his judgement is about' (Evans 1982: 89). In the context of (D1), this principle is important for two reasons. The first is that it provides a basis for the discrimination requirement. It is a quite general truth that the ascription of experiences to an identical subject turns on the existence of some means of distinguishing the subject of such ascriptions as one object among others, because it is an even more general truth that a thinker will not count as having latched on to a particular item in the world and predicated something of it unless she has a capacity to distinguish the object of her judgement from all other things. The second reason for the importance of Russell's Principle is that the demand for discriminating knowledge need not be understood as a verificationist demand. The problem with the suggestion that one can grasp a judgement about an object without knowing which object the judgement is about is not that one would be unable to verify the judgement. The problem is rather that if one does not satisfy the 'knowing which' requirement, one will not even count as knowing what it is for the judgement to be true.

When one self-ascribes an experience, what is it to be able to delineate that to which the experience is ascribed? One influential suggestion is that one cannot, in general, know *which* thing one has referred to without knowing what *sort* of thing one has referred to. To delineate an object in thought is to draw its boundaries, and it makes no sense to suppose that one can draw the boundaries of something in thought if one does not know what it is. The next stage of the argument is the proposal that for one to know what kind of object a judgement is about, one must know the object's criterion of identity.[1] What the first concept version of the Identity Argument refers to as the empirical criteria requirement can be seen as a reflection of this entirely general thesis about reference and predication, but the empirical criteria requirement goes further than is warranted by the general thesis.

The sense in which the empirical criteria requirement goes too far may be brought out by drawing upon the frequently remarked distinction between 'evidential' and 'constitutive' criteria of identity.[2] In the evidential sense, a criterion of identity is a way of telling whether some object x and some object y are numerically identical. In the constitutive sense, a criterion of identity specifies what it is for x and y to be numerically identical. This distinction raises the following question about the preceding 'knowing what' requirement on reference: is it criteria of identity in the evidential or in the constitutive sense which must be invoked in reference to objects? If reference to objects must be underpinned by

---

[1] It is in this sense that, as Dummett puts it, 'any reference to objects, properly so called, and any predication of objects, involves the tacit or explicit invocation of a criterion of identity' (Dummett 1981: 218).

[2] Wiggins (1980: 53–5) gives a good account of this distinction.

evidential criteria,[3] then good sense can be made of the empirical criteria requirement. For if an empirical criterion of identity for x is such that it is possible for sensible intuition to present us with an object which satisfies it, then it is also one which enables us to decide whether or not x and y are identical. So being in possession of an empirical criterion of identity would be one way of meeting the 'knowing what' requirement.

The problem with this defence of the empirical criteria requirement is that it is not clear why reference to objects should need to be underpinned by criteria of identity in the evidential sense. It would seem that as long as one knows what the singularity and identity of something consists in, one has delineated it in thought, even if the criterion is not such that it is possible to experience or perceive its satisfaction. Given something like the principle of significance, such a sharp distinction between constitutive and evidential considerations would be unacceptable, but the object of the exercise at present is to avoid dependence upon the principle of significance. What has yet to be explained, therefore, is how the physical object requirement can be justified on the basis of a 'constitutive' reading of the 'knowing what' requirement.

This challenge may be met in the following way: it is one thing to accept a distinction between constitutive and evidential criteria of identity, but there must be some restrictions on what counts as an acceptable constitutive criterion in this context if the 'knowing what' requirement is not to be trivialized. In the first place, whether or not the criterion of identity which underpins reference to some object x is empirically applicable, it must be coherent and it must be a substantive criterion. To describe a criterion of identity for x as substantive is to say that it places empirical constraints on what it is to grasp the supposition that x and y are identical (cf. Evans 1982: 116). Moreover, the criterion must be accurate, that is, it must be faithful to what x actually is. Since knowledge requires truth, someone with false or incoherent beliefs about the nature of x can scarcely be said to have known what x is.

When these constraints are applied to our understanding of the workings of self-reference, the result is the following anti-Cartesian argument: self-reference involves the tacit invocation of a criterion of personal or subject–identity, and the invoked criterion must be coherent, substantive, and accurate. In other words, it must be faithful to what persons actually are. The problem with the idea that A and B are the same person if and only if they have the same immaterial soul is that it satisfies none of these

---

[3] This appears to be Dummett's view. See, for example, Dummett 1973: 73.

requirements. To take the requirement of coherence, for example, the Cartesian criterion is incoherent not because immaterial souls cannot be sensibly intuited, but because it is not possible to give a proper account of what the singularity and identity of immaterial souls consists in. This anti-Cartesian argument is not a verificationist argument, as it does not turn on the stipulation that an acceptable criterion of personal identity must be empirically applicable in Strawson's sense. By focusing on the question of whether Cartesian souls can be objects of sensible intuition, the first Identity Argument puts the emphasis in the wrong place and unnecessarily makes itself vulnerable to accusations of verificationism.

The revised anti-Cartesian argument suggest the following non-verificationist argument for (D1): for one to be self-conscious, one must be capable of ascribing experiences to oneself and of grasping the identity of that to which the different experiences are ascribed (the self-ascription requirement). For one to be in a position to understand one's self-ascriptive judgements, one must know which thing these judgements are about (Russell's Principle). This means that one must have some means of distinguishing oneself as an object among others in the world (the discrimination requirement) and so must have a coherent, substantive, and accurate conception of what one's singularity and identity consists in (the 'knowing what' requirement). Persons or subjects of experience are physical objects. A coherent, substantive, and accurate conception of what one's singularity and identity consists in must therefore be the conception of oneself as a physical object (the physical object requirement). Since physical objects cannot be individuated without reference to their spatio-temporal location, to have adequate means of distinguishing oneself as an object among others in the world is to have a practical capacity to determine one's spatio-temporal location (the self-location requirement). This is the second concept version of the Identity Argument.

This argument for (D1) has a number of attractions. On the one hand, it makes no use of the principle of significance. On the other hand, it still provides a compelling explanation of the link between self-consciousness and grasp of criteria of subject-identity, and it does so in a way which is no more congenial to a Cartesian account of self-consciousness than the first concept version of the Identity Argument. This helps to strengthen the earlier suspicion that the verificationist framework of the first argument is dispensable, although questions remain about the assertion that persons are physical objects. Before addressing these questions, however, it would be worth exploring the bearing of the second concept version of the Identity Argument on one frequently quoted criticism of Descartes.

Lichtenberg is reported to have claimed that Descartes should have said 'It thinks' or 'There is some thinking going on' rather than 'I think'.[4] According to the second Identity Argument, the force of this objection may be brought out by considering so-called 'feature-placing' sentences, such as 'Now it is raining' and 'Snow is falling', which do not involve reference to particulars (Strawson 1959: 202). It has sometimes been suggested that underlying the level of language at which we refer to objects and predicate things of them is a more primitive level of language consisting of feature-placing sentences.[5] Consider, for example, a case in which a child says 'Cat' in the presence of a cat, but in which she has no grasp of the (constitutive) criteria of singularity and identity for cats. Without such criteria, it would not be correct to interpret the child's utterance as referring to an object; it simply reports the presence of cat somewhat in the way that 'It's raining' reports the presence of rain. The transition from this primitive level to the level of language at which there is reference to objects therefore involves the acquisition of the appropriate criteria of singularity and identity (cf. Dummett 1981: 217).

The relevance of all of this for Lichtenberg's criticism is as follows: Descartes took it that even in the predicament of the first two Meditations, he was capable of understanding 'I' as a referring expression. The second Identity Argument points out, however, that the use of 'I' as a referring expression is subject to the 'knowing which' and 'knowing what' requirements. At this stage in his investigation, the only answer which Descartes is in a position to give in response to his question 'What then am I?' is that he is a thinking thing; the nature of this thing has yet to be determined. As Gassendi pointed out, however, the problem with this account of the nature of the 'I' is not that it is false or incoherent but that it is purely 'formal' and so does not yield substantive criteria of subject-identity.[6] In other words, Descartes does not satisfy the 'knowing what' requirement and is, to this extent, unable to draw his own boundaries. Since he does not satisfy the discrimination requirement, he is not in a position to understand 'I' as a referring expression; the most that he is left with is 'It thinks'. Thus Descartes would be confined to reporting the contents of consciousness in the form of feature-placing sentences.

How convincing is the second Identity Argument? There are at least two major objections to it, one of which is an objection to it on its own

---

[4] Lichtenberg's criticism of Descartes is quoted in Williams 1978: 95.

[5] For a version of this proposal, see Dummett 1981: 216–18.

[6] This appears to be the point of Gassendi's comments in Cottingham, Stoothoff, and Murdoch 1984: ii. 234–5.

terms, while the other objection calls into question the entire framework within which it operates. The objection on its own terms accepts that self-reference is subject to a 'knowing what' requirement but questions its conception of the nature of persons. For example, if Locke was right to claim that the '*personal Identity* consists . . . in the Identity of *consciousness*' (1975: 342), then persons are not individuated by reference to spatio-temporal location. If Locke's account is incoherent, insubstantial, or inaccurate, this has yet to be established. Since the second argument does not say anything in support of the account of the nature of persons upon which it relies, it fails to establish that knowledge of what one is requires the conception of oneself as a physical object.

Suppose, next, that this gap in the second Identity Argument can be filled in, and that those who employ this argument are entitled to its conception of the nature of persons. Even if persons are in fact physical objects, it does not follow that self-consciousness requires the conception of oneself as a physical object unless it is also accepted that self-consciousness requires a coherent, accurate, and substantive conception of what one is. That there is such a requirement on self-consciousness is precisely the point of the 'knowing what' requirement, but this requirement is open to dispute. Consider, once again, the Cartesian dualist who regards the persisting subject of her thoughts as an immaterial substance. This belief may well be philosophically indefensible for the reasons given earlier, but this surely has no bearing on her ability to think first-personally. In other words, even if it is true that self-conscious subjects or persons are physical objects among physical objects, it is not a necessary condition of their being self-conscious that they *believe* that this is so. Hence, (D1) cannot be correct. This will be referred to as the *problem of misconception*.[7]

To the extent that the problem of misconception calls into question the 'knowing what' requirement on self-reference, it calls into question a requirement which lies at the heart of the second Identity Argument. Later it will be argued that while the problem of misconception represents a serious challenge to the Identity Argument, the resources for

---

[7] Campbell (1994: 126) also discusses the possibility of a self-conscious subject having false beliefs about the kind of thing she is, but his examples are not ones in which the subject conceives of herself as incorporeal. Indeed, Campbell's own view seems to be that a self-conscious subject must 'conceive of itself as one physical object among many' (1993: 92). So the problem of misconception is also a problem for Campbell's position, despite the many differences between it and the second concept version of the Identity Argument. The issue is not clear-cut, however, because Campbell has a different conception of what a physical object is from the one employed in formulating the problem of misconception.

dealing with this challenge can be found in the intuition version of the Identity Argument. To anticipate, self-conscious subjects who have seriously misguided self-conceptions are still able to refer to themselves, while satisfying a robust discrimination requirement, in virtue of their intuitive awareness of themselves, *qua* subjects, as physical objects among physical objects. The moral of the problem of misconception is not that self-consciousness does not require the ability to discriminate oneself from other things in the world but rather that one can discriminate oneself from other things in the world, in the sense required for consciousness of self-identity, even if one has an inaccurate self-*conception*. It will also turn out that this point holds the key to understanding why Lichtenberg's challenge is unthreatening from a non-Cartesian perspective.

Before developing this line of thought, it would be worth relating the problem of misconception to a wider question concerning transcendental arguments. Suppose that S is a proposition which is the target of sceptical attack. On one reading, the aim of a transcendental argument is to establish that the truth of S is a necessary condition of something which is not and cannot coherently be doubted by the sceptic. Transcendental arguments in this sense are 'truth-directed' (Peacocke 1989: 4). In reply, it has often been suggested that the most that a transcendental argument can hope to establish is that we must believe that S is true, not that S is actually true. Transcendental arguments in this sense are 'belief-directed'. The challenge which belief-directed transcendental arguments face, however, is that if S is a proposition which the sceptic herself claims not to believe, then she is hardly likely to concede that believing that S is true is a necessary condition of the possibility of, say, experience or language. It is, of course, always open to the transcendental arguer to argue that the sceptic's claims about what she believes are insincere or mistaken, but the latter response seems difficult to reconcile with the idea that we are authoritative with respect to our own beliefs. So while belief-directed transcendental arguments escape some of the difficulties which face truth-directed transcendental arguments, they give rise to difficulties of their own. Indeed, viewed from the perspective of the problem of misconception, the thesis that a self-conscious subject must believe that S is true is, in a way, more ambitious than the thesis that the mere truth of S is a necessary condition of self-consciousness. Whereas the former thesis is threatened by the problem of misconception, the latter is not.

The significance of the problem of misconception in this context is that it is an excellent illustration of this quite general challenge to belief-directed transcendental arguments. The concept version of the Identity Argument is just such an argument, on the assumption that to conceive of oneself as a corporeal object among corporeal objects is to believe that one is just such an object. If S is the proposition that the subject of thought and experience is a physical object among physical objects, then someone who claims that her thinking self is incorporeal is presumably going to want to deny that belief in the truth of S is a necessary condition of the self-ascription of thoughts and experiences. To the extent that the problem of misconception is an instance of a more general objection to belief-directed transcendental arguments, it is one which cannot be ignored by anyone with an interest in Kantian epistemology.

4. *The Problem of Misconception*

One way of bringing out the full force of the problem of misconception would be to reflect on the fact that it is a rule of the ordinary practice of personal reference by the use of personal pronouns that, as Strawson puts it, 'the first personal pronoun refers, on each occasion of its use, to anyone who then uses it' (1994: 210). It is a consequence of this reference rule that the use of 'I' to refer does not require knowledge of *who* one is. Even someone who is wholly deluded as to his own identity and who thinks, say, 'I wrote the *Tractatus*' does not fail to refer to himself. He has simply thought something false, but this is so precisely because 'the reference to himself is unshaken' (ibid.).

This mild version of the problem of misconception has no direct bearing on the question of whether conceiving of one's thinking self as corporeal is a necessary condition of self-conscious self-reference, since the deluded subject who believes that he wrote the *Tractatus* might still be conceiving of himself *qua* subject as shaped, located, and solid. On the other hand, once it is understood that a use of 'I' always refers to its user, then it must presumably also be granted that when a person P asserts 'I believe that my thinking self is immaterial', this use of 'I' refers to P. In making this assertion, P has self-ascribed a belief, but it would surely be unacceptable to insist that this self-ascription is underpinned by P's conception of herself *qua* subject as corporeal, since the self-ascribed belief is precisely the belief that she is incorporeal.

It might be objected that this argument is too hasty. It is one thing to say that the comprehending self-ascription of thoughts and experiences is compatible with one's having *some* false beliefs about the nature of that

to which these thoughts and experiences are ascribed, but there are limits
to how much confusion and misconception can be made sense of if someone is to be credited with the capacity to think first-personally. Mini-
mally, the subject must think of herself as the kind of thing to which it at
least makes sense to ascribe thoughts and experiences. It might also be
held to be necessary that she thinks of herself as someone to whom
thoughts could be ascribed by others, and so as someone who is identifiable by an 'outer observer' (Kant 1929: A362). The moral is that self-
ascribers must have, in the words of Carol Rovane, 'enough true beliefs
about themselves in virtue of which they are quite clear about their iden-
tities even though they have some false beliefs as well' (1987: 154). Hence,
there is no objection in principle to the use of belief-directed transcendental arguments in theorizing about self-consciousness.

It would certainly be difficult to dispute the suggestion that there are
limits to the extent to which a genuinely self-conscious subject can be
confused about the kind of thing she is; beyond a certain point, say in the
case of a subject who claims that she is a steam locomotive,[8] it would perhaps be more appropriate to raise questions about her sanity than to see
it as confirmation of the thesis that self-conscious self-reference does not
require an accurate self-conception. In the present context, however, the
important question is whether the true beliefs required for self-
consciousness must include the belief that that to which one ascribes
one's thoughts and experiences is shaped, located, and solid. If not, then
the conclusion of the Identity Argument is still in doubt. If so, then the
question of what is to be made of the Cartesian remains unresolved, since
proponents of the Identity Argument are presumably not in the business
of raising questions about the sanity of Cartesian dualists. Indeed, there
is no reason for the sophisticated dualist to deny that she is identifiable
by others on the basis of bodily criteria. What the dualist wishes to deny
is that any of this commits her to the conception of herself *qua* subject as
a physical object among physical objects. So this version of the problem
of misconception continues to pose a threat to the Identity Argument.

There are at least five possible responses to the problem of misconception which, unlike the responses considered so far, address themselves
directly to the threat posed to the Identity Argument by self-conscious
subjects with allegedly Cartesian self-conceptions. The first response,
anticipated above, would simply be to deny that the dualist actually
believes that her thinking self is immaterial. There are two points that

---

[8] This example is taken from Campbell 1994: 126.

might be made in this connection. The first is that in ascribing proposi-
tional attitudes to others, there must be a presumption against the attribution of beliefs that are manifestly false or incoherent, such as the belief
that $2 + 2 = 5$. The second is that while it may be true that the Cartesian
assents to sentences in which the subject of her thoughts and experiences
is said to be incorporeal, the sentences to which someone assents are not
an infallible guide to what she believes. What people actually believe
about the nature of the self is not settled by what they are willing to say
when in the grip of philosophical reflection; rather, it is to be conceived
as determinable by reference to their ordinary, unreflective use of personal pronouns as well as their non-linguistic behaviour. The fact is that
in ordinary discourse, 'we can and do ascribe to one and the same individual human being things as various as actions, intentions, sensations,
thoughts, feelings, perceptions, memories, physical position, corporeal
characteristics, skills or abilities, traits of character and so on' (Strawson
1974b: 169). As long as the dualist continues to speak in these ways, there
are good grounds for insisting that she does in fact conceive of herself
qua subject as corporeal in the sense that matters for the Identity
Argument. More generally, it is never enough to undermine a belief-
directed transcendental argument simply to observe that there are actual
subjects who do not believe what the argument claims they must believe,
for if the argument is independently plausible then such subjects do not
believe what they claim to believe.

Earlier it was hinted that this line of argument is incompatible with
the idea that we are authoritative with respect to our own beliefs. The
suggestion is presumably that the Cartesian believes that she believes that
that to which she ascribes her thoughts and experiences is incorporeal,
yet if the first response to the problem of misconception is correct then
this second-order belief is false and so incompatible with first-person
authority. Those who are sympathetic to the first response are, however,
unlikely to be moved by this line of argument. They will insist that the
very considerations which support the denial that the Cartesian believes
in the immateriality of herself *qua* subject also support the denial that
she believes that she believes this.[9] So the first response can be reconciled
with the phenomenon of first-person authority.

The question of whether or not this reconciliation is successful will
not be pursued here since there are other difficulties with the first

---

[9] One way of defending this response would be to argue that in such cases the content
of the second-order belief is 'logically locked' (Burge 1994: 75) on to the content of the
first-order belief.

response that seem more decisive than the objection from first-person authority. Firstly, the general presumption against the attribution of manifestly incoherent beliefs is of little value in the present context, given that the incoherence of Cartesian dualism is arguably not as transparent as the incoherence of the idea that $2 + 2$ might be 5. Secondly, it is not obvious what kind of non-linguistic behaviour is supposed to manifest the Cartesian's (alleged) belief that the subject of her thoughts is corporeal, as distinct from the belief that her incorporeal thinking self 'has' a body. As for the significance of ordinary ways of talking in this connection, it can hardly be appropriate to take these as providing decisive evidence one way or another, in view of the fact that the Cartesian regards these ways of talking as disguising the real nature of the subject. Even if there are cases in which there is, as it were, a mismatch between the sentences to which people are prepared to assent and the propositions which they actually believe, it must surely be accepted that what people say provides the best evidence for what they believe. The fact that some of what is said is said in the context of philosophical reflection is not a good reason for attaching less significance to it than to other forms of discourse whose status is very much at issue. When this point is combined with the earlier observation concerning the religious and ethical implications of immaterialism, the suggestion that the best neo-Kantian response to the problem of misconception is to deny that the misconception is genuine begins to look increasingly unattractive.

This might prompt the following suggestion: suppose that a particular belief-directed transcendental argument aims to show that for a subject S to have a certain conceptual capacity C she must also have a certain belief, say the belief that p. The first response tries to deal with examples in which S supposedly has C without believing that p by arguing that they are cases in which the S does in fact believe that p. An alternative response would be to argue that they are cases in which S does not actually have the capacity C. This is the second response to the problem of misconception. Thus, in connection with the Identity Argument, what needs to be shown is that examples in which a subject genuinely does not believe that she is a physical thing are also examples in which she is incapable of grasping her own identity as the subject of different thoughts and experiences.

One way of developing the second response would be to draw upon Evans's remark that 'the central concept is not that of making a reference of such-and-such a kind, but that of *understanding* one' (1982: 142 n.). The significance of this remark is that neo-Kantian self-consciousness is to be understood as requiring a capacity for the *comprehending* self-ascription of thoughts and experiences, and a thoroughly confused 'subject' who does not know which thing or what kind of thing she is cannot properly be said to be in a position to understand thoughts whose conventional expression would require the employment of the first person pronoun. If someone who is not in a position to understand such thoughts is not self-conscious in the neo-Kantian sense, then the question of whether her self-conscious beliefs about herself are misguided simply does not arise, since she has no such beliefs.

Whatever the attractions of the second response in the context of other transcendental arguments, in the present context there seems little to be said for it. In the first place, denying self-consciousness to dualists is simply not an option. Indeed, the suggestion that someone who conceives of herself *qua* subject as incorporeal must be incapable of the comprehending self-ascription of thoughts and experiences, is not just implausible but also profoundly paradoxical. For on a neo-Kantian view of self-consciousness, someone who is incapable of the comprehending self-ascription of thoughts and experiences is not self-conscious; but how can self-consciousness be denied to a subject who has the ability to think thoughts about the nature of the subject of her thoughts? According to the second response, however, those who do not satisfy the self-knowledge requirements on self-conscious self-reference can only *try* to think of themselves as incorporeal. Since, strictly speaking, their attempts at I-thinking 'fail to net any object at all' (Evans 1982: 253), there is no question of denying self-consciousness to a subject who can actually think about herself *qua* subject.

The suggestion that the so-called dualist fails to think of herself as incorporeal is reminiscent of the first response to the problem of misconception, but only results in the substitution of one paradox for another. Instead of the paradox of a non-self-conscious subject engaging in thought about the nature of the subject of her thoughts, there is now the paradox of a subject trying but failing to think first-personally. There are two points to be made in this connection. The first is that there might be an objection in principle to the idea of a subject trying but failing to think first-personally. The second is that the denial of self-consciousness to alleged dualists remains extremely difficult to swallow. This should come as no surprise when it is recalled that belief-directed transcendental arguments such as the Identity Argument are, after all, concerned with the necessary conditions of forms of self-consciousness our possession of which is especially secure.

At this point, it would be worth exploring the suggestion that the preceding discussion of the problem of misconception is based upon a straightforward misunderstanding of what belief-directed transcendental arguments set out to achieve. So far it has been assumed that the sense in which, according to the Identity Argument, a self-conscious subject must conceive of herself as a corporeal object is that this is a belief which self-conscious subjects must actually have. This is the 'actual belief' reading of the Identity Argument. According to the third response to the problem of misconception, this reading of the argument is incorrect. On the face of it, there are at least two alternatives to the 'actual belief' reading, a dispositional and a normative alternative. According to the dispositional alternative, the point of the Identity Argument is to insist that a subject who is self-conscious in the neo-Kantian sense must simply be disposed to think of herself *qua* subject as corporeal. The fact that some self-conscious subjects do not actually think of themselves in this way therefore poses no threat to the Identity Argument as long as they have the disposition to regard the subject of their thoughts and experiences as shaped, located, and solid. According to the normative alternative, the force of the Identity Argument is not even that self-conscious subjects must have this disposition; the point is rather that they are rationally committed to regarding themselves as corporeal in the neo-Kantian sense. Since people are not always rational, they do not always believe what they are rationally committed to believing, but it is a mistake to suppose that belief-directed transcendental arguments make no allowance for irrationality or eccentricity. As long as the conclusion of the Identity Argument is understood as being essentially normative, it is not undermined by the fact that some subjects do not believe what they ought to believe about themselves.

Unfortunately, the 'actual belief' reading of the Identity Argument cannot be so easily dismissed. In the first place, the assertion that even a committed dualist can be said to be disposed to regard herself *qua* subject as shaped, located, and solid lacks any independent basis and so is in danger of trivializing the dispositional version of the Identity Argument. Secondly, and more importantly, it will be recalled that the fundamental basis of the Identity Argument was the idea that in order to make and understand a judgement about something one must know which thing one's judgement is about. If 'knowing which' requires 'knowing what', then it is difficult to see how one can be said to be in a position to delineate that to which one ascribes one's thoughts and experiences simply in virtue of being disposed to have a certain belief about oneself, or in virtue of the fact that this is a belief to which one is rationally committed. The epistemological framework employed by the Identity Argument implies that self-consciousness requires actual knowledge of what one is, and this is the force of the 'actual belief' reading. If one does not actually regard oneself *qua* subject as a corporeal object among corporeal objects, then the Identity Argument must surely insist that one does not know what kind of thing one is.

This might prompt the thought that the problem of misconception only seems so intractable because the epistemological presuppositions of the Identity Argument have not been subjected to the critical scrutiny which they deserve. According to the fourth response to the problem of misconception, the obvious moral of the discussion so far is that these presuppositions are unacceptable. Instead of denying the possibility of misconception, the fourth response concludes that this possibility shows that self-reference is not subject to the discrimination requirement. If first-person reference does not require knowledge of which thing one is or of the criteria of personal identity, then there is simply no reason to try to explain away cases of misconception. At the same time, however, the abandonment of the discrimination requirement also amounts to the abandonment of the Identity Argument. For some versions of the fourth response, the very fact that uses of 'I' invariably refer to the person who produced them means that the 'I'-user's self-conception has no work to do in fixing the reference of such uses (cf. Campbell 1994: 127). Other versions of the fourth response take things a step further and argue that since genuine reference is subject to the discrimination requirement, 'I' is not a genuine referring expression.[10] Either way, self-consciousness does not require the conception of the subject of one's thoughts and experiences as corporeal.

On the face of it, both versions of the fourth response are profoundly unattractive. Contrary to what the first version suggests, it does indeed appear to be a quite general truth that in order to make a judgement about something one must be able to discriminate the object of one's judgement from all other things, and it is quite mysterious how first-person judgements are supposed to be able to escape this requirement. As for the suggestion that 'I' is not a referring expression at all, this is so counter-intuitive that everything possible should be done to avoid it. This leads on to the fifth and final response to the problem of misconception. This response accepts that the comprehending self-ascriptions

[10] This is Anscombe's view. See Anscombe 1994: 153.

of thoughts and experiences is subject to a discrimination requirement but questions the idea that the ability to discriminate the object of a judgement from all other things requires substantive knowledge of the kind of thing it is. So the possibility to be considered is that although there is indeed a sense in which someone who conceives of the subject of her thoughts as incorporeal does not meet the 'knowing what' requirement, she might still count as knowing which thing she is. The sense in which she knows which thing she is need not involve the belief that the subject of her thoughts is corporeal, but must nevertheless be bound up with intuitive awareness of that to which she ascribes her representations as shaped, located, and solid. So the fifth response to the problem of misconception amounts to an intuition version of the Identity Argument, an argument for (D2) rather than (D1).

5. The Intuition Version of the Identity Argument

One way of developing the intuition version of the Identity Argument would be to consider how someone who is committed to the discrimination requirement should respond to something like the problem of misconception in connection with perceptual-demonstrative reference. Suppose that a subject S judges 'That is F' in connection with a currently perceived physical object which is in fact a tadpole. The discrimination requirement states that for S to be in a position to understand the judgement she must be able to delineate or single out the object which she judges to be F. To single out an object x is, as Wiggins puts it, to 'isolate x in experience; to determine or fix upon x in particular by drawing its spatio-temporal boundaries and distinguishing it in its environment from other things of like and unlike kinds' (1980: 5). What is it, then, for S to meet the discrimination requirement with respect to the object of her demonstrative judgement? One possibility is this: she is able to single out the object which she judges to be F in virtue of her perceptual or intuitive awareness of its shape and location. In perceiving the solid shape and location of the object, she literally perceives the boundary between it and other objects in the environment, and perceives the object as a *physical* object.[11] This awareness of the object as a shaped, located,

---

[11] This account of perceptual individuation draws upon Ayers 1974 and Hirsch 1982: 72–112.

and solid 'articulated unity' (Hirsch 1982: 107) is what puts S in a position to 'isolate' it and predicate something of it.

An extremely important feature of this account is that it does not require the assumption that S knows what kind of thing she is judging to be F. On one reading, to know what kind of thing it is would be to know that it is a tadpole, that is, the larva of a frog or toad. It makes sense to suppose that S can isolate the tadpole in her experience even if she has never come across tadpoles before and does not know what a tadpole is. To the extent that she is prepared to speculate about the object, she may arrive at a grossly inaccurate conception of its nature, but this will typically not prevent S from perceiving the tadpole as a distinct object in its environment. In an important sense, therefore, she knows which thing she is judging to be F even if she does not satisfy a substantive 'knowing what' requirement with respect to it. If this is correct, then the Identity Argument was too hasty in its transition from the discrimination to the 'knowing what' requirement.

Another way of putting this point would be to employ the terminology of 'sortal concepts',[12] for the claim that it is possible to isolate something in experience even if one lacks substantive knowledge of what it is may be understood as the claim that it is possible to single something out even if one is in a state of sortal ignorance with respect to it. According to what might be called a *moderate* anti-sortalist account of individuation, it is one thing to say, with Hirsch, that 'someone's sortal ignorance with respect to a given object will typically not prevent the object from presenting itself as an articulated unity' (Hirsch 1982: 107), but this is not to say that this kind of singling out would be possible for someone who does not possess any sortal concepts at all. According to an *extreme* anti-sortalist account, perceptual singling out is compatible with one's not possessing any sortal concepts at all, not just with sortal ignorance.[13] Either way, perceptual individuation does not require a sortal identification of what has been singled out.

It might be objected that this line of argument has little direct bearing on the original problem of misconception, since the sortally ignorant subject might still be conceiving of the object of her demonstrative thought as a physical object. Unlike 'person' and 'tadpole', which are sortal

[12] Following Wiggins, I take it that a sortal concept is what a sortal predicate stands for, and that a sortal predicate is one whose extension consists of 'all the particular things or substances of one particular kind' (Wiggins 1980: 7).

[13] Ayers (1974) defends an extreme anti-sortalist account of perceptual individuation.

concepts, 'physical object' is categorial concept, and sortal ignorance or confusion is not the same thing as categorial ignorance or misconception.[14] In contrast, the immaterialist who claims to regard the subject of her thoughts as non-physical is guilty of a categorial misconception. So for the two examples to be analogous, the question that needs to be asked is not whether someone who is sortally ignorant with respect to a given object can still think about it demonstratively, but whether it is possible for one to think perceptual-demonstrative thoughts about a physical object even if one does not regard it as a physical object. Given the distinction between sortal and categorial concepts, anti-sortalist views of individuation do not show that knowledge of the ontological category to which something belongs is not a necessary condition for one to be able to think perceptual-demonstrative thoughts about it.

What would it be for someone who possesses the concept 'physical object' not to regard a perceived physical object as a physical object? One possibility is this: since physical objects are objects in the 'weighty' sense, to regard something as a physical object is, at least, to regard it as something that is capable of unperceived existence. Hence, an idealist who thinks of 'physical objects' as collections of ideas might be said not to regard the 'objects' in her environment as physical objects. A less extreme example would be the following: since physical objects must be solid, a hologram is not a physical object. So someone who sees what is in fact a boulder in the middle distance but who has been led to believe that what she sees is a perfect hologram of a boulder does not believe that this object is a physical object.[15] Yet, both in this case and in the case of the idealist, it would be natural to extend the anti-sortalist view of individuation by arguing that just as one's sortal ignorance with respect to something need not prevent one from perceiving it as an articulated unity, so the fact that one does not believe that the boulder is a physical object need not prevent one from perceiving it as an articulated unity. As long

---

[14] Even an extreme anti-sortalist such as Ayers insists that 'if a speaker indicates something demonstratively, then in order for other people to catch his reference, and to understand what he is indicating, they must know, at some level of generality, *what kind of thing* he is intending to indicate. They must certainly know what *category* of thing it is: whether it is an event, a physical object, a quality or whatever' (1974: 113–14). Presumably, the speaker will know what category of thing he is *intending* to indicate, but the important question in the present context is whether he has failed to refer if he is mistaken about the category to which the purported object of reference belongs.

[15] This example is the reverse of the example discussed in Peacocke 1993: 174. Peacocke's example is one in which a creature is in fact surrounded by holograms, but conceives of them as material objects. Peacocke's conception of a material object is, however, different from the Lockean conception employed in the present discussion.

as the idealist or the subject in the hologram example perceive objects in this way, they know which things their thoughts are about when they think about them demonstratively. Since the subjects in these examples are not conceiving of the objects in question as physical objects, their misconception is similar to the dualist's misconception with respect to the self.

Just as the first response to the original problem of misconception insisted that the dualist does not actually believe that her thinking self is immaterial, so an analogous response to the case of the idealist would be to insist that she does in fact believe that her world is a world of physical objects. On the assumption that her behaviour is the same as everyone else's, the idealist has simply adopted a peculiar notation in describing the world, but the adoption of a notation in which one is not allowed to say that objects can exist unperceived is not the same thing as genuinely believing that they cannot exist unperceived. Indeed, what someone believes about the nature of objects in her environment is arguably more directly manifested in her interactions with them than what she believes about the nature of her thinking self is manifested in her non-linguistic behaviour. In this respect, something like the first response to the problem of misconception may be more compelling in connection with the idealist than it is in connection with the immaterialist about the thinking self.

However plausible this response to the idealist may be, it has no direct bearing on the subject in the hologram example, who need not be an idealist. What manifests her belief that what she sees is a hologram is not just the fact that this is what she says, but also, for example, the fact that she is not disposed to avoid walking into it in the way in which she would be disposed to avoid walking into what she takes to be a genuine boulder. On the plausible assumption that the subject would still be capable of thinking about the boulder demonstratively, the belief that the object of a given demonstrative thought is a physical object does not appear to be a strictly necessary condition of the possibility of thinking such a thought. What remains plausible, however, is that grasp of a perceptual–demonstrative thought requires perceptual or intuitive awareness of the boundaries of object referred to; the belief that it is a physical object is neither necessary nor sufficient. When all is said and done, even the most committed idealist is intuitively aware of objects *as* shaped, located, and solid, and so of the boundary between one physical object and another. It is in virtue of this fact that perceptual-demonstrative reference to physical objects in cases of categorial misconception need not violate a sane version of the discrimination requirement.

This discussion helps to bring into focus the peculiarity of the idea of a feature-placing level of thought or language at which there is no discernment of objects. The problem with this idea, and with the thesis that the transition from this level to the level of singular reference involves the acquisition of criteria of identity, is that there seems to be no level of experience that is more fundamental than that at which we are aware of discrete physical objects whose boundaries are given boundaries.[16] The point of taking a child's utterance 'That is F' as genuinely subject–predicate is not to attribute a grasp of the appropriate criterion of identity to the child but to bring out the fact that the structure of the judgement corresponds to the structure of the awareness upon which it is based. The object of reference is perceived as an articulated unity that has a certain property, so there is no question of the application of a criterion of identity enabling the child to articulate something which she is not already aware of as articulated. The question of how the transition from the feature-placing level to the level of object-awareness is one which simply does not arise.

The fifth response to the problem of misconception in connection with self-reference is exactly parallel to the account which has just been given of how it is possible for someone who is sortally or even categorially ignorant to satisfy the discrimination requirement on demonstrative reference. The dualist satisfies a substantive 'knowing which' requirement on self-reference because and only because she is intuitively aware of that to which she ascribes her experiences as an articulated physical unity. Like the idealist, the dualist claims not to take appearances at face value, but this only shows that the content of intuitive awareness is belief-independent. The dualist's false beliefs about her own nature need not deprive her of a sense of her own boundaries *qua* physical object among physical objects, any more than the fact that one has false beliefs about the object of a perceptual-demonstrative thought need deprive one of a sense of its location and boundaries. As long as the dualist is intuitively aware of her boundaries *qua* physical object, she satisfies a substantive 'knowing which' requirement on self-reference, and this is the point of (D2).

This response to the problem of misconception draws upon aspects of

---

[16] As E. J. Lowe points out, research on infant perception suggests that 'human infants perceptually individuate discrete objects in their environment and do so in a predictively selective way which indicates the exercise of an innate cognitive capacity' (1989: 16–17).

our intuitive self-awareness which Descartes himself emphasized. One is not in one's body as a sailor is in a ship precisely because one's spatial boundaries are, in a sense, felt as one's own boundaries. The distinction between mind and body is one drawn at the level of philosophical reflection rather than one that is given in ordinary self-awareness.[17] To the extent that one is intuitively aware of oneself *qua* subject as a bounded physical object, such awareness embodies an illusion, by Descartes's lights, about the true nature of the thinking subject. Yet, if (D2) is correct, even the most committed dualist's concrete grasp of which thing is the subject of her experiences cannot help but draw upon such intuitive awareness. This is what makes the Cartesian position so paradoxical; it is committed to dismissing as illusory the very mode of self-awareness which underpins its own ability to use 'I' as a referring expression.

This casts fresh light on Lichtenberg's challenge. Since, as Hume and Kant stressed, there is no such thing as intuitive awareness of oneself as an immaterial substance, it might be tempting to conclude that the 'I' of the Cartesian *cogito* cannot be a genuine referring expression. From the perspective of (D2), the right response to Lichtenberg's challenge is to point out that the subject–predicate structure of mental self-ascriptions is quite unproblematic, since it corresponds to the structure of one's intuitive awareness of the presented subject of thought and experience as a bounded physical object. There is therefore no question of the use of the first person pronoun going 'beyond' what is given in intuitive self-awareness or of its needing to be grounded in an accurate conception of the nature and identity-conditions of the object of reference. To insist upon such a grounding would simply be to make oneself vulnerable to the problem of misconception.

This account of how (D2) helps to disarm the problem of misconception will be unconvincing unless more is said about the precise sense in which intuitive awareness of oneself as a physical object provides one with a sense of one's own boundaries. It has already been explained what intuitive awareness of oneself as a physical object amounts to: to be aware of oneself in this sense is to be intuitively aware of oneself *qua* subject as shaped, solid, and located. In the context of the Objectivity Argument, much was made of the role of awareness of one's own location and solidity in spatial perception. In the present context, more needs to be made of the sense which each of us has of his or her own shape. To be aware of

---

[17] See Descartes's letter to Princess Elizabeth, dated 28 June 1643, in Cottingham, Stoothoff, Murdoch, and Kenny 1991: 226–29.

the shape of objects distinct from oneself is to be aware of their boundaries. By the same token, intuitive awareness of one's own shape provides
one with a sense of one's own boundaries *qua* subject; to have a sense of
oneself as determinately shaped is therefore to have a concrete sense of
where one ends and where the rest of the world begins.[18] Awareness of
the subject of one's experiences as something with a determinate shape,
as well as solidity and location, is a necessary condition of consciousness
of self-identity because it is in being aware of one's spatial properties
that one satisfies the discrimination requirement on self-reference.

6. Objections to (D2)

How convincing is this defence of (D2)? The first objection to the intuition version of the Identity Argument is that what one is intuitively
aware of as a physical object in bodily self-awareness is the shape of one's
body, and that awareness of the boundaries of one's body does not
explain how one satisfies the discrimination requirement on self-reference unless body and self are assumed to be identical. This line of attack
will be familiar from Chapter 2, where it was explained why it fails. The
point, it will be recalled, is that the bodily self is not a 'mere' object but a
'subject-object'; it is the *presented* subject of perception and thought, so
awareness of its boundaries is at the same time awareness of one's own
boundaries *qua* subject of perception of thought. It is true that the
account given in Chapter 2 of the idea that the bodily self is the presented subject of perception took it for granted that our perceptions present
themselves as perceptions of physical objects that are distinct from ourselves. So if the Identity Argument is understood as an attempt to establish that self-conscious experience must satisfy the objectivity-condition,
the present account of how bodily self-awareness enables one to discriminate oneself from other things in the world would be question-begging.
It has already been remarked, however, that this is not how the Identity
Argument should be understood.

The next objection is that intuitions without concepts are blind, so
unless conceptual capacities are in some way operative in experience

---

[18] Michael Martin also emphasizes the role of bodily awareness in providing one with a
'sense of our limits and boundaries with the rest of the world, some sense of the contrast
between what is oneself and what is other' (1993: 211). Martin's account of the aspects of
bodily awareness which are important in the present connection is, however, rather different from the account given here.

itself, it makes no sense to suppose that intuitive awareness puts one in a position to delineate an object of judgement. The underlying point here is that experience is, in Kant's words, 'a knowledge which determines an object through perceptions' (A176/B218), and knowledge requires both intuitions and concepts. Thus knowledge of which thing one is cannot be conceived of as something 'non-conceptual'. This objection will also be familiar from Chapter 2, where it was seen to rest upon a misunderstanding of the notion of intuitive self-awareness. At least for the moderate anti-sortalist, intuitive awareness of the boundary between one object and another need not be non-conceptual. The fifth response to the problem of misconception takes it that intuitive self-awareness is belief-independent, but the thesis that conceptual capacities are operative in experience is not obviously equivalent to the thesis that one must believe that things are as experience represents them as being.

An apparently more threatening objection to the fifth response to the problem of misconception is that it is at odds with what has been described as the 'Sortal Dependency of Individuation' (Wiggins 1980: 15). When the second Identity Argument was first introduced into the discussion, it was represented as being committed to the following: to delineate an object in thought is to draw its boundaries, and it makes no sense to suppose that one can draw the boundaries of something in thought if one does not know what kind of thing it is. This was rapidly abandoned in the light of the problem of misconception, but it was never properly explained why the Identity Argument maintains that there is such a close connection between 'knowing which' and 'knowing what'. The explanation is this: to single out some object x is, as Wiggins puts it, to put oneself into a position to 'specify what it turns on whether or not an arbitrary object w, referred to whatever way . . . is or is not the same as the object singled out' (1995: 221). If one has no idea what it would be for the judgement 'x is w' to be true, then it is indeterminate which entity one has singled out. The core of the thesis of the sortal dependency of individuation is that for a judgement such as 'x is w' to be true, there must be a sortal concept f such that x is the same f as w. Since sortal concepts determine identity and persistence conditions for members of their extension, a sortal identification of x puts one in a position to address typical identity questions concerning x. Unless one is able to address such questions, one has failed to make it clear which object is at issue.

In the light of this account of individuation, it might be objected that the problem with the fifth response to the problem of misconception is that it fails to explain how one's intuitive awareness of something as an 'articulated unity' is supposed to be able to put one in a position to address questions about its identity. In the case of a continuant, one must understand what its diachronic identity consists in, yet the fifth response fails to explain how, without an accurate sortal identification of x, one can have a proper conception of what it is for x to persist. This gap in the fifth response is all the more surprising because questions about the nature of consciousness of self-identity, which is what is at issue in the present context, are most naturally understood as questions about consciousness of the identity of the self through time. Yet it would surely be quite implausible to suppose that, in the absence of a grasp of constitutive criteria of subject-identity, intuitive awareness of one's spatial properties puts one in a position to understand that the presented subject of one's current experience is the same as the subject of some past experience.

One reaction to this argument would be to claim that while the fifth response does not yield an adequate account of consciousness of self-identity over time, consciousness of the subject of one's representations as an articulated unity does amount to consciousness of its identity at a time. The problem with this response, however, is that the notions of synchronic and diachronic identity cannot be so sharply separated.[19] A better response would be to question the idea that individuation is sortally dependent to an extent which the fifth response cannot accommodate. Consider, in this connection, Strawson's observation that 'one has not sensibly discriminated, or distinguished, or "picked out" something unless one has some reason for counting what one is attending to at some subsequent moment as the same, or not the same thing, as what one discriminated at an earlier moment' (1974c: 97). The question which now arises is whether having such a reason requires an accurate sortal identification of the object. Just as it is possible to become aware of an object's spatial boundaries without knowing what kind of object it is, so there seems no reason why one should not be aware of its continuity over a period of observation even if one lacks a sortal identification of it. So when the sortally ignorant or misguided subject judges 'That is F', she knows which thing her judgement is about both because she is intuitively aware of the object judged to be F as an articulated synchronic unity and because she can, with good reason, count it as numerically identical through time.

Indeed, it is not clear that there is anything in what has just been said

[19] On this point, see Wiggins 1980: 70.

with which the sortalist would wish to disagree. Even by Wiggins's own lights, 'it is perfectly possible for a thinker to qualify as singling something out, as being in the right *rapport* for that, without *knowing* what he is singling out or having any in the context informative answer to the question what he has singled it out *as*' (Wiggins 1980: 218). In such cases, the thesis of sortal dependence reduces to the claim that when a strange thing is singled out, its perceived persistence cannot help but provide the thinker with the assurance that the item is a member of a 'well defined thing kind' (ibid.). The main question raised by this account is the following: even if one has such an assurance, what work is it supposed to be doing in the singling out? On the face of it, the thought that the item singled out belongs in some well defined kind presupposes and so cannot explain the singling out; the thought is, in this sense, extraneous to the drawing of a boundary around the strange thing. Even if the sortalist is not persuaded by this argument, the fact remains that the concession that discrimination without actual sortal identification is possible is all that is needed by the moderate anti-sortalist version of the fifth response. Given this concession, the fifth response can continue to maintain that intuitive awareness of something as a synchronic and diachronic physical unity puts one in a position to predicate something of it even if one is in a state of sortal ignorance with respect to it or has false beliefs about its ontological nature.

While the fifth response might be thought to explain how it is possible to satisfy a substantive 'knowing which' requirement on demonstrative judgement even if one does not know what kind of thing the judgement is about, it might be objected that this has little bearing on first-person judgements. In the case of demonstrative judgements, one's awareness of the object of judgement as an articulated synchronic and diachronic unity involves the exercise of an ability to keep track of the object. In contrast, it is distinctive of the 'cognitive dynamics'[20] of I-thoughts that, as Evans puts it, such thoughts do not require 'any skill or *care* (not to lose track of something) on the part of the subject' (Evans 1982: 237). Someone in a state of sortal ignorance with respect to the object of a demonstrative thought may have good reason for counting what she is attending to at a given time as the same as an object discriminated at an earlier moment, but this model cannot be applied to consciousness of the

---

[20] Following Kaplan, Evans describes 'cognitive dynamics' as being concerned with 'how a person's belief system is organized to take account of the passage of time' (1982: 235).

self for the simple reason that the subject of one's thoughts is something which one does not normally 'attend to' at all. This is not to say that I-thoughts are not subject to Russell's Principle. The point is rather that an adequate account of how such thoughts conform to Russell's Principle must also respect the differences between first-person and demonstrative thoughts. The problem with (D2), it might be argued, is that it ignores these differences. Intuitive awareness of oneself as a physical object cannot explain how I-thoughts satisfy the 'knowing which' requirement because such awareness would have to involve some form of perceptual 'self-tracking'. Since there is a 'no tracking' requirement on first-person thought, (D2) is a non-starter.

Of all the objections to (D2) considered so far, this is the most serious. The appropriate response to it is similar to the response in Chapter 2 to a parallel objection to the intuition version of the Objectivity Argument. The suggested response combines two features: it accepts the 'no tracking' requirement but argues that there is no conflict between this requirement and (D2). To be intuitively aware of something as a persisting physical object is to be intuitively aware of it as a shaped, solid, and located synchronic and diachronic unity, and one can be aware of oneself as a physical object in this sense even if such awareness does not require any skill or care 'not to lose track of something'. Just as one is intuitively aware of the presented bodily subject of one's thoughts and experiences as shaped, solid, and located, so one is intuitively aware of it as temporally extended. This is the core of consciousness of one's own identity as the subject of temporally separate representations. Intuitive awareness of oneself as the temporally extended subject of different representations no more requires an accurate conception of what one's own identity consists in than intuitive awareness of the object of a demonstrative thought as a diachronic unity requires an accurate conception of what its identity consists in. If this were not so, it would be difficult to understand how someone who regards her own identity as consisting in the identity of her immaterial soul can still be conscious of her own identity as the subject of temporally diverse representations.

In the light of these remarks, what significance should be attached to the fact that there is a 'no tracking' requirement on consciousness of oneself as temporally extended? If one were to accept the stipulation that one can only be intuitively aware of something as a physical object if one has to keep track of it or attend to it, then the 'no tracking' requirement would be fatal for (D2), but, to echo a point made in Chapter 2, the considerations which support (D2) are arguably more powerful than the case for such a stipulation. Thus, the fact that one is intuitively aware of one-self as the numerically identical subject of temporally diverse represen-tations without having to keep track of oneself should not be taken to show that one is not intuitively aware of oneself *qua* subject as an object at all. Rather, it helps to bring out the importance of insisting that in intuitive self-awareness one is presented to oneself not as a 'mere' object but as a persisting, physical *subject*-object. Since this is a point insisted upon by the intuition version of the Identity Argument itself, (D2) can hardly be accused of failing to respect the cognitive dynamics of I-think-ing. While the 'no tracking' requirement marks an important difference between the basis of a first-person and a demonstrative thought, there is still a perfectly respectable sense in which one satisfies the discrimination requirement on first-person thought in virtue of one's intuitive aware-ness of oneself *qua* subject as a persisting physical object among persist-ing physical objects.

All the objections to (D2) considered so far have been concerned with its coherence or intelligibility. The remaining objection accepts the coherence of (D2) but disputes the suggestion that intuitive awareness of oneself as a physical object is necessary for consciousness of self-identity. A popular argument against the necessity claim is an argument from the possibility of total sensory deprivation. Anscombe writes:

And now imagine that I get into a state of 'sensory deprivation'. Sight is cut off, and I am locally anaesthetized everywhere, perhaps floating in a tank of tepid water; I am unable to speak, or to touch any part of my body with another. Now I tell myself, 'I won't let this happen again!' If the object I meant by 'I' is this body, this human being, then in these circumstances it won't be present to my senses; and how else can it be 'present to' me? But have I lost what I mean by 'I'? Is that not present to me? Am I reduced to, as it were, 'referring in absence'? I have not lost my 'self-consciousness'; nor can what I mean by 'I' be an object no longer present to me. (1994: 152)

Although, contrary to what Anscombe suggests, support for (D2) does not commit one to the thesis that 'I' *means* 'this body', her example clear-ly constitutes a threat to (D2). The implicit objection to (D2) is this: someone in a state of total sensory deprivation would not be intuitively aware of herself as a physical object but would still be capable of think-ing first-personally, conscious of her own identity as the subject of dif-ferent I-thoughts. So intuitive awareness of oneself as a physical object is not a necessary condition of consciousness of self-identity.

One response to this objection would be to point out that total sensory deprivation need not deprive one of the *conception* of oneself as a physical object, and that it is this background understanding which sustains the sensorily deprived subject's ability to think first-personally. However, this will not satisfy critics of (D2) who are also critics of (D1). If conceiving of oneself as a physical object is, as opponents of (D1) maintain, not a necessary condition of self-consciousness, then the sensorily deprived subject need not regard herself as a physical object. So while a sensorily deprived subject's conception of herself as a physical object might be what is sustaining her ability to think first-personally, it need not be.

Since the intuition version of the Identity Argument is, in part, a reaction to doubts about the concept version, it would be inappropriate for supporters of (D2) to respond to this line of argument by insisting on the correctness of (D1). On the other hand, while the problem of misconception shows that (D1) is not unproblematic, the point of the intuition version of the Identity Argument is to offer a response to this problem which respects the 'knowing which' requirement on first-person thinking. Thus, the two versions of the Identity Argument share a commitment to Russell's Principle. This raises the following question about the sensory deprivation scenario: if the deprived subject is not intuitively aware of herself as a physical object and does not conceive of herself as a physical object, then why should it not be concluded that she would be unable to discriminate herself from other things in the world and so would be incapable of thinking first-personally? This does not amount to suggestion that the subject's I-thoughts somehow fail to refer to herself. Since she cannot think first-personally, the question of reference-failure does not arise.

Perhaps this is too hasty. It might be held, for example, that the deprived and misguided subject is capable of thinking first-personally as long as she was intuitively aware of herself as a physical object before being placed in the deprivation tank.[21] In other words, what the sensory deprivation example shows is that self-consciousness is possible in a given stretch of experience even if one is not intuitively aware of oneself as a physical object in that stretch of experience, but it does not show that one would be in a position to think first-personally if one has never been presented to oneself as a physical object. This, it might be claimed, is the force of (D2).

---

[21] According to McDowell, for example, the moral of Anscombe's example is simply that 'one's bodily being need not always impress itself on one' (McDowell 1994: 104 n. 25).

Critics of (D2) will presumably be unconvinced by all of this. They will object that consciousness of self-identity in a given stretch of experience can only be parasitic upon the subject's history of bodily self-awareness if she remembers having been presented to herself as a physical object, but it makes sense to suppose that the sensorily deprived subject can think first-personally even if she suffers from amnesia.[22] If it is possible to think first-personally despite the fact that one is no longer intuitively aware of oneself as a physical object, does not conceive of oneself as a physical object, and has lost one's memories, then one would have to conclude that first-person thought does not require knowledge of which thing one is. On the other hand, if one is already committed to Russell's Principle, then the case which has just been described would not be a case of first-person thinking not conforming to this principle; rather, it would be a case of a subject who is incapable of such thinking. So the question which now needs to be addressed is whether the burden of proof lies with the intuition version of the Identity Argument or with proponents of the radical sensory deprivation objection.

When the question is put in these terms, the remarkably popular assumption that the burden of proof lies entirely with the argument for (D2) seems incredible. For it is a familiar point in discussions of a wide range of philosophical issues that intuitions about far-fetched cases may be unreliable and might need to be rejected in the light of broadly 'theoretical' considerations. When a well-supported theory conflicts with the deliverances of intuition in the ordinary, non-Kantian sense, it is not always rational to abandon the theory. This methodological observation applies with equal force in the present context. The sensory deprivation argument begins with the case of an ordinary subject and progressively abstracts from everything which provides the subject with a sense of herself as a physical object among physical objects. At each stage, the argument appeals to the brute intuition that the subject would still be capable of thinking first-personally, but this is not enough to warrant the rejection of (D2). Indeed, it might be held that the very theoretical considerations which support the intuition version of the Identity Argument also constitute grounds for suspecting that the sensory deprivation case is one in which, as Snowdon writes in a different context, 'we find ourselves with what, in the light of all the evidence, has to be recognized as a deviant, although recalcitrant, intuition' (1991: 126). By the lights of the Identity Argument, to imagine a subject who has absolutely no sense of

---

[22] O'Brien presses this point in 1995: 239.

herself as a bodily presence in the world is to imagine a subject who is incapable of thinking first-personally. While it would be unwise to claim that the sensory deprivation example has no force at all, it would be equally unwise to allow one's thinking about the nature of self-consciousness to be disproportionately influenced by examples whose intelligibility is, to put it mildly, not beyond question.

7. The Fifth Response and (D1)

The fifth response to the problem of misconception is a response to an objection to (D1). Yet what the fifth response actually achieves is to provide a basis for (D2) rather than (D1). This may create the impression that the fifth response is an irrelevance from the perspective of (D1), since it does nothing to support the concept version of the Identity Argument. Such an impression would not be entirely accurate. To see why not, more needs to be said about the question of whether intuitive awareness of oneself as a physical object is sufficient for consciousness of self-identity. The suggestion to be considered is that when it is seen why it is not sufficient, and what more is required, it will become apparent that (D1) can be at least partially vindicated.

Consider once again what is involved in grasping a perceptual-demonstrative thought about a physical object. It was argued above that intuitive awareness of an object as an articulated synchronic and diachronic unity puts one in a position to predicate something of it in a demonstrative thought even if one is in a state of sortal ignorance with respect to it. This cannot, however, be a complete account of the matter for someone who is committed to Russell's Principle. Since physical objects cannot be individuated without reference to their positions in space and time, it would seem that even in cases of sortal ignorance one does not know which object a demonstrative judgement is about unless one either knows its spatio-temporal location or has the practical ability to discover it. To have this ability is to be able to engage in certain patterns of reasoning which involve the conception of the object as one among others in a spatially ordered world. So the sense in which intuitive awareness of an object as an articulated unity is not sufficient for 'knowing which' is that it is possible for one to perceive something as a unity even if one is incapable of engaging in patterns of reasoning which would enable one to determine its objective spatio-temporal location. Infants, after all, appear to be capable of perceiving objects as articulated unities, but are incapable of engaging in reasoning of this sort (see Spelke and Van de Walle 1993).

These considerations also have a bearing on first-person thought. If, as the concept version of the Identity Argument assumes, 'a fundamental identification of a person involves a consideration of him as the person occupying such-and-such a spatio-temporal location' (Evans 1982: 211), then while knowledge of which thing one is does not require actual knowledge of one's spatio-temporal location, it does require that one has the practical capacity to determine one's location. To have this capacity is to be capable of engaging in certain patterns of reasoning which involve the conception of oneself as 'one object among others' (ibid.). In particular, one must regard oneself as moving continuously through space, and must think of one's location as determinable on the basis of one's perceptions. So the sense in which intuitive awareness of oneself *qua* subject as an articulated synchronic and diachronic unity is insufficient for knowledge of which thing one is, is therefore that such awareness is no guarantee that one will be capable of engaging in the relevant patterns of reasoning.

Further support for this argument is provided by the following line of thought: on the face of it, we are capable of grasping thoughts about ourselves which we are incapable of verifying. In Evans's terminology, this is to say that our thinking about ourselves conforms to the 'Generality Constraint'.[23] The connection between this point and the earlier discussion of consciousness of self-identity is that for I-thinking to conform to the Generality Constraint is, in part, a matter of the thinker being able to grasp the ascription of a range of different predicates to one and the same 'I'. The next stage of the argument is the claim that for one's I-thinking to conform to the Generality Constraint, one must regard oneself as 'something whose career is a substantial continuity in the objective world' (McDowell 1994: 102), a third person as well as a first person. Once again, the moral is that intuitive awareness of oneself as a physical object is not sufficient for consciousness of self-identity. Awareness of oneself as a synchronic and diachronic unity is not sufficient to provide one with the conception of oneself as a substantial continuity in the objective world, and so cannot account for the fact that one's I-thoughts conform to the Generality Constraint.

These considerations might be read as an attempt to rehabilitate the

---

[23] The Generality Constraint states that 'if a subject can be credited with the thought that a is F, then he must have the conceptual resources for entertaining the thought that a is G, for every property of being G of which he has a conception' (Evans 1982: 104).

first response to the problem of misconception. Since intuitive awareness of oneself as a physical object is not sufficient for knowledge of which thing one is, the question to press in connection with someone who claims to regard the subject of her thoughts as incorporeal is whether she satisfies the further requirements that have just been identified. If, in addition to being intuitively aware of her spatiality, she conceives of herself as a spatio-temporally located object among others in the world, a third person as well as a first person, then there is no difficulty with the idea that her first-person thinking conforms to Russell's Principle and the Generality Constraint. On the other hand, it might seem that to say that someone conceives of herself in these terms is to say that she conceives of herself as a physical object. Thus, reflection on the limitations of (D2) appears to have reopened the case for (D1).

While there is undoubtedly something to be said for this line of argument, it goes too far in one familiar respect. For it is one thing to say that one must regard oneself as spatio-temporally located, but it does not follow that one must regard oneself *qua* subject as a physical object. As was argued in Chapter 2, the possibility of regarding oneself as located in the world only geometrically or as an embodied immaterial soul shows that there is a gap between thinking of oneself as spatio-temporally located and conceiving of oneself *qua* subject as shaped and solid. For example, the Cartesian can think of her location as the location of her body, and can think of this location as determinable on the basis of her perceptions; she can think of herself as a third person as well as a first, and can agree that her thinking self is a 'substantial continuity in the objective world', though not a physical substantial continuity.[24] To the extent that her first-person thought is *de facto* sensitive to what actually distinguishes the corporeal subject of her thoughts from everything else in the world—namely, its spatio-temporal location—she might still be said to know in practice which thing in the world she is despite her misguided self-conception.

The position, then, is this: while intuitive awareness of oneself as an articulated synchronic and diachronic unity is insufficient for consciousness of self-identity, the further conditions do not amount to a complete

---

[24] Unlike the Cartesian dualist, someone who claims to regard herself as a merely geometrically located point of view purports not to be thinking of herself *qua* subject as a persisting substance. To this extent, there is still a question about how her thinking manages to conform to the Generality Constraint. On the other hand, it is not obvious why it would not be sufficient for one's I-thoughts to conform to this constraint that one thinks of oneself as located in the world only geometrically.

vindication of (D1). On the other hand, the threat posed to (D1) by the problem of misconception no longer seems as serious now as it did at the outset. For while the Identity Argument does not establish that a self-conscious subject must, as it were, get quite as far as conceiving of herself *qua* subject as a physical object, the two versions of this argument do establish that such a subject must go a considerable distance in this direction. Crucially, a subject who is capable of consciousness of her own identity must in general be presented to herself as a physical object and must at least think of herself as spatio-temporally located. There is no better way of bringing out the importance of these claims than to reflect on the contrast between them and the Self-Consciousness Argument for the Exclusion Thesis. The fact that it is possible for a fully self-conscious subject to resist the final transition from conceiving of herself as located in the world to conceiving of herself *qua* subject as a physical object is not without interest, but should not be allowed to obscure the extent to which both versions of the Identity Argument call into question the idea that the perspective of self-consciousness is one from which one cannot conceive of oneself as 'in' the world at all. To the extent that the Identity Argument provides an insight into the incoherence of the Exclusion Thesis, it has established something of lasting importance.

8. *Kant and the Identity Argument*

Since the Identity Argument is broadly Kantian in inspiration, it would be pertinent to examine its bearing on Kant's own account of consciousness of self-identity in the first *Critique*. In the Transcendental Deduction, Kant claims that a priori consciousness of 'the complete identity of the self in respect of all representations which can ever belong to our knowledge' is 'a necessary condition of the possibility of all representations' (A116). He then argues that a necessary condition of consciousness of the identity of the self as the subject of diverse representations is the employment of categories such as those of substance and causality in the conceptualization of these representations. There is, however, no suggestion that consciousness of self-identity requires awareness (in either sense) of the self as a physical object. Indeed, by Kant's lights, the self whose identity one must be capable of grasping when attaching an 'I think' to one's representations is not to be conceived of as an object at all, corporeal or incorporeal. So Kant is committed to the Exclusion Thesis. In that case, is Kant's theory threatened by the Identity Argument? Or might it be that the Identity Argument is undermined by Kant's theory? As there are several different versions of the Identity Argument, the best way of pursuing these questions would be to consider in turn the relationship between what Kant has to say about consciousness of self-identity and each version of the Identity Argument.

To begin with the first concept version of the Identity Argument, its starting-point is the self-ascription requirement. On the face of it, this requirement corresponds to Kant's claim that 'it must be possible for the "I think" to accompany all my representations' (B131). Just as satisfaction of the self-ascription requirement requires an ability on the part of the subject to grasp the numerical identity of that to which she ascribes, or can ascribe, her experiences, so Kant insists that one must be capable of thinking of the diverse representations to which the 'I think' is attached or is attachable as belonging to one and the same self. Despite these similarities, however, it may well be a mistake to interpret Kant's remarks about the 'I think' as giving expression to the first Identity Argument's self-ascription requirement. To begin with, Kant is concerned in the Deduction with transcendental consciousness of self-identity or 'transcendental apperception'. The significance of this is that it is not clear that attaching the 'I' of transcendental consciousness to a representation is a way of self-ascribing it. Kant repeatedly describes this 'I' as entirely empty, as meaning 'a something in general' (A355); it is 'not a representation distinguishing a particular object, but a form of representation in general' (A346/B404). Attaching to a representation an expression which fails to distinguish a particular object cannot be, in any straightforward sense, a means of ascribing that representation to one particular subject rather than another.

As for the identity component of the self-ascription requirement, it is striking that while Kant does sometimes refer to the relation of representations to the identity of the subject in transcendental apperception, he more usually characterizes transcendental apperception as involving consciousness of the identity of *self-consciousness*. By the lights of the first Identity Argument, to grasp the identity of that to which experiences are ascribed by attaching an 'I think' to them would be to grasp the numerical identity of the substantial subject of one's experiences, an object among others in the world. In contrast, the identity of self-consciousness is a 'logical identity' and 'in no way proves the numerical identity of my subject' (A363). It remains to be seen what Kant has in mind here, but the apparent gap between consciousness of the 'logical' identity of self-

consciousness and consciousness of the identity of the subject *qua* substantial continuity in the objective world is further evidence that Kant's
remarks about the 'I think' do not amount in any straightforward sense to
acceptance of the self-ascription requirement.

The fact that transcendental self-consciousness involves no more than
consciousness of the identity of apperception or self-consciousness also
suggests that there is no place in Kant's account for the empirical criteria
requirement. It will be recalled that an empirical criterion of identity is
such that it is possible for sensible intuition to present us with an object
which satisfies it, but there is no question of the identity of self-consciousness being sensibly intuitable. In Kant's words, 'this identity of the
subject, of which I can be conscious in all my representations, does not
concern any intuition of the subject, whereby it is given as object' (B408).
To demand empirical criteria of identity for the 'I' of transcendental
apperception would be to commit some sort of category mistake, so even
if it is true that there can only be empirical criteria of subject-identity if
subjects are physical objects, this has no bearing on transcendental apperception. From the perspective of transcendental apperception, the question of whether the self *qua* object must be conceived of as corporeal is
simply irrelevant.

Despite his rejection of the physical object requirement in connection
with transcendental apperception, Kant shares some of the first Identity
Argument's doubts about the Cartesian account of self-consciousness. In
particular, the fact that Cartesian egos cannot be sensibly intuited is taken
by Kant as a decisive objection to the rational psychologist's thesis that
the numerical identity of the self *qua* thinking substance can be known
with a priori certainty. For Kant, knowledge of an object requires both
an intuition and a concept of it. The 'self' of rational psychology is supposed to be an object among others in the world, despite its immateriality. So when the rational psychologist claims knowledge of her numerical
identity *qua* thinking substance, this claim has no chance of being acceptable unless it has the appropriate conceptual and intuitive backing. In
contrast, since transcendental apperception involves a logical rather than
a substantial identity, knowledge of this identity is not subject to the same
epistemological requirements as knowledge of the identity of the subject
qua object. For this reason, Kant can consistently endorse the first
Identity Argument's criticism of rational psychology while maintaining
that this criticism leaves untouched his own denial of (D1) in connection
with transcendental self-consciousness.

With regard to the second concept version of the Identity Argument, the key to this argument is the discrimination or 'knowing which' requirement, the thesis that the ascription of different states or determinations to an identical subject turns on the existence of some means of distinguishing or identifying the subject of such ascriptions as one object among others. This requirement also plays a part in the first concept version of the Identity Argument, as the basis of the empirical criteria requirement. The difference between the two versions of the Identity Argument is that the first version sees the discrimination requirement as flowing from a verificationist principle of significance, whereas the second version presents it as a consequence of a non-verificationist 'knowing which' requirement. Despite this difference, the discrimination requirement is no more relevant to transcendental self-consciousness than the empirical criteria requirement. Once again, the key to understanding Kant's position is the fact that the numerical identity of apperception is a logical rather than a substantial identity. There is no question of transcendental self-consciousness depending upon the availability of some means of distinguishing the subject of this form of self-consciousness as an object among others in the world because the 'I' of apperception cannot be thought of as an object at all. To repeat, this 'I' is a 'form of representation in general' rather than a 'representation distinguishing a particular object' (A346/B404). Just as the demand for empirical criteria of identity for the form of representation embodies a kind of category mistake, so the formal 'I' of transcendental apperception cannot intelligibly be regarded as something of which it is possible to have discriminating knowledge.

According to the second concept version of the Identity Argument, knowledge of which thing is referred to by one's uses of 'I' requires knowledge of the kind of thing one is. Assuming that one's uses of 'I' refer to a person, and that persons are individuated in spatio-temporal terms, it follows that first-person thought requires the conception of oneself as the person occupying such-and-such a spatio-temporal location. Given Kant's rejection of the discrimination requirement on transcendental apperception, none of this has any bearing on his account of self-consciousness in the Transcendental Deduction. It is a difficult question whether Kant conceived of the 'I' of transcendental apperception as a referring expression at all, but it does appear that in attaching this 'I' to our thoughts we do not designate a person; at best we 'designate' the transcendental subject, but 'without knowing anything of it either by direct acquaintance or otherwise' (A355). The question of whether persons are physical things cannot therefore have the same significance for the argument of the Transcendental Deduction as it has for the second Identity Argument. As far as Kant's account of transcendental apperception is concerned, (D1) is unwarranted.

As for the intuition version of the Identity Argument, Kant would no doubt have regarded the suggestion that intuitive awareness of oneself as a physical object is necessary for one to be able to think the logical identity of the 'I' as scarcely intelligible. In contrast, there is some evidence in the 'Refutation of Idealism' that Kant would have agreed that bodily awareness is a necessary condition of *empirical* self-consciousness.[25] Empirical self-consciousness is the consciousness of one's existence as determined in time. The determination of one's existence in time is only possible through the perception of objects in space outside one, and spatial perception requires bodily self-awareness. There are, however, important differences between this argument and the intuition version of the Identity Argument. Questions about time-determination do not figure in the latter, and the 'Refutation' does not appear to concern itself with the conditions under which it is possible for an empirically self-conscious subject to discriminate herself from other things in the world. Rather, bodily self-awareness is significant in the context of the 'Refutation' because empirical self-consciousness requires that one's experience satisfies the objectivity condition, and the latter involves bodily self-awareness. In this respect, the argument of the 'Refutation' is closer to the intuition version of the Objectivity Argument than it is to the intuition version of the Identity Argument.

This illustrates a more general point about Kant's position in relation to the Identity Argument. If one's theory of self-consciousness is deeply influenced by the discrimination requirement, then one might be persuaded that intuitive awareness of oneself as a physical object is necessary for one to be able to delineate the subject of one's thoughts. The discrimination requirement is, however, motivated by a theory of singular reference which it would be a mistake to read into the first *Critique*. For this reason, it is highly unlikely that the intuition version of the Identity Argument is any more faithful to Kant's account of empirical self-consciousness than it is to his account of transcendental self-consciousness. Thus, although it would not be correct to claim that Kant did not attach any weight to bodily self-awareness in his thinking about self-consciousness, the intuition version of the Identity Argument is not the argument of the 'Refutation' and appears to be at odds with Kant's account of transcendental apperception.

[25] For a defence of this reading of the 'Refutation', see Cassam 1993a.

In the light of these remarks, it would be appropriate to return to the question of whether Kant's theory of transcendental self-consciousness is a threat to, or is undermined by, the Identity Argument. This question is difficult to answer because it is extremely difficult to understand the thesis that the numerical identity of the 'I' of transcendental apperception is a 'logical' rather than a 'substantial' identity. In the next part, an attempt will be made to explain this thesis in a way which makes it clear why it might be thought to entail that transcendental apperception is not subject to the discrimination or empirical criteria requirements. It will then be argued that Kant's position is indefensible. To anticipate, even the logical identity of transcendental apperception cannot be grasped without awareness of oneself as an object among others in the world.

9. *The 'Logical' Identity of the 'I'*

Kant attributes the following characteristics to the 'I think' of transcendental apperception:

(i) *Identity*: the 'I think' is 'one and the same in all consciousness' (B132), and its identity is '*a priori* certain' (A113).

(ii) *Universality*: the 'I think' is a 'universal proposition' (A398) 'which I can apply to every thinking subject' (A355).

(iii) *Emptiness*: the 'I' of the 'I think' is neither an intuition nor a concept (A382). It has no special designation and is 'not a representation distinguishing a particular object' (A346/B404). It is an 'entirely empty expression' (A355).

(iv) *Formality*: the 'I' is 'the mere form of consciousness' (A382), a 'form of representation in general' (A346/B404).

(v) *Non-Determinativeness*: although the 'I think' is an empirical proposition which contains within it the proposition 'I exist', it does not itself determine the manner of one's existence 'whether it be as substance or as accident' (B420).

Consider, in the light of this list, Kant's remarks about the logical identity of the 'I'. Having described this 'I' as a representation which accompanies 'with complete identity, all representations at all times in *my* consciousness' (A363), he goes on to argue that 'despite the logical identity of the "I", such a change may have occurred in it as does not allow the retention of its identity, and yet we may ascribe to it the same-sounding "I"' (ibid.). This passage may be understood as follows: suppose that p and q are representations each of which is accompanied by an 'I think'. Since this 'I' is, by definition, the form of consciousness rather than a representation distinguishing a particular object, to think its identity is to grasp the fact that the form of consciousness in 'I think p' is the same as the form of consciousness in 'I think q'. The 'logical identity' of the 'I' is this identity of form. The important point about this identity is that it is insensitive to the boundary between one thinker and another, however that boundary is drawn. Even if the subject A who thinks 'I think p' is numerically distinct from the subject B who thinks 'I think q', the form of A's consciousness of p is the same as B's consciousness of q. According to the Third Paralogism, it is this insensitivity to differences between individual subjects that makes it illegitimate to argue from the identity of the form of consciousness in different 'I think' instances to the numerical identity of the substantial subject of those instances.

This account of the logical identity of the 'I' suggests the following gloss on the five Kantian theses about the 'I think':

(i) *Identity*: the assertion that the 'I think' is one and the same in all consciousness may now be understood as giving expression to the fact that (a) all conscious representations, 'no matter whose' (Strawson 1987: 207), must be capable of being accompanied by an 'I think', and (b) all 'I think' instances,[26] no matter in whose consciousness they occur, are instances in which representations are apprehended as belonging to an 'I'. The numerical identity of the 'I' is a priori certain because it can be known with a priori certainty that the form of all 'I think' instances is the same.

(ii) *Universality*: the universality of the 'I think' consists in the fact that the 'I' in the universal proposition 'I think' is 'the one condition which accompanies all thought' (A398) and therefore 'announces itself as a universal proposition valid for all thinking beings' (A405)

(iii) *Emptiness*: the thesis that the 'I' of the 'I think' does not distinguish a particular object is based on the fact that it makes no sense to suppose that the form of consciousness, which is common to different I-thinkers, picks out a particular object in the world. In Peacocke's Fregean terminology (see Peacocke 1983: 108), when Peter thinks 'I think p' and Paul thinks 'I think q', the modes of presentation which they each express by 'I' must be different

[26] The phrase ' "I think" instance' is taken from Henrich 1989: 272.

since they determine different objects. Nevertheless, they think of themselves in the same type of way, the type denoted by '[self]'. The constituent of all Peter's first-person thoughts is a token mode of presentation which consists of the type [self] indexed by Peter. The constituent of all Paul's first-person thoughts is a token mode of presentation which consists of the type [self] indexed by Paul. The identity of the form of Peter's consciousness and the form of Paul's consciousness consists in the fact that their thoughts are both of the [self] type. Since it is token modes of presentation which pick out particular objects, to ask which object is picked out by the type [self] would be to commit a kind of category mistake. By Kant's lights, this is the sort of mistake that one would be making if one were to think of the 'I' of apperception—the mere form of consciousness—as distinguishing a particular object. This also helps to bring out the fact that Kant's argument is a version of what was referred to in Chapter 1 as the Abstraction Argument, for when one talks of the 'I' of apperception, one is abstracting from any reference to individual thinkers in different 'I think' instances.

(iv) *Formality*: the 'I think' is the form of conscious representation because it is only in virtue of one's ability to attach an 'I think' to one's representations that one can be said to be conscious of them at all. The 'I' of apperception 'forms the correlate of all our representations in so far as it is to be at all possible that we should become conscious of them' (A123).

(v) *Non-determinativeness*: Kant claims that the 'I think' is non-determinative, in part, because it does not constitute an intuition of the self, whereas the determination of the mode or manner of one's existence is only possible on the basis of self-intuition.

It is now at least intelligible why the 'I' of transcendental self-consciousness cannot be a point of application for empirical criteria of identity. It only makes sense to speak of empirical criteria in connection with what can be given as an object of sensible intuition, but the form of consciousness is something abstract, and it makes no sense to suppose that it can be sensibly intuited or distinguished as one object among others. It is also worth remarking that empirical criteria of identity are criteria for the 'numerical identity through time . . . of an identical thing'(Strawson 1966: 162), but the form of consciousness is not a temporal item, even if particular instances of this general form are temporally located. So once again, the 'I' of apperception turns out to be something for which it would not be intelligible, even by the lights of the Identity Argument, to demand empirical criteria of identity. By the same token, knowledge of the logical identity of the 'I' of transcendental apperception does not require knowledge of which thing in the spatio–temporal world this 'I' is because it would be senseless to describe the form of consciousness as spatially located. As for the question of whether it would be possible to distinguish oneself *qua* subject of transcendental apperception without intuitive awareness of oneself as a physical object, this question does not arise if the subject of transcendental apperception is not an object among others in the world at all.

This account of Kant's position might prompt the following reaction: the impression that there is any conflict between Kant's theory of transcendental apperception and the Identity Argument is based upon the assumption that the two accounts are accounts of the same thing. It now appears, however, that this assumption is incorrect. When the Identity Argument speaks of consciousness of the identity of the self *qua* subject of diverse representations, what it means by this is consciousness of the identity of the self *qua* concrete individual subject of diverse representations. In contrast, self-consciousness or the 'form of consciousness' is not an individual subject in this sense; strictly speaking, therefore, consciousness of its identity can hardly be described as, in any ordinary sense, consciousness of the identity of a *self*. The fact that the identity of self-*consciousness* can be thought without awareness of oneself as a physical object therefore does nothing to undermine the idea that consciousness of one's own identity *qua* individual subject of diverse experiences requires awareness of oneself as a physical object.

There is something right about the idea that Kant's account of transcendental apperception and the Identity Argument are not straightforward rivals, but the extent to which the two views can be reconciled should not be exaggerated. In the first place, although it was presumably not Kant's view that his notion of transcendental self-consciousness captures the full force of the ordinary notion of consciousness of self-identity, it presumably was his view that the concept of transcendental apperception in some sense captures the essential core of the ordinary notion. So the first question to be considered below is this: is the ability to think the identity of the form of consciousness in different 'I think' instances, if not sufficient, then at least a necessary condition of consciousness of self–identity in the ordinary sense?

Suppose that consciousness of the identity of apperception is a part of consciousness of self-identity in the ordinary sense. Kant's position would still be under threat for the following reason: the claim, made several times above, that the discrimination requirement has no bearing on Kant's notion of transcendental self-consciousness assumes that transcendental apperception is intelligible independently of the notion of consciousness of oneself as an object among others in the world. Since self-consciousness in the latter sense is subject to the discrimination requirement, this 'independent intelligibility' thesis is extremely important for the purposes of showing that the requirements which drive the different versions of the Identity Argument do not apply to Kant's account. In Chapter 3, it was noted that Strawson's suggestion that the concept of transcendental self-consciousness as he understands it might be 'intelligible quite independently of the empirically applicable concept of the identity of a subject of experience' is indefensible (Strawson 1966: 108). By the same token, it might be wondered whether Kant's 'independent intelligibility' thesis is correct. One possibility is that consciousness of the numerically identical subject of different 'I think' instances as an object among others in the world is essential for consciousness of the form of those instances. If this were so, there would be no escape for transcendental self-consciousness in Kant's sense from the demands of the Identity Argument. So the second question to be considered below is this: is consciousness of oneself as an object among others in the world, and therefore as a point of application for the discrimination or empirical criteria requirements, a necessary condition of consciousness of the identity of self-consciousness as Kant understands it?

In connection with the question whether the ability to think the form of consciousness is a part of consciousness of self-identity in the ordinary sense, it will be objected that while the concept of the 'form of consciousness' is one which might be employed by an external analyst in giving an account of the nature of first-person thought, there is no reason to suppose that it must be understood or employed by every subject who is conscious, in the ordinary sense, of his or her own identity. To suppose that such subjects must be able to think in terms of the identity of the form of consciousness in different 'I think' instances is to suppose that in order to be self-conscious one must be able to 'do the philosophy of one's own situation' (Harrison 1970: 219). Being able to do the philosophy of one's own situation is, however, not a necessary condition of self-consciousness. There is therefore every reason to reject the 'form of consciousness' account of transcendental apperception, on the grounds that it collapses the distinction between the perspective of an external analyst of self-consciousness and the perspective of self-consciousness itself.

This objection goes to the heart of one of the most difficult aspects of Kant's method in the Transcendental Deduction, since there are good grounds for thinking that Kant rejected the idea of a sharp distinction between the perspective of an external analyst and that of self-consciousness itself.[27] In the terminology of Chapter 3, Kant regarded transcendental self-consciousness as essentially self-reflexive; roughly, to be self-conscious one must be able to think of oneself as self-conscious. To be able to think of oneself as self-conscious, one must have some understanding of what it is to be self-conscious, and to have this understanding is, in a non-trivial sense, to be able to 'do the philosophy of one's own situation'. For Kant, self-consciousness is intimately connected with the capacity for reflection; if, for example, self-consciousness requires the employment of the categories, then this is something which must be known—at least implicitly—by self-conscious subjects themselves.[28]

On this interpretation of Kant's position, it gives rise to several related difficulties. The first is that attributions of implicit knowledge always need to be carefully justified, and it is not clear that the attribution of, say, implicit knowledge of the 'form of consciousness' to self-conscious subjects respects plausible general constraints on the attribution of knowledge in this sense. The second difficulty concerns the status and plausibility of the claim that self-consciousness must be self-reflexive. It might be plausible that being self-conscious involves being able, in some sense, to do the philosophy of one's own situation, but it is a further question whether it involves being able to do as much of the philosophy of one's own situation as Kant requires. In particular, it is a further question whether self-conscious subjects must have the ability to think the identity of the form of consciousness in different 'I think' instances.

Although the second of these difficulties is undoubtedly one which

---

[27] This point is emphasized in Henrich 1989.

[28] As Henrich puts it, Kant's deduction of the categories 'cannot confine itself to proving, from the distance of an external analyst, that self-consciousness could not come about without the use of the categories. For this would not be to show the internal connection between the consciousness which is self-conscious and the natural consciousness of the validity and functioning of the categories' (1989: 253). According to what Henrich calls Kant's 'Rousseauian' criterion, the deduction must justify 'the ordinary person in claiming the right to have experiences in a well-founded way at any time and to use the principles which are indispensable to this. It does not establish any claims to exclusive knowledge on the part of a few' (ibid.). On my reading, it is this 'Rousseauian' criterion which underpins the idea that a subject who is self-conscious in the ordinary sense must be capable of doing the philosophy of his own situation.

deserves to be taken seriously, it is nevertheless less hostile to Kant's approach than the original Harrisonian objection. Even if Kant's 'form of consciousness' proposal is ultimately unacceptable, its unacceptability is no longer to be thought of as capable of being established by appeal to a blanket distinction between the perspective of an external analyst and that of self-consciousness itself. From a Kantian standpoint, such blanket distinction fails to respect the thesis that transcendental self-consciousness is essentially self-reflexive; the question is not whether self-consciousness requires the ability to do the philosophy of one's own situation, but whether the particular form of reflection demanded by the form of consciousness proposal is part and parcel of self-consciousness.

The most straightforward reason for doubting whether being able to think the identity of the form of consciousness in different 'I think' instances is necessary for consciousness of self-identity in the ordinary sense is this: suppose that one does conceive of oneself as an 'objective continuant' (McDowell 1994: 101), an object among others in the world. If one is aware of one's experiences as belonging to the career of such a continuant, it would be implausible to deny that one is, in the ordinary sense, conscious of one's own identity through the diversity of experience. Whether or not the conception of one's experiences as belonging to the career of an objective continuant is necessary for consciousness of self-identity, it is surely sufficient. Yet one can have the latter conception without being able to think the identity of the form of consciousness in an 'I think' instance. So what the form of consciousness proposal identifies as a necessary condition of consciousness of self-identity is wholly dispensable.

This leads on to the second and most important question about Kant's position: if the ability to think the form of consciousness is not an essential element of self-consciousness in the ordinary sense, might it be that consciousness of the numerically identical subject of different 'I think' instances as a substantial object among others in the world is necessary for consciousness of the form of these instances? If this suggestion is correct, then what was referred to above as Kant's 'independent intelligibility' thesis is unacceptable. The moral would be that there is no conceptual space for Kant's notion of transcendental self-consciousness other than as a peculiar abstraction from consciousness of self-identity properly so called. Since consciousness of the identity of the self as an objective continuant is subject to the discrimination requirement, one would have to conclude that it is an illusion that Kantian transcendental apperception escapes the demands which drive the Identity Argument.

One way of developing this point would be to consider the suggestion that Kant's position lacks the resources to disarm a Lichtenbergian objection. The Lichtenbergian objection is that, by rejecting the idea that transcendental apperception involves being able to think of one's representations as belonging to a subject who is an object among others in the world, one is left with no clear sense in which transcendental apperception is a genuine form of *self*-consciousness rather than consciousness of subjectless mental episodes. A Kantian reply to this objection would presumably be to argue that there is a middle way between thinking of consciousness as consciousness of subjectless mental episodes and the Identity Argument's conception of self-consciousness; from the fact that transcendental self-consciousness is consciousness of the form of consciousness in 'I think' instances, it does not follow that it is simply consciousness of subjectless occurrences. The problem with this middle way, however, is that it ultimately makes no sense to suppose that self-consciousness, properly so called, can be anything other than the consciousness of oneself as a concrete individual subject. Since neither self-consciousness itself nor the form of 'I think' instances is, in the relevant sense, an individual subject, it is an illusion to suppose that Kant has the resources to respond to the Lichtenbergian challenge.

The problem with these remarks is that while they cast doubt on the notion of transcendental apperception, they do not amount to a demonstration that the 'independent intelligibility' thesis is false. A less impressionistic objection to this thesis would be something along the following lines: in order to think the identity of the form of consciousness in 'I think p' and 'I think q', one must abstract from the reference of 'I' in these 'I think' instances; one must simply think of these thoughts as I-thoughts. The perspective of transcendental apperception is, in this sense, impersonal. It is, however, an important characteristic of I-thoughts that the content of a particular thought of this form cannot adequately be specified without ascribing it, or drawing upon the possibility of ascribing it, to a particular person. This might be described as the *relativization requirement*. This requirement holds the key to understanding why Kant's position is untenable, on the assumption that persons are objects among others in the world.

Consider the following analogy: suppose that it is reported that at time t someone thought 'That tree is burning'. On the face of it, the content of the thought has not been fully specified unless it is made clear which tree was thought to be burning. Since thoughts are individuated by their truth-conditions, it is only possible to fix the truth-condition and hence the content of a demonstrative thought once it is clear which object the demonstrative term refers to. By the same token, if 'I think p' is genuinely subject–predicate in form, then it would be natural to say that it is true if and only if the person to whom this use of 'I' refers thinks that p. Just as the content of a demonstrative thought depends in part on the object referred to by the demonstrative term, so the content of a first-person thought depends in part on the reference of the first person pronoun. If one failed to grasp this point, one could not be said to know what a first-person thought is. Since persons are objects among others in the world, grasp of the relativization requirement and therefore the ability to think the form of consciousness in different 'I think' instances requires the conception of their subjects, including oneself, as objects among others in the world.

It is not being denied by this argument that the occurrence of 'I think' instances can be reported in impersonal terms. For example, the statement 'It is thought: I think that p' is an impersonal report of a first-person thought since it does not ascribe the embedded I-thought to a thinker (cf. Williams 1978: 98). The point being made here is that even if it is possible to report 'I think' instances in this way, one must nevertheless understand that they are all instances of the 'I think' form. In order to understand this, one must understand that they are at least subject to the relativization requirement, since being subject to this requirement is part of what makes them thoughts of the 'I think' form. Given the way in which I-thoughts are relativized or particularized, in order to think 'the identity of apperception itself' (B134), one must conceive of 'I think' instances as ascribable to subjects who are objects among others in the world. This is the sense in which transcendental apperception is not intelligible independently of the concept of the subject of one's 'I think' instances as just such an object.

The same point can be made using Peacocke's terminology. In order to grasp the form of consciousness in 'I think p' and 'I think q', one must understand that these are both thoughts of the [self] type. Although the [self] type does not itself pick out a particular object in the world, part of what makes this type of thinking what it is is the fact that when 'indexed' by a particular person (Peacocke 1983: 108), the result is a token of the type which does pick out a particular object. It is not possible to have a proper understanding of what the [self] type is without having some conception of what tokens of this type consist of. Since tokens of the [self] type consist of the type indexed by a particular person, grasp of the form of consciousness cannot coherently be detached from a conception of how persons are distinguished from each other. This is the force of the claim that Kantian transcendental apperception is subject to the discrimination requirement. If one has no conception of the subjects of 'I think' instances as objects among others in the world, one will not have a proper understanding of how such instances are indexed. In the absence of a proper understanding of the principles governing the indexing of 'I think' instances, one would scarcely be in a position to grasp the 'form' of these instances.

Those who are persuaded by this argument against Kant's 'independent intelligibility' thesis might be tempted to take matters even further by suggesting that it shows how Kant's account of transcendental apperception actually leads to (D1). So far all that has been claimed is that the ability to think the form of 'I think' instances requires an understanding of the relativization requirement, and that this requirement embodies the conception of the subjects of 'I think' instances as persons who are objects among others in the world. This leaves open the question of how persons are individuated, but supposes that persons are, as a matter of fact, physical objects. This might prompt the following line of thought: for one to be in a position to grasp the form of consciousness, one must grasp the relativization requirement. In order to grasp this requirement, it is not enough simply that one thinks of persons as 'objective continuants'; one must also know or understand the nature of those objective continuants by reference to which thoughts of the 'I think' form are particularized. Since persons are physical objects, this means that one must conceive of the subjects of 'I think' instances, including oneself, specifically as physical objects.

As with the original concept versions of the Identity Argument, this latest defence of (D1) faces the problem of misconception. A Cartesian might agree, for example, that the thinking subjects by reference to which 'I think' instances are relativized are substantial continuants, but deny that they are physical objects. On the assumption that this position embodies a misconception, the question which arises is whether it is one which calls into question the Cartesian's grasp of the form of the 'I think'. As before, the problem with saying that grasp of the form of the 'I think' requires an accurate conception of the nature of persons is that it is just implausible to deny self-consciousness to someone simply because her conception of persons is inaccurate. Yet this is precisely what one would be committed to doing if one insists both that the ability to think the form of consciousness is an essential element of self-consciousness in the ordinary sense and that the latter ability requires the conception of I-thinkers as physical objects.

One reaction to this version of the problem of misconception would be to argue that the Cartesian's grasp of the form of the 'I think' is not in question because she does in fact conceive of the subjects of 'I think' instances as physical objects. Another response would be to argue that one counts as being able to think the form of the 'I think' as long as one is intuitively aware of the subjects of such instances, including oneself, as physical objects. Since transcendental apperception involves being able to do the philosophy of one's own situation, the first of these responses is arguably more compelling in this connection than in connection with the second concept version of the Identity Argument. It would not be worth pursuing this point, however, since it has already been argued that there is little to be said for the proposal that being able to think the form of the 'I think' is an essential element of self-consciousness in the ordinary sense. The important point for present purposes is this: if it is true that consciousness of self-identity involves consciousness of the identity of self-consciousness, then it is also true that consciousness of self-identity requires the conception of oneself as an object among others in the world. This is all that is needed to undermine the 'independent intelligibility' thesis. The Cartesian version of the problem of misconception does not affect this central point because the Cartesian is not in the business of arguing that I-thinkers are not substantial or objective continuants.

In order to defend the 'independent intelligibility' thesis against this line of attack, one would need to argue either that grasp of the form of 'I think' instances does not require an understanding of how such instances are relativized or that 'I think' instances need not be relativized or indexed by reference to subjects who are objects among others in the world. In connection with the second of these possibilities, what one is trying to capture when one speaks of the 'indexing' of 'I think' instances is the idea that such instances can occur at, as it were, the same or different 'places' (Williams 1978: 100). The difficulty with the bare notion of the 'place' at which an 'I think' instance occurs is, however, that it is totally figurative. As Williams remarks, when one tries to find a less figurative replacement for this notion, 'it is natural to conclude that nothing less than a personal name, or some such, will do as a replacement' (1978: 99). It is this last step which the 'independent intelligibility' thesis needs to avoid. What it requires is 'some replacement for figurative "places" which serves the purposes of effective relativization', but one which does not 'go so far as introducing a subject who thinks', that is, one whose existence is a 'substantial fact' (Williams 1978: 100).

On the face of it, there is an objection in principle to the idea that something whose existence is not a 'substantial fact' can serve the purposes of effective relativization. The objection is that the capacity for first-person thought is not something which can exist in isolation; it can only be present in the context of a range of other cognitive abilities. Determining the precise nature of the abilities required to sustain first-person thought is not a straightforward matter, but there must be some non-trivial constraints on what it is to be an I-thinker. It might be held, for example, that for one to be capable of first-person thought, one must have special ways of gaining knowledge of one's past and present physical and mental properties, and one's thoughts must have the appropriate connections with one's actions (cf. Evans 1982: 262). The problem with the suggestion that it is possible to relativize I-thoughts by 'ascribing' them to something whose existence is not a substantial fact is that it is difficult to understand how something that is not an object among others in the world can have the cognitive abilities required to sustain the capacity for first-person thought.

This argument against the 'independent intelligibility' thesis will not be convincing without a more detailed account of the precise nature of the cognitive abilities required for I-thinking, and an explanation of the connection between the idea that something possesses these abilities and the idea that it is an object among others in the world. These are matters which will be discussed in Chapter 5, which will focus on the question of whether it is possible to give a complete description of reality without claiming that persons exist. If first-person thoughts must be mentioned in a complete description and are essentially events in the lives of persons, then it is difficult to see how a complete description of reality can fail to mention persons.[29] Since persons are objects among others in the world, this argument has a direct bearing on the 'independent intelligibility' thesis. So much of our understanding of the cognitive abilities required to sustain I-thinking draws upon the conception of thoughts of this form as occurrences in the lives of substantial persons that it is scarcely intelligible how the indexing of 'I think' instances can avoid ascribing them to thinkers whose existence is a substantial fact.

If this claim about our understanding of the nature of first-person thought turns out to be sound in the light of Chapter 5, then it is time to

---

[29] This line of argument is developed in Cassam 1992.

abandon once and for all the suggestion that Kant has a coherent alterna-tive to the idea of consciousness of self-identity as consciousness of the subject of one's representations as an object among others in the world. Kant's alternative depends on two ideas both of which have turned out to be deeply problematic. The first is that an essential element of con-sciousness of self-identity is grasp of the form of consciousness in dif-ferent 'I think' instances. The second is that grasp of the form of the 'I think' is detachable from the conception of the subjects of 'I think' instances, including oneself, as substantial points of application for the discrimination requirement. The moral of this chapter is that there is no getting around the fact that consciousness of the identity of the self as the subject of diverse representations is consciousness of one's identity *qua* object among others in the world. The 'logical' identity of the Kantian 'I' is an abstraction from the identity of an objective continuant, but one should not be misled by such abstractions into thinking that self-consciousness has nothing to do with a concrete sense of the presented subject of one's thoughts, experiences, and sensations as a physical object among physical objects.

5

REDUCTIONISM

1. *Reductionism and the Exclusion Thesis*

The Exclusion Thesis claims that the subject that thinks or entertains ideas is not an object among others in the world. According to the 'robust response' outlined in Chapter 1, the Exclusion Thesis cannot be right, since thinking subjects are or include persons, and persons evidently belong to the world. Two reactions to this robust response to the Exclusion Thesis were then examined in Chapter 1. The first consisted of the denial that persons are objects in the world. The second consisted of the denial that the thinking subject can properly be identified with a person. It emerged that neither of these reactions is acceptable, but it was also noted that this leaves open the possibility of a more moderate and arguably more persuasive reaction to the robust response. The more moderate reaction accepts that thinking subjects include persons and that persons belong to the world, but goes on to argue that the existence of persons in the world is, as it were, only a derivative fact about the world. The aim of the present chapter is to criticize this line of thinking, which arguably represents the best that can be done for the Exclusion Thesis.

One way of understanding the assertion that the existence of persons is derivative would be to understand it as claiming that though persons exist, 'we could give a *complete* description of reality without claiming that persons exist' (Parfit 1987: 212). This *impersonal description thesis* is one element of Derek Parfit's 'Reductionist' account of persons. Reductionism is an ontological rather than conceptual or linguistic thesis. Its central negative claim is that a person is not a separately existing entity, distinct from her brain, body, and experiences. Its least controversial positive claim is that 'a person's existence just consists in the existence of a brain and body, and the occurrence of a series of interrelated physical and mental events' (Parfit 1987: 211). Since persons are not separately existing entities, they need not be mentioned in a complete description of reality. In other words, the impersonal description thesis is supposed to be a consequence of Parfit's ontological reductionism. A closely related consequence of his ontological reductionism is an impersonal account of the unity of consciousness. The unity of consciousness at a time and over time must both be explained by describing the relations between a person's experiences and their relations to the person's brain. The sense in which it is possible to give an impersonal account of the two unities is that 'we can refer to these experiences, and fully describe the relations between them, without claiming that these experiences are had by a person' (Parfit 1987: 217).

Apart from the impersonal description thesis, the other element of Reductionism about persons is the following reductionist thesis about personal *identity*: the fact of a person's identity over time 'just consists in the holding of certain more particular facts' which can be 'described without presupposing the identity of this person' (Parfit 1987: 210). This thesis is of fundamental importance for Reductionism, which may therefore be understood as a combination of *reductionism about personal identity* and the *impersonal description thesis*. An immediate complication is that reductionism about personal identity and the impersonal description thesis are not of equal importance for Reductionism. Whereas the former is essential to Reductionism, the latter is presented as an optional extra.[1] Nevertheless, given that the impersonal description thesis is one which the Reductionist regards as true, and that it is at the heart of the moderate reaction to the robust response, it would not be inappropriate in the present context for one to continue to treat it as an integral part of Reductionism.

The truth of Reductionism would not vindicate the Exclusion Thesis, since Parfitian persons are 'in' the spatio-temporal world. On the other hand, Reductionism does help to make sense of the claim that the existence of persons is a 'derivative' fact about the world. Since, according to the moderate reaction to the robust response, this claim represents the best that can be done for the Exclusion Thesis, the question of whether Reductionism is defensible ought to be of interest to those with any sympathy for the Exclusion Thesis. This point is related to the distinction drawn in Chapter 1 between the question of whether persons are 'in' the empirical world at all and the question of whether persons are *substantial* constituents of empirical reality. For Reductionism, the ontological status of persons is akin to the ontological status of nations, and nations are

---

[1] To be more precise, the impersonal description thesis is presented as an optional extra in Parfit 1987: 210, but not in earlier printings of *Reasons and Persons*.

not substances. This suggests that although Parfitian persons are 'in' the world, they are not substantial elements of objective reality.[2] According to the moderate reaction to the robust response, this is what is right about the Exclusion Thesis, even if it goes too far in attempting to exclude thinking subjects from the world altogether.

One way of approaching the question of whether Reductionism, understood in this way, is defensible, would be to ask whether it is compatible with the successful elements of the Objectivity, Unity, and Identity Arguments. This may seem like a somewhat surprising approach since Reductionism is, in contrast to these arguments, primarily an account of the nature of persons rather than of self-consciousness. As Locke emphasized, however, questions about the nature of persons and the nature of self-consciousness cannot be sharply separated, and it will emerge in due course that someone who is persuaded by certain aspects of the concept versions of the Objectivity and Identity Arguments ought not to be a Reductionist about persons. To the extent that these arguments can be shown to undermine Reductionism, then they also undermine the last hope for the Exclusion Thesis.

2. Reductionism and the Objectivity Argument

It is not immediately obvious why there should be any conflict between Reductionism and the concept version of the Objectivity Argument. The conclusion of the concept version of the Objectivity Argument is that a subject whose experience satisfies the objectivity condition must think of herself as a physical object. If Reductionism were in the business of denying that persons are corporeal, then there would be a mismatch between what Reductionism has to say about the actual nature of persons and the self-conception demanded by the Objectivity Argument. As has already been remarked, however, Reductionism itself insists that the existence of a person consists in the existence of, among other things, a brain and body. To say this is, presumably, to be committed to the thesis that persons are corporeal entities, so there is no mismatch. Despite this, Parfit himself suggests that something like the Objectivity Argument is at odds with Reductionism (see Parfit 1987: 225). The first question, then, is whether anything can be made of this suggestion.

In order to make anything of the idea that Reductionism is threatened

---

[2] See Ayers 1991: ii. 281 and Cassam 1993b for a defence of this reading of Parfit.

by the concept version of the Objectivity Argument, it is important to remember that this argument incorporates two elements. The first step of the argument claims that *objectivity requires unity of consciousness* (ORU). The second step consists of the *physical object requirement*. What has just been established is that there is no obvious conflict between Reductionism and the second of these requirements, but it is less clear that Reductionism can accommodate the first requirement. There are therefore two questions to consider. The first is whether the 'objectivity requires unity' thesis is compatible with reductionism about personal identity. The second is whether ORU is compatible with the impersonal description thesis. To simplify matters, it will be assumed here that the Reductionist is committed to psychological reductionism about personal identity, which maintains that personal identity consists in non-branching psychological continuity.

An indirect but illuminating way of approaching the first of these questions would be to begin by examining the objection that psychological reductionism is unacceptably circular. This is the objection that psychological continuity presupposes personal identity and so cannot explain it. Psychological continuity includes continuity of memory, but is part of our concept of memory that we cannot be said to remember 'from the inside' past experiences that were not our own past experiences. If this is correct, then the particular facts in the holding of which a person's identity over time consists cannot be described without presupposing the identity of this person.

A familiar Reductionist response to the circularity objection is to introduce the notion of quasi-memory. Since a veridical quasi-memory need not be of one's own past experience, psychological continuity can be described in a way that does not presuppose personal identity, as long as it is thought of as involving continuity of quasi-memory. As was remarked in Chapter 2, the introduction of the notion of quasi-memory appears to raise a question about the 'objectivity requires unity' component of the concept version of Objectivity Argument. The force of the ORU thesis is that for one to be capable of thinking of distinct perceptions as perceptions of one and the same enduring *object*, one must be capable of self-ascribing them and of representing to oneself the numerical identity of *subject* to which they are ascribed, a subject who must also be conceived of as tracing a continuous spatio-temporal route through the world. The 'quasi-memory objection' to the ORU thesis is that there might be circumstances in which one would be justified in regarding one's present perception and an apparently remembered past perception

as perceptions of the very same object even if one's apparent memory is a
veridical quasi-memory of someone else's past perception. If one knows
that the apparently remembered past perception 'belonged' to someone
else, one will not self-ascribe it, but this need not prevent one from
anchoring the past and present perceptions to one and the same enduring
object. Since perceptions which are not ascribed to a single subject can
properly be conceptualized as perceptions of a single object, objectivity
does not require unity of consciousness.

In response to this objection, it was argued that mere quasi-memories
could only yield inferential knowledge of past experiences that were not
one's own, and they would only be capable of yielding such inferential
knowledge against a background in which ordinary memory is the primary form of access 'from the inside' to past experiences. For quasi-
memories to provide knowledge of past experiences one must know
'roughly how they have been caused' (Parfit 1987: 221), but an investigation into the causal origin of a given apparent memory could never get
off the ground if it were always in question whether one's apparent
memories were of one's own or someone else's past experiences. The significance of ordinary experiential remembering in this context is, to
quote Wiggins once again, that its epistemological role is to 'help to provide us with a starting-point for any further inquiry about how things are
in the world . . . a place I can start out from without making an inference
from something else' (1992: 348). In other words, even if it makes sense
to suppose that one might quasi-remember someone else's past experiences, ordinary memories necessarily have what might be called *epistemological primacy* over mere quasi-memories.

In Chapter 2, this epistemological primacy thesis was used to defuse
the quasi-memory objection to the ORU component of the Objectivity
Argument, but the primacy thesis can now also be seen as explaining the
precise sense in which the Objectivity Argument threatens reductionism
about personal identity. The explanation is that the epistemological primacy thesis, which does important work in the ORU component of the
Objectivity Argument, establishes the illegitimacy of the reductionist's
response to the problem of circularity. The suggestion, to be more precise, is that if the primacy thesis is correct, then one will be guilty of fal-
sifying the actual nature of psychological continuity if one describes it as
involving anything other than continuity of memory. It is not acceptable
to regard psychological continuity as involving continuity of quasi-memory rather than continuity of memory, given that experiential remembering must be, for someone who is in a position to conceptualize her

experiences as experiences of an objective world, the primary form of access 'from the inside' to past experiences.

It would be a mistake to object to this line of argument on the grounds that it leaves supporters of the Objectivity Argument without the resources to deal with the circularity objection. Circularity only matters if one is committed to reductionism about personal identity, but supporters of the Objectivity Argument may regard the epistemological primacy thesis as a powerful reason for rejecting any attempt to define a person's identity over time in terms of the holding of more particular facts which can be described without presupposing the identity of this person. The fact that the psychological continuity of persons whose experience satisfies the objectivity condition necessarily involves continuity of memory, together with the idea that memory 'presupposes' personal identity, suggests that personal identity neither calls for nor permits explanation in reductive terms.

The Reductionist has two choices at this point. The first would be to dispute the epistemological primacy thesis. The second would be to challenge the assertion that this thesis calls into question the psychological reductionist's response to the circularity objection. In the light of the points made in Chapter 2, the prospects for the first of these options do not appear to be bright; the reductionist must find a way of accommodating the primacy thesis. The second option seems more promising, and may be developed as follows: reductionism is primarily concerned with the question of what the continued existence of a person consists in, where this is understood as what might be called an external rather than an internal question. The 'internal' question about personal identity is this: from a standpoint within the life of a person, what does the person's own awareness of his or her own numerical identity as the subject of perceptions of independent objects involve? This is a question about the nature of consciousness of self-identity. In contrast, the 'external' question may be understood as follows: when the life of a person is viewed from a detached standpoint, is it possible to explain or analyse what the continued existence of the person consists in by reference to facts which do not presuppose this person's identity? This is the question asked by the reductionist, who is an 'external analyst' of personal identity (Henrich 1989: 253). Whereas the 'internal' question is an epistemological or, perhaps, psychological question, the 'external' or 'sideways on' question is a metaphysical or ontological question (McDowell 1981: 150). The epistemological primacy thesis is compatible with reductionism about personal identity because the primacy thesis has no bearing on the metaphysical issue, which is the issue with which reductionism is primarily concerned.

This distinction between 'internal' and 'external' is not very precise, but it does appear to be of fundamental importance for reductionism about personal identity. It may well be true, the reductionist will argue, that persons are typically self-conscious, and that for a person to be conscious of her experience as experience of an objective world, she cannot always regard it as an open question whether her apparent memories are of her own past experiences. It does not follow, however, that from the perspective of the external analyst of personal identity, the relation between a given experience and a later apparent memory of it cannot legitimately be described in terms which leave open the question whether the earlier and later state are states of the same person. To suppose that it does follow is to be guilty of confusing an epistemological with a metaphysical issue. The value of the notion of quasi-memory is that it provides the external analyst with the technical resources to defuse the circularity objection; from this standpoint, the only question that matters is whether it is possible to describe the facts in which a person's identity consists without presupposing the identity of that person. The 'external' approach is, of course, compatible with allowing that most of the person's apparent memories are in fact ordinary memories, since ordinary memories are a sub-class of quasi-memories. The fact that the person whose identity is being explained cannot but regard her apparent memories as, by and large, providing her with knowledge of her own past may be true but is irrelevant from the reductionist's external perspective.

The problem with this attempt to downplay the significance of the epistemological primacy thesis in the present context is that it is not enough for the purposes of reductionism about personal identity that introduction of the notion of quasi-memory should constitute a formally adequate external response to the circularity problem. Although it would be implausible to insist that the concepts employed by the external analyst must the same as those employed from a standpoint within the life of a person, it is nevertheless important that an external description of psychological continuity should do justice to a person's 'subjective take' on his or her own persistence (McDowell 1994: 101). One reason is this: a major motivation for the psychological continuity account of personal identity is that persons are typically aware of themselves as, in Locke's words, 'the same thinking thing, in different times and places' in virtue of 'that consciousness which is inseparable from thinking' (Locke 1975: 335). To claim that personal identity has to do with psychological continuity is therefore to give an account of personal identity which in some sense matches a person's subjective take on his or her own persistence. From this inner perspective, however, apparent memories cannot by and large be regarded as anything other than ordinary memories, so when psychological continuity is described as involving continuity of quasi-memory, the reductionist can no longer claim to be explaining personal identity in terms which correspond to a person's own sense of being the same thinking thing at different times. This removes one of the major attractions of psychological reductionism, and creates the following dilemma for the psychological continuity account: without the idea that psychological continuity involves continuity of quasi-memory, the account is circular; with this idea in place, the account cuts itself off from one of its central motivations. The way out is to agree with Locke that part of what it is to be a person is to have a subjective take on one's own persistence but to disagree with the psychological reductionist that a person's identity over time can be analysed in terms of this subjective take (cf. Wiggins 1980: 151).

The reductionist about personal identity will, no doubt, claim to be unmoved by this argument. In the first place, it might be argued that the notion of quasi-memory cannot be merely a technical fix introduced to deal with the circularity objection, since it is also essential if a proper account is to be given of familiar problem cases, such as those involving fission or memory-trace transplants. Even more importantly, the reductionist will reject the demand that an external analyst's account of the facts in which personal identity consists must 'match' a person's 'inner' sense of his or her own identity. Consider the following analogy: a theorist who is trying to explain what it is for objects to be coloured may need to acknowledge that colours present themselves as non-dispositional properties of external objects, but this is surely not enough to refute the metaphysical thesis that colours are reducible to the powers or dispositions of objects to produce the appropriate experiences in us. The dispositionalist about colour is trying to explain what possession of colour properties consists in, and it would be excessively restrictive to stipulate that she must confine herself to providing an explanation in terms which correspond to the content of ordinary colour experience. By the same token, Reductionism is in the business of trying to explain what the identity of a person consists in and need not confine itself to providing an explanation in terms which correspond to the content of 'that consciousness which is inseparable from thinking'. It would also be worth remarking that since the reductionist is happy to accept that most apparent memories are, and present themselves as being, ordinary memories, it is not even obvious that reductionism cannot do justice to a person's 'inner' perspective on his or her own persistence. The epistemology of quasi-memory may well be different from the epistemology of ordinary memory but this does not make it illegitimate to analyse personal identity as consisting in continuity of quasi-memory.

These remarks suggest that reference to the epistemological role of experiential remembering in the context of the life of a person whose experience satisfies the objectivity condition will not be enough to refute psychological reductionism in any straightforward sense. They also suggest that reductionists about personal identity and those who believe that the epistemological primacy thesis is a problem for reductionism have, in effect, quite different conceptions of the adequacy conditions on the explanation or elucidation of personal identity. The anti-reductionist will argue that giving an account of personal identity which does not correspond to the inner perspective on personal identity might be legitimate if there are good independent grounds for seeking a non-circular 'analysis' of personal identity, but that there are no such grounds. As for the analogy with the dispositional account of colour, this is in some respects an unfortunate analogy for the reductionist, since the dispositional 'analysis' appears to be unashamedly circular. To all of this, the reductionist will reply that it is always a legitimate metaphysical question whether the identity of a continuant can be given a non-circular analysis, and that this is a good enough reason for exploring the prospects for reductionism about personal identity.

In order to resolve these issues, it would be necessary to enter into questions about the nature of philosophical explanation which are well beyond the scope of the present discussion. All that can safely be said on the basis of the discussion so far is that although the epistemological points made by the Objectivity Argument may not be straightforwardly incompatible with reductionism about personal identity,[3] they do at least raise questions about the philosophical—as distinct from narrowly technical—adequacy of this approach, and about the respectability of its motivation. At the very least, it remains an open question whether an 'external' account of personal identity which detaches itself from the 'inner' perspective on personal identity can plausibly claim to be well-grounded. This may seem a disappointingly weak conclusion for those who were hoping that the epistemological primacy thesis would yield a

---

[3] This contrasts with the conclusion reached in Cassam 1995b.

decisive objection to reductionism about personal identity, but it is arguably the best that can be done. For a less impressionistic argument against Parfitian Reductionism, those convinced by the Objectivity Argument would be better advised to question its other component, namely, the impersonal description thesis.

As has already been remarked, Parfit himself presents something like the Objectivity Argument as posing a threat to the impersonal description thesis. He outlines a neo-Kantian view of persons which, like Reductionism, accepts that 'the existence of a person just consists in the existence of his brain and body, and the doing of his deeds, and the occurrence of various other physical and mental events' (1987: 225). The neo-Kantian is also represented as maintaining that 'we could not have knowledge of the world about us unless we believe ourselves to be persons, with an awareness of our identity over time' (ibid.). This is the point at which the neo-Kantian view seems to part company with Reductionism. The suggestion is that it might be a consequence of the neo-Kantian conception of what is required for knowledge of the world that our lives cannot be redescribed in an impersonal way. If this is a consequence of the neo-Kantian position, then it is incompatible with Reductionism as well as with the Cartesian view that persons are separately existing entities.

The relationship between the neo-Kantian position as characterized by Parfit and the Objectivity Argument is not entirely straightforward, since the latter does not explicitly claim that satisfaction of the objectivity condition requires the belief that the subject of experience is a person. Nevertheless, the thesis that awareness of the identity of the self is required for knowledge of the world is similar to the ORU component of the concept version of the Objectivity Argument. This suggests that the best way of exploring the suggestion that Reductionism might be at odds with the neo-Kantian position would be to explore the suggestion that there is a conflict between the 'objectivity requires unity' argument and the impersonal description thesis.

Suppose that the Objectivity Argument is right to insist that for perceptions to be conceptualizable as perceptions of objects in the weighty sense, their subject must be capable of self-ascribing them, conscious of the numerical identity of that to which the perceptions belong. Suppose, in other words, that objectivity requires unity of consciousness in Kant's sense. This might be held to undermine the impersonal description thesis for the following reason: for the impersonal description thesis to be correct, it must be possible to describe our perceptions and the relations

between them 'without claiming that they are had by a subject of experiences' (Parfit 1987: 225). The moral of the 'objectivity requires unity'
argument is, however, that if we abstract from the fact that diverse perceptions belong to a subject who can self-ascribe them, then the possibility of conceptualizing the perceptions as perceptions of objects in the
weighty sense will no longer have been provided for. If the explanation of
the unity of consciousness, and therefore of the fact that our experience
satisfies the objectivity condition, involves the ascription of experiences
to persons or subjects of experience, then a description of reality which
fails to mention persons or subjects could not be complete.

In connection with the relationship between the 'objectivity requires
unity' argument and reductionism about personal identity, it was suggested above that one way of reconciling them would be to press the
point that they are answers to different questions, an 'internal' and an
'external' question. A similar 'compatibilist' move might seem appropriate in the present context. When we as external analysts are concerned to
describe a given mental life and to explain its unity, we can acknowledge
that the life under consideration includes the thinking of self-ascriptive
thoughts, and that the thinking of such thoughts does important work in
helping to make it intelligible, from within the life, that it includes perceptions of objects in the weighty sense. None of this requires the ascription of self-ascriptive thoughts to subjects by the external analyst. From
the external standpoint, it is possible, as Parfit puts it, to 'describe what,
at various different times, was thought and felt and observed and done,
and how these various events were interrelated. Persons would be mentioned here only in the description of the content of many thoughts,
desires, memories, and so on. Persons need not be claimed to be the
thinkers of any of these thoughts' (1987: 251). Even if it is true that this
impersonal framework could not be adopted from an 'internal' standpoint, it does not follow that our lives cannot be redescribed in impersonal terms from 'sideways on'.

If this compatibilist argument is successful, then, contrary to the
impression given by Parfit, it is not the case that the 'objectivity requires
unity' view cannot be reconciled with the impersonal description thesis.
When the 'objectivity requires unity' argument claims that it is not possible to understand how experience can be thought of as including perceptions of independent objects if 'we' abstract from the ownership of
experiences by a self-conscious subject, the compatibilist will want to
know who the 'we' refers to. If the claim is that the external analyst cannot abstract from considerations of ownership, then the compatibilist

will object that this is false. The external analyst can explain the unity of consciousness at a time by reference to the possible co-consciousness of experiences, and the unity of consciousness over time by reference to the R-relatedness of experiences, that is, relations of psychological continuity or connectedness with the right kind of cause. Among the experiences unified by such relations, some will be accompanied by self-ascriptive thoughts and some by the further thought that they are experiences of independent objects. But these are just more thoughts, each of which 'occurs within some life in virtue of its relations to many other mental and physical events which, by being interrelated, constitute this life' (Parfit 1987: 252). In this way, the occurrence of self-ascriptive I-thoughts can be acknowledged in a 'sideways on' explanation of the unity of consciousness without ascribing them to persons. So the Reductionist can accept the Objectivity Argument's 'internal' self-ascription requirement without giving up the impersonal description thesis.

This attempt to reconcile the ORU component of the Objectivity Argument with the impersonal description thesis raises some of the same questions as the earlier attempt to reconcile it with reductionism about personal identity. Opponents of Reductionism will once again protest that if the idea that thoughts and experiences 'belong' to subjects or persons is part of what makes our lives intelligible 'from the inside', then a description of our thoughts and perceptions which abstracts from considerations of ownership cannot be adequate. To this, the familiar Reductionist response will be to deny that for an external description to be adequate it must correspond to what makes our lives intelligible from an internal perspective. As long as the unity of consciousness can be explained by reference to impersonal relations between experiences, there is nothing missing from the Reductionist's impersonal description.

There is, however, at least one powerful reason for thinking that the unity of consciousness cannot be adequately explained in impersonal terms even from 'sideways on'. The reason is this: for an impersonal account of the unity of consciousness to be acceptable, it must be capable of explaining the relations between thoughts and experiences in a way which does justice to the contents of thoughts and experiences, including self-ascriptive thoughts. The objection to the impersonal description thesis is that there is no perspective, internal or external, from which it is possible to specify the content of a self-ascriptive thought without ascribing it to a subject or person. Since, according to the Objectivity Argument, the ability to think such thoughts is essentially involved in the capacity to think of one's perceptions as perceptions of objects in the weighty sense, this amounts to the suggestion that the impersonal description is at least indirectly at odds with one important aspect of the Objectivity Argument.

This objection to Reductionism is based upon the idea that first-person thoughts constitute a special problem for the impersonal description thesis. This idea is based upon points made in Chapter 4 in connection with the concept version of the Identity Argument. Strictly speaking, therefore, it is the ORU argument in conjunction with these points which threatens to undermine the impersonal description thesis. Unlike the earlier doubts about reductionism about personal identity, the present objection to the impersonal description thesis does not leave it an open question whether the Reductionist's 'external' account of the unity of consciousness is ultimately acceptable; the proposal to be considered below is that the impersonal description thesis yields a demonstrably inadequate account of self-consciousness.

3. Reductionism and the Identity Argument

Lichtenberg's objection to the Cartesian *cogito* argument is that Descartes should have said 'There is thinking' rather than 'I think'. In contrast, the Reductionist is not in the business of denying that some of our thoughts are genuinely first-personal. Indeed, if Reductionism were to agree with Lichtenberg on this point, then it would hardly be in a position to accommodate the ORU component of the Objectivity Argument. Instead, Parfit's response to Lichtenberg is to follow Williams in maintaining that a Lichtenbergian substitute for the *cogito* need not be wholly impersonal. Instead of saying 'I think', perhaps Descartes should have said 'It is thought: I think'. The usefulness of this formulation is that it acknowledges the occurrence of a first-person thought, but does so in a way which does not involve the ascription of the thought to a subject. As Parfit writes, 'since the subject of experiences is here mentioned only in the *content* of the thought, this sentence does not ascribe this thought to a thinker' (1987: 225). If it is possible to acknowledge the occurrence of a self-ascriptive thought without ascribing it to a thinker, then the occurrence of such thoughts does not prevent Reductionism from being able to explain their unity with other thoughts and experiences in impersonal terms.

In Chapter 4, it was suggested that some of the points made in opposition to Kant's 'form of consciousness' account of transcendental apperception were closely related to an objection to the impersonal description thesis. It will be recalled that the objection to Kant's account was something along the following lines: the truth-condition and hence the content of a particular I-thought cannot be specified without ascribing it, or drawing upon the possibility of ascribing it, to a particular person. Just as the content of a demonstrative thought such as 'That tree is burning' depends upon which tree is being referred to, so the content of a particular 'I think' instance depends in part upon who the thinker is. Since 'I think' instances are subject to this relativization requirement, grasp of the form of consciousness in an 'I think' instance requires the conception of its subject as an object among others in the world.

This raises the following question about the claim that the occurrence of a self-ascriptive thought can be acknowledged in impersonal terms: if the content of such a thought depends upon who the thinker is, then how can a report of the form 'It is thought: I think that p', which fails to specify the thinker of the embedded thought, count as a complete specification of its content? The impersonal description reports the occurrence of a thought of the 'I think' form, but fails to make it clear which particular thought of this form has been or is being thought. In this sense, the Reductionist's 'sideways on' account of the unity of consciousness fails to explain the relations between thoughts and experiences in a way which fully captures their contents, since thinkings of I-thoughts will be among those physical and mental events which, by being interrelated, constitute a particular life.

The Reductionist's response to this challenge is to agree that when I-thoughts are reported impersonally, it needs to be 'made clear whether these thoughts occurred within the same or different lives' (Parfit 1987: 225), but to argue that this can be made clear without ascribing the reported thoughts to persons or subjects. In opposition to Williams, Parfit argues that an impersonal alternative to ascribing an I-thought to a person would be to 'place' thoughts of this form by reference to the bodies upon which they are causally dependent. For example, it might be reported that it is thought 'I think p' in the life which is directly causally dependent upon body A, and 'I think q' in the life that is directly causally dependent upon body B. The idea is that relating thoughts to bodies is not the same thing as ascribing them to persons, and so meets the impersonal description requirement. Another possibility would be to report that it is thought 'I think p' in 'the particular life that contains the thinking of the thought expressed by the occurrence of this sentence' (Parfit

1987: 226). Once again, the suggestion is that a report of this form places the I-thought without ascribing it to a person.

The position, then, is this: the objection to the impersonal description thesis is that there is no level at which it is possible to abstract from the ownership of a first-person thought while maintaining a fix upon its content. In other words, the fact that I-thoughts are subject to the relativization requirement shows that in the case of I-thoughts, the ascriptive and content-specifying levels of description are inseparable. The Reductionist's response to this objection is, in effect, to accept that I-thoughts are subject to some form of relativization requirement, but to deny that relativization must take the form of ascribing them to persons. One way of putting this would be to say that for Reductionism, I-thoughts are subject to a *weak* relativization requirement, according to which they can be adequately relativized or 'indexed' by being related to a particular body or 'life'. Opposed to this view is the claim that if one is interested in specifying the content of an 'I think' instance, then nothing short of satisfaction of a *strong* relativization requirement will do, that is, the ascription of it to a particular person. If, as the Reductionist claims, the strong relativization requirement is too demanding, then the fact that our lives include thinkings of I-thoughts does not show that the unity of consciousness cannot be explained impersonally.

It should now be clear that the question of whether I-thoughts are subject to a strong or weak relativization requirement is of fundamental importance in the context of discussion of the impersonal description thesis. In defence of the strong requirement, it is important to begin by separating two questions. Firstly, there is the question of what makes it the case that a thought belongs to the first-person type. Secondly, there is the question of what makes it the case that a thought of this type has the particular first-person content which it has. For example, when two people A and B both think thoughts expressed by the words 'I am F', they think of themselves in the same type of way, but their thoughts concern different objects and so have different truth conditions. How are these questions related? Given that particular I-thoughts are 'tokens' of the first-person type, what makes it the case that a token of this type has the particular content which it has cannot be unrelated to what makes it the case that the token is of the first-person type. Thus, it would seem a proper account of that in virtue of which an I-thought has the particular content which it has must adequately reflect what is distinctive of this type of thinking. In particular, an account of the relativization requirement on I-thoughts must be informed by an underlying conception of what it is for token thoughts to belong to the first-person type.

Suppose, next, that there are grounds for maintaining that it is distinctive of first-person thinking that thoughts of the first-person type are only properly ascribable to persons. In other words, to regard a form of words as giving expression to a thought of the first-person type is to be prepared to think of it as an occurrence in the life of a person. If this is correct, then it is plausible that the only way of specifying fully the content of a particular I-thought is to ascribe it to a particular person. The truth or falsity of the thought expressed by 'I am F' depends upon whether the person who thinks this thought is F because only persons can think thoughts of this form. This is the point of the strong relativization requirement. This defence of the strong requirement meets the constraint that it should be informed by a conception of what is distinctive of thoughts of the 'I'-type. As long as token I-thoughts are, as it were, essentially occurrences in the lives of persons, impersonal reports of their occurrence are bound to be incomplete.

In sharp contrast, the weak relativization seems to rest upon no plausible account of what a first-person thought is. It simply helps itself to the idea that a given thought belongs to the first-person type, and then relativizes or indexes it by relating it to a particular body or life. If these are legitimate ways of 'locating' I-thoughts, it can only be because of the assumption that the lives or bodies to which such thoughts are related are the lives or bodies of persons. Given this assumption, Parfit's two alternatives to Williams's account of the relativization of I-thoughts are 'impersonal' only in a superficial sense. This becomes especially clear when an attempt is made to specify the truth-condition of an I-thought using only the weak relativization requirement. If the truth or falsity of the thought expressed by 'I am F' is not claimed to depend upon whether the person to which its use of 'I' refers is F, then it is not clear how else the truth-condition can be specified in a manner which accords with our usual understanding of the nature of I-thoughts. It is, after all, scarcely intelligible that the truth or falsity of the thought 'I think that p' should depend upon whether the body upon which it is directly dependent thinks that p, unless this is simply a peculiar way of ascribing the thought to the person whose body this is.

The most controversial premiss of this defence of the strong relativization requirement is the claim that it is distinctive of first-person thinking that thoughts of the first-person type are only properly ascribable to persons. This would explain the incompleteness of strictly impersonal reports of I-thoughts, but it might be wondered whether this pre-miss is correct. It has been assumed so far that the concepts of 'person' and 'subject' are more or less interchangeable, but suppose that this is not the case. For example, certain non-human animals might be thought to be 'subjects of experience', but are not persons. Some might wish to go further by arguing that there is no reason in principle why suitably sophisticated non-human animals or even non-animals should be inca-pable of I-thinking, even if they are not persons. If subjects that are not persons are capable of I-thinking, then specifying the content of a par-ticular of I-thought need not involve the ascription of it to a person, con-trary to what is claimed by the strong relativization requirement.

One response to this line of argument would be to maintain that any being that is capable of I-thinking is by definition a person. This response might be motivated by the Lockean thesis that the concept of a person is the concept of a thinking intelligent being, that has reason and reflection, and can consider itself as itself, the same thinking being, in different times and places. On this view, there is simply no gap between the idea that a being, animal or otherwise, is self-conscious and the idea that it is a person. The important point, however, is that even if subjects of I-thinking need not be persons, this does not really help Parfit's im-personal description thesis or, for that matter, Kant's position. It simply shows that instead of claiming that the content of a particular I-thought cannot be specified without ascribing it, or drawing upon the possibility of ascribing it, to a particular person, the strong relativization require-ment should be understood as claiming that the content of a particular I-thought cannot be specified without ascribing it, or drawing upon the possibility of ascribing it, to a particular subject.

The fact that this modified strong relativization requirement does not help the impersonal description thesis or Kant's position may be explained as follows: although Parfit allows that some 'subjects' are not persons (see 1987: 250), Reductionism requires not just that it should be possible to explain the unity of consciousness without ascribing thoughts and experiences to persons but also that we could fully describe our expe-riences, and the connections between them, without claiming that they are had by a subject of experiences. On this reading of the impersonal description thesis, nothing turns on the possibility of drawing a distinc-tion between persons and subjects who are not persons; the claim that I-thoughts must be 'placed' by being ascribed to subjects, if not to persons, is still incompatible with this component of Reductionism. Equally, as long as subjects who are not persons are, as is undoubtedly the case with

non-human animals, still objects among others in the world, the possibility of relativizing an 'I think' instance by ascribing it to a subject who is
not a person does not show that grasp of the form of the 'I think' does
not require the conception of I-thinkers as objects among others in the
world.

It might be objected that this appeal to a modified strong relativization requirement as a means of undermining the impersonal description
thesis and Kant's notion of transcendental apperception, does not really
advance matters. Whereas the defence of the unmodified version of the
requirement assumed that it is distinctive of first-person thinking that
thoughts of the first-person type are only properly ascribable to persons,
it is now being assumed that it is distinctive of first-person thinking that
thoughts of the first-person type are only properly ascribable to subjects
who may or may not be persons but who are objects among others in the
world. Once again, it might be wondered whether this assumption is correct. With this assumption in place, it is difficult to escape the conclusion
that a complete specification of the content of a particular I-thought
must make it clear who the subject is and so cannot be 'impersonal'; but
why should it be supposed that only subjects whose existence is a 'substantial fact' are capable of thinking of the first-person type (Williams
1978: 100)?

The obvious reply to this question would be to argue that anything
that is capable of I-thinking is by definition, if not a person, then at least
a substantial subject, an object among objects. From a Kantian perspective, however, such an argument begs the central question. As was noted
in Chapter 4, Kant's view is that the capacity to attach an 'I think' to
one's representations leaves the 'manner' of one's existence undeter-
mined, 'whether it be as substance or as accident' (B420). Against this
background, it is not enough to stipulate that only substantial subjects
are capable of I-thinking; what is required is an explanation of the connection between substantial subjecthood and possession of an ability to
think thoughts of the 'I'-type. If such an explanation can be given, it
would serve two purposes. On the one hand, it would raise a question
about the alleged 'non-determinativeness' of the 'I think'. On the other
hand, it would provide a basis for the modified strong relativization
requirement, in such a way as to explain the essential incompleteness of
strictly impersonal reports of I-thoughts.

In his work on reference, Evans provides what he calls a 'functional'
characterization of various Idea-types, including 'I-Ideas' (1982: 262). In
general, an Idea of an object is 'something which makes it possible for a

subject to think of an object in a series of indefinitely many thoughts, in each of which he will be thinking of the object in the same way' (p. 104). A functional account of an Idea-type characterizes it in terms of the special relation of thoughts involving it to certain sorts of evidence and to behaviour, although such an account does not constitute a complete account of the Idea-type in question. In the case of I-Ideas, the functional account includes an informational and an action component. A thinker of an I-thought must realize the relevance to such thoughts of various special ways of gaining knowledge of his mental states and physical properties, and his I-thoughts must have the appropriate connection with his actions.[4] A particularly important feature of I-Ideas is the way in which they give rise to thoughts dependent upon information received over a period of time. As Evans remarks, 'it is possible to regard this feature of I-Ideas as part of the informational component of a functional characterization. A possessor of an I-Idea has a capacity to ascribe past-tense properties to himself on a special basis: namely the memory of the basis appropriate for an earlier present-tense judgement' (1982: 238).

It was remarked in earlier chapters that unlike demonstrative thought, first-person thought does not rest upon an ability on the part of the subject to keep track of the object of thought. This is a central element of what Evans calls the 'cognitive dynamics' of I-Ideas, where 'cognitive dynamics' is defined as the way in which a subject's belief-system deals with the passage of time. As Evans writes:

if a subject has at t a belief which he might then manifest in judging 'I am now F', then there is a non-negligible probability of his having, at a later time $t1$, a disposition to judge 'I was previously F' . . . so far as the I-Idea is concerned, the later dispositions to judge flow out of the earlier dispositions to judge, without the need for any *skill* or *care* (not to lose track of something) on the part of the subject. (1982: 237)

This account of the cognitive dynamics of I-Ideas suggests the following way of connecting the capacity for I-thinking with substantial subject-hood: to begin with, it is important to recognize that the functional account of I-Ideas is intended as a constitutive account. The claim is that for a thought to count as an I-thought, it must be a thought one of whose components is a particular I-Idea, where an I-Idea is one which possesses the various characteristics set out in the functional account. This suggests that even from 'sideways on' it will only be correct to ascribe I-thoughts to a being whose thoughts, perceptions, and actions are organized in a

---

[4] The importance of the action component is made vivid by Perry 1994.

certain way. To be more precise, they must be organized in such a way that its I-thoughts stand in the appropriate relations to each other, to perceptual evidence, and to action, where the 'appropriate' relations are just those set out in the functional account. How should such a being be characterized? At this point, it would be tempting to claim that a being which has what it takes to count as an I-thinker must be, if not a person, then at least a subject that is an object among others in the world. In other words, the external analyst's willingness to ascribe token thoughts of the I-type to a being must go hand in hand with a willingness to ascribe to it a certain kind of internal organization, and this is in effect to regard it as a subject whose existence is a 'substantial fact'.

One objection to this argument is that it does not really explain the connection between a capacity for I-thinking and substantial subject-hood, since it resorts to arbitrary stipulation at the crucial point. It might be tempting to say that beings who meet the Evansian conditions on I-thinking must be subjects who are objects among others in the world, but is this really a temptation to which one ought to succumb? The charge of arbitrary stipulation might be resisted as follows: on the one hand, it is plausible that the concepts of self-consciousness, rationality, and agency form the core of the concept of a substantial subject, where self-consciousness is understood as involving a capacity to conceive of oneself as temporally extended and spatially located. On the other hand, it would seem that no being could satisfy the constraints set out in the functional account of I-Ideas without being, in the relevant sense, self-conscious, rational, and capable of acting in the world. So it should come as no surprise that the ascription of I-thoughts necessarily goes hand in hand with the conception of that to which such thoughts are ascribed as a substantial subject, an object among objects.

This might prompt the following reformulation of the charge of stipulation: the point of this charge is not to deny that in ascribing I-thoughts to something, one must also be prepared to ascribe to it the appropriate surrounding capacities. It may even be that in practice, I-thinking and substantial subject-hood are ascribed as elements of a single package, but it does not follow that the elements of the package are, in principle, inseparable. There are, in fact, several ways of taking this objection. It may be denying that the Evansian account of the background required for I-thinking is the right account. If it were the right account, then I-thinking would indeed only be possible for substantial subjects, but perhaps the objection is that something far less rich is required to sustain thinking of the I-type. Alternatively, the objection may be accepting the Evansian account of the cognitive dynamics of I-Ideas but denying that a something that satisfies the Evansian constraints *must* be a substantial subject. Finally, and most subtly, the objection may be understood as accepting these constraints and accepting that something that satisfies them must be a substantial subject, but as denying that the latter fact does any explanatory work. The suggestion, in other words, is that it is possible for the external analyst to maintain a grip on the constraints on I-thinking while abstracting from the fact that anything capable of sustaining thinking of this type counts as a substantial subject. This is possible because an understanding of the constraints need not derive from an understanding of how the lives of substantial subjects are organized; the constraints are independently intelligible.

In support of the first of these points, it might be held that the Evansian account of what it takes to be an I-thinker is too demanding because we do, after all, ascribe I-thoughts to amnesiacs and people who are paralysed despite the fact that they do not satisfy all of the 'functional' constraints. There are two things to be said about this. The first is that our willingness to ascribe I-thoughts in such cases may be a reflection of the fact that the subjects in question are such that *typical* members of their kind—other human beings—do display the kind of internal organization set out in the functional account.[5] Even if it makes sense to suppose that impaired individuals are capable of I-thinking, this does not make it intelligible that I-thinkers in general do not need to be capable of acting in the world or of self-ascribing past-tense properties on a special basis. The second point about such marginal cases is that the subjects in question are still objects among others in the world. Reflection on such cases, therefore, does nothing for the idea that I-thoughts can intelligibly be ascribed to something whose existence is not a substantial fact.

A more difficult question is whether anything that satisfies the Evansian constraints on I-thinking must be a substantial subject. It has been taken for granted so far that the substantiality of an I-thinking subject is equivalent to its being an object among others in the world, which is in turn equivalent to its existence being a 'substantial fact'. This might prompt the objection that this formulation ignores a number of important distinctions. For example, the existence of nations is, in a sense, a perfectly 'substantial' fact about the world, but nations are not substances. There are also questions about what it means to describe something as an 'object among others in the world' and about the relationship

---

[5] A suggestion along these lines can be extracted from Wiggins 1980: 171.

between a subject's being such an 'object' and its being a substantial sub-ject. Without greater clarity on these terminological questions, it is diffi-cult to understand, let alone assess, the thesis that it is distinctive of first-person thinking that thoughts of the first-person type are only properly ascribable to 'substantial subjects' who are objects among others in the world.

The appropriate response to these difficulties in the present context would be to return to the central assumption of previous chapters, name-ly, that for something to be an 'object among others in the world' is for it to be a physical object. It will also be assumed that only physical objects are genuine substances, and that to describe something's existence as a 'substantial fact' is to be committed to regarding it as a substance. The claim that only substantial subjects can fulfil the Evansian conditions on I-thinking is therefore equivalent to the claim that only subjects that are physical objects among physical objects can have what it takes to be capa-ble of first-person thought. The explanation is simple: to be capable of I-thinking, one's I-thoughts must stand in certain relations to perception and action, and one must also be capable of remembering the basis of earlier present-tense judgements. Only something with shape, location, and solidity can perceive, act, or remember, so only subjects with shape, location, and solidity can have the internal organization required to sus-tain I-thinking. Since anything with shape, location, and solidity is a physical object, another way of putting this point would be to say that it only makes sense to ascribe I-thoughts to subjects who are physical objects among others in the world. This is a claim about the actual nature of I-thinkers, not a claim about how I-thinkers must conceive of them-selves.

Those who regard subjects of experience as separately existing enti-ties will no doubt reject the claim that only something with shape, loca-tion, and solidity can perceive, act or remember, but Reductionism denies that subjects are separately existing entities. For Reductionism, persons or subjects are thinkers and agents, and the existence of such thinkers and agents consists in the existence of a brain and body and a series of interrelated mental and physical events. Since Reductionism ought to accept that subjects of thought, perception, memory, and action are physical objects, it should also accept that they are substances; it should therefore abandon the claim that persons or subjects are 'like nations' (Parfit 1987: 275). The problem for Reductionism, however, is that once it concedes that the functional constraints on I-thinking are such that only substantial subjects can have what it takes to be I-thinkers, then it is difficult to see how it can object to the modified strong relativization requirement. It would seem, therefore, that the only remaining option for Reductionism is the third of the three options set out above. Instead of denying that I-thinkers must be subjects who are objects among others in the world, the Reductionist should argue that it is possible for an external analyst to grasp the constraints on I-thinking while abstracting from the fact that anything capable of sustaining such thinking must be a substantial subject. In other words, the Reductionist is now to be understood as maintaining that the 'functional' constraints on first-person thought can be understood in impersonal terms, and that it is because this is so that it is possible to maintain a fix on the content of an I-thought without ascribing it to a subject or person.

One way of developing the idea that the constitutive constraints on I-thinking can be understood in impersonal terms would be to appeal to functionalism, the view that mental states are individuated by reference to their place in a complex causal network. Some functionalists such as Shoemaker regard functionalism as calling Parfitian Reductionism into question, on the grounds that the existence of the kind of network that has just been described amounts to the existence of a person. The suggestion, then, is that functionalism is incompatible with the impersonal description thesis because functional definitions are quite explicit in drawing upon the concept of a person. As Shoemaker puts it, 'it is in conjunction with other mental states *of the same person* that a mental state produces the effects it does; and its immediate effects, those the having of which is definitive of its being the mental state it is, will be states (or behaviour) on the part of the *very same person* who had the mental state in question' (1984a: 93).

The problem with this account of an alleged conflict between Reductionism and functionalism is that even if what makes it the case that a given state is the belief that p is its causal relations to inputs, outputs, and other mental states, it is not clear why functionalism must conceive of such content-yielding causal relations as relations that obtain between states of a person. Functionalism is certainly committed to an 'anti-isolationist' conception of content, but the reference to persons in Shoemaker's specification of the form of a functional definition seems unnecessary. In essence, functionalism is the view that something counts as the realization of a given state if, in conjunction with other states in what might be called the same 'psychological space', it produces certain effects in that same space. What makes it the case that given states belong in a single space is, in turn, just the fact that they have the functionally

appropriate effects. As is illustrated by cases of 'divided minds', psychological spaces cannot be equated outright with persons. A belief and a
desire may be assigned to distinct spaces or 'sub-systems'[6] on the
grounds that they do not have the effects that one would expect if they
were elements in the same space, but such spaces or subsystems may be
too transient to count as persons or subjects. Thus, it would appear that
the concept 'same person' is doing no special work in functional definitions, work which could not be done just as well by the more neutral and
abstract concept of a 'psychological space' within which various states
are appropriately functionally related.

Another way of pressing the question about the role of reference to
persons or subjects in functional definitions would be to examine the
prospects for a functionalist, rather than merely 'functional', account of
the cognitive dynamics of I-thoughts. It is true that in Evans's characterization of the cognitive dynamics, use was made of the idea that when a
subject judges 'I am F', there is a non-negligible probability that he—the
very same subject—will later be disposed to judge 'I was F', but how
much explanatory work is being done by this reference to the sameness of
subject? Consider, in this connection, Shoemaker's notion of a 'successor
state' (Shoemaker 1984a: 95). The proposal is that while the content of a
person's belief or intention will depend to a certain extent upon all of
her preceding states, there will often be a particular preceding state upon
whose content its content especially depends. It is of that earlier state
that the current state is the 'successor state'. With this notion of a 'successor state' in place, functionalism maintains, in Shoemaker's words,
that 'a mental state is defined in part in terms of what successor state it is
liable to give rise to in combination with various other states' (ibid.).

This suggests the following functionalist account of the cognitive
dynamics of I-thinking: part of what makes a thought a present-tense
self-ascriptive thought of the form 'I am F' is the fact that it typically
causes a particular type of successor state, namely, a thought with the
content 'I was F'. This is not Shoemaker's proposal, but it is a recogniz-
ably functionalist way of handling the cognitive dynamics. If it is claimed
that the successive 'states' must be states of the same person, it may be
replied that it is only necessary that they occupy the same 'psychological
space', a space which is itself delineated in functional terms. There is an
element of circularity here, but there are familiar functionalist strategies
for defusing the circularity of functional definitions. If it turns out that

the successive states are *de facto* causally related as events in the life of a single person, this fact is doing no special explanatory work. It is in this sense that functionalism may be seen as accommodating the 'functional' constraints on I-thinking in impersonal terms.

The problem with this impersonal account of the cognitive dynamics of first-person thought is that it describes but does not explain the relations between I-thoughts and their successor states. It is one thing to say that if someone judges 'I am F' then there is a non-negligible probability that she will later be disposed to judge 'I was F', but the external analyst of I-thinking also needs to be able to explain why thoughts of the form 'I am F' typically cause later thoughts of the form 'I was F'. The explanation is this: to be a person or subject is, at least, to have the conception of oneself as temporally extended. As Bennett puts it on Kant's behalf, 'the notion of oneself is necessarily that of a possessor of a history: I can judge that this is how it is with me now only if I can also judge that this is how it was with me then' (Bennett 1966: 117). There is a non-negligible probability that someone who judges 'I am F' will later be disposed to judge 'I was F' because these thoughts are occurrences in the life of a subject who conceives of herself as temporally extended, and because part of what it is to regard oneself as temporally extended is for one's past-tense I-thoughts to flow out of earlier present-tense I-thoughts without the need for any skill or care not to lose track of oneself. In other words, a proper explanation of the dynamic relations between temporally separate I-thoughts must draw upon the way in which I-thoughts that are related in the appropriate manner help to sustain the idea of their subject as the possessor of a history.

This is only a rough indication of how a 'sideways on' understanding of what a self-conscious subject is helps to ground and render intelligible a particular constraint on I-thinking. An understanding of the structure required to sustain I-thinking needs to be properly anchored, and what provides the anchoring is the fact that it only makes sense to ascribe I-thoughts to substantial subjects or persons whose lives are organized in such a way as to enable them to regard themselves as temporally extended. Other aspects of the cognitive dynamics may be explicable by reference to the fact that the substantial subjects of I-thoughts must also be able to think of themselves as spatially located, and of their experience as experience of an objective world. In contrast, the bare concept of a 'psychological space' cannot explain the cognitive dynamics or what might be described as the 'normative' relations between I-thoughts. Only if such spaces are modelled on the lives of subjects is it possible to capture the full force of the idea that a given element in the space not only does but, as it were, ought to give rise to specific further elements. If functionalism can accommodate this point, then, as Shoemaker suspects, it is of no help to Reductionism. If, on the other hand, functionalism cannot allow any special explanatory work to be done by the concept of a subject in its account of I-thinking, then it stands accused, along with Reductionism, of failing to provide the dynamic constraints on such thinking with an adequate explanatory foundation. Either way, Reductionism is in trouble. To say that it is not possible to explain the cognitive dynamics of I-thinking without regarding I-thoughts as occurrences in the lives of substantial subjects is to say that the 'functional' constraints on first-person thought cannot be understood in impersonal terms. In that case, it remains a mystery how it is supposed to be possible to maintain a fix on the content of an I-thought without ascribing it to a subject or person.

4. Reductionism and the Unity of Consciousness

The time has come to bring together the various strands of the extremely complex anti-Reductionist argument of the preceding section. It will be recalled that the argument began with the observation that the acceptability or otherwise of Reductionism depends, in part, upon the acceptability or otherwise of the impersonal description thesis, together with the claim that the unity of a person's life can be described in impersonal terms. It was objected that the impersonal description is incompatible with the ORU argument, since the thinking of self-ascriptive I-thoughts is a necessary condition of being able to think of one's experience as experience of an objective world. In reply, the Reductionist was envisaged as arguing that this objection overlooks the distinction between the perspective of self-consciousness itself and the perspective of the external analyst of self-consciousness. The external analyst may need to refer to persons in describing the content of many thoughts, desires, and memories, but need not ascribe any of these mental 'events' to persons.

The difficulty with this argument is that there is no perspective, internal or external, from which it is possible to capture the content of an I-thought without ascribing it to a person or subject. This is a reflection of the strong relativization requirement, which poses a serious threat to the impersonal description thesis. In defence of this requirement, it was argued that thoughts of the 'I'-type are only properly ascribable to persons or subjects who are objects among others in the world. If only persons or subjects can grasp I-thoughts then it is plausible that the truth-condition and hence the content of a thought of this form will depend upon who the thinker or subject is.

Why it should be accepted that only persons or substantial subjects can be the thinkers of I-thoughts? This is a question for the external analyst, and the answer to it is that I-thoughts can only be grasped in the context of a range of other abilities. These abilities are such that they can only be possessed by persons or other subjects who are physical objects among physical objects. This, in turn, is a reflection of the fact that a proper understanding of the dynamic constraints on I-thinking must be informed by the conception of such thoughts as having a distinctive role in the lives of subjects who have a sense of themselves as temporally extended. Once it is understood that thoughts of the I-type are essentially events in the lives of substantial subjects or persons, it is difficult to see how the 'indexing' or relativization of such thoughts can involve anything less than their ascription to subjects or persons. And once it is understood that I-thoughts are subject to the strong relativization requirement, not even an external analyst can capture their contents in impersonal terms. If it is not possible fully to capture the content of an I-thought in impersonal terms, then the unity of a life which includes thinkings of thoughts of this form also cannot be described or explained in impersonal terms. Since the unity of consciousness cannot be explained impersonally, an impersonal description of reality cannot be complete.

Reductionists who regard the impersonal description thesis as inessential to their position may not be troubled by this argument, but the same cannot be said for those who regard the impersonal description thesis as the best hope for the Exclusion Thesis. As was remarked at the outset, the idea that the existence of persons is a 'derivative' fact about the world is easier to understand than the idea that persons or subjects are not 'in' the world at all. From this standpoint, the interest of the impersonal description thesis is that saying that persons need not be mentioned in a complete description of reality is the best way of making sense of the thesis of derivative existence. Thus, the failure of the impersonal description thesis does indeed have the consequence predicted earlier; it removes the last hope for the Exclusion Thesis.

In addition to undermining the impersonal description thesis, the defence of the strong relativization requirement also deepens the argument given in the last chapter against Kant's claim that transcendental consciousness of self-identity is intelligible independently of the notion of the self, *qua* subject of 'I think' instances, as an object among others in the world. It was objected in Chapter 4 that Kant's position is indefensible, since transcendental apperception is consciousness of the identical form of 'I think' instances, and even consciousness of this 'logical' identity requires awareness of the subjects of such instances, including oneself, as objects among others. It is now possible to see the full force of this objection. Kant's 'independent intelligibility' thesis fails because in order to think of 'I think' instances as 'I think' instances, one must understand their cognitive dynamics, and this requires the conception of such instances as occurrences in the lives of substantial subjects. This is the sense in which, as remarked in the last chapter, our ability to think the 'form of consciousness' is not detachable from a sense of ourselves as substantial and not merely 'formal' subjects.

In the Paralogisms, Kant gives the following account of the fundamental error of rational psychology:

The unity of consciousness, which underlies the categories, is here mistaken for an intuition of the subject as object, and the category of substance is then applied to it. But this unity is only unity in *thought*, by which alone no object is given, and to which, therefore, the category of substance, which always presupposes a given *intuition*, cannot be applied. Consequently, this subject cannot be known. (B421–2)

Kant was only partly right. The unity of consciousness certainly does not involve an intuition of the subject as object, if this means an intuition of the subject as an immaterial thinking substance. Kant's mistake was to conclude from this that the unity of consciousness does not involve being presented to oneself as an object at all. The right conclusion is that self-consciousness, and so the unity of consciousness, is intimately bound up with awareness of the subject 'as an object'—not as an 'immaterial' substance but as a physical object in a world of physical objects.

BIBLIOGRAPHY

Allison, H. (1983), *Kant's Transcendental Idealism* (New Haven: Yale University Press).

Ameriks, K. (1982), *Kant's Theory of Mind: An Analysis of the Paralogisms of Pure Reason* (Oxford: Clarendon Press).

Anscombe, G. E. M. (1994), 'The First Person', in Cassam (1994), 140–59.

Aquila, R. (1979), 'Personal Identity and Kant's "Refutation of Idealism"', *Kant-Studien*, 70: 257–78.

Armstrong, D. M. (1984), 'Consciousness and Causality', in Armstrong and Malcolm (1984), 103–91.

Armstrong, D. M., and Malcolm, N. (1984), *Consciousness and Causality* (Oxford: Basil Blackwell).

Ayers, M. R. (1974), 'Individuals Without Sortals', *Canadian Journal of Philosophy*, 4: 113–48.

—— (1991), *Locke*, 2 vols. (London: Routledge).

Baldwin, T. (1988), 'Phenomenology, Solipsism, and Egocentric Thought', *Proceedings of the Aristotelian Society*, Supp. Vol. 62: 46–60.

Bell, D. (1990), *Husserl* (London: Routledge).

Bennett, J. (1966), *Kant's Analytic* (Cambridge: Cambridge University Press).

Berkeley, G. (1975), *Philosophical Works including the Works on Vision*, introd. by M. R. Ayers (London: J. M. Dent & Sons Ltd.).

Bermúdez, J. L., Marcel, A., and Eilan, N. (1995) (eds.), *The Body and the Self* (Cambridge, Mass.: MIT Press).

Bird, G. (1996), 'Kantian Myths', *Proceedings of the Aristotelian Society*, 96: 245–51.

Brewer, B. (1992), 'Self-Location and Agency', *Mind*, 101: 17–34.

Burge, T. (1994), 'Individualism and Self-Knowledge', in Cassam (1994): 65–79.

Campbell, J. (1993), 'The Role of Physical Objects in Spatial Thinking', in Eilan, McCarthy, and Brewer (1993), 65–99.

—— (1994), *Past, Space, and Self* (Cambridge, Mass.: MIT Press).

Carruthers, P. (1992), *Human Knowledge and Human Nature: A New Introduction to an Ancient Debate* (Oxford: Oxford University Press).

Cassam, Q. (1987), 'Transcendental Arguments, Transcendental Synthesis, and Transcendental Idealism', *Philosophical Quarterly*, 37: 355–78.

—— (1989), 'Kant and Reductionism', *Review of Metaphysics*, 43: 72–106.

—— (1992), 'Reductionism and First-Person Thinking', in Charles and Lennon (1992), 361–80.

—— (1993a), 'Inner Sense, Body Sense, and Kant's "Refutation of Idealism"', *European Journal of Philosophy*, 1: 111–27.

Cassam, Q. (cont.) (1993b), 'Parfit on Persons', *Proceedings of the Aristotelian Society*, 93: 17–37.

—— (1994) (ed.), *Self-Knowledge* (Oxford: Oxford University Press).

—— (1995a), 'Introspection and Bodily Self-Ascription', in Bermúdez, Marcel, and Eilan (1995), 311–36.

—— (1995b), 'Transcendental Self-Consciousness', in Sen and Verma (1995), 161–78.

Charles, D., and Lennon, K. (1992) (eds.), *Reductionism, Explanation, and Realism* (Oxford: Clarendon Press).

Chisholm, R. (1994), 'On the Observability of the Self', in Cassam (1994), 94–108.

Cockburn, D. (1991), *Human Beings* (Cambridge: Cambridge University Press).

Cole, J. (1991), *Pride and a Daily Marathon* (London: Duckworth).

Cottingham, J. (1986), *Descartes* (Oxford: Basil Blackwell).

Cottingham, J., Stoothoff, R., and Murdoch, D. (1984) (eds. and trans.), *The Philosophical Writings of Descartes*, 2 vols., (Cambridge: Cambridge University Press).

Cottingham, J., Stoothoff, R., Murdoch, D., and Kenny, A. (1991) (eds. and trans.), *The Philosophical Writings of Descartes*, iii: *The Correspondence* (Cambridge: Cambridge University Press).

Cramer, K., Fulda, H., Horstmann, R-P., and Pothast, U. (1987) (eds.), *Theorie der Subjectivität* (Frankfurt am Main: Suhrkamp).

Dancy, J. (1988) (ed.), *Perceptual Knowledge* (Oxford: Oxford University Press).

Dummett, M. (1973), *Frege: Philosophy of Language* (London: Duckworth).

—— (1981), *The Interpretation of Frege's Philosophy* (London: Duckworth).

Eilan, N., McCarthy, R., and Brewer, B. (1993) (eds.), *Spatial Representation* (Oxford: Basil Blackwell).

Evans, G. (1980), 'Things Without the Mind—A Commentary upon Chapter Two of Strawson's *Individuals*', in Van Straaten (1980), 76–116.

—— (1982), *The Varieties of Reference*, edited by J. McDowell (Oxford: Oxford University Press).

—— (1985), *Collected Papers* (Oxford: Oxford University Press).

Gill, C. (1990) (ed.), *The Person and the Human Mind: Issues in Ancient and Modern Philosophy* (Oxford: Clarendon Press).

Grayling, A. (1995) (ed.), *Philosophy: A Guide Through the Subject* (Oxford: Oxford University Press).

Harrison, R. (1970), 'Strawson on Outer Objects', *Philosophical Quarterly*, 20: 213–21.

Hatfield, G. (1990), *The Natural and the Normative: Theories of Spatial Perception from Kant to Helmholtz* (Cambridge, Mass.: MIT Press).

Henrich, D. (1989), 'The Identity of the Subject in the Transcendental Deduction', in Schaper and Vossenkuhl (1989), 250–80.

Hirsch, E. (1982), *The Concept of Identity* (New York: Oxford University Press).

Holtzman, S., and Leich, C. (1981) (eds.), *Wittgenstein: To Follow a Rule* (London: Routledge & Kegan Paul).

Hume, D. (1978), *A Treatise of Human Nature*, ed. L. A. Selby-Bigge, revised by P. H. Nidditch (Oxford: Oxford University Press).

Husserl, E. (1989), *Ideas Pertaining to a Pure Phenomenology and to a Phenomenological Philosophy, Second Book: Studies in the Phenomenology of Constitution*, trans. R. Rojcewicz and A. Schuwer (Dordrecht: Kluwer Academic Publishers).

—— (1991), *Cartesian Meditations: An Introduction to Phenomenology*, trans. D. Cairns (Dordrecht: Kluwer Academic Publishers).

Janaway, C. (1989), *Self and World in Schopenhauer's Philosophy* (Oxford: Clarendon Press).

Joske, W. (1967), *Material Objects* (London: Macmillan).

Kant, I. (1929), *Critique of Pure Reason*, trans. N. Kemp Smith (London: Macmillan).

—— (1974), *Anthropology from a Pragmatic Point of View*, trans. M. J. Gregor (The Hague: Martinus Nijhoff).

—— (1977), *Prolegomena to Any Future Metaphysics*, original trans. P. Carus, revised by J. Ellington (Indianapolis: Hackett Publishing Company).

—— (1993), *Opus Postumum*, trans. E. Förster and M. Rosen (Cambridge: Cambridge University Press).

Locke, J. (1975), *An Essay Concerning Human Understanding*, ed. P. H. Nidditch (Oxford: Clarendon Press).

Lowe, E. J. (1989), 'What is a Criterion of Identity?', *Philosophical Quarterly*, 39: 1–21.

McDowell, J. (1981), 'Non-Cognitivism and Rule-Following', in Holtzman and Leich (1981), 141–62.

—— (1982), 'Criteria, Defeasibility, and Knowledge', *Proceedings of the British Academy*, 68: 455–79.

—— (1994), *Mind and World* (Cambridge, Mass.: Harvard University Press).

McGinn, C. (1993), *Problems in Philosophy: The Limits of Inquiry* (Oxford: Basil Blackwell).

Martin, M. (1993), 'Sense Modalities and Spatial Properties', in Eilan, McCarthy, and Brewer (1993), 206–18.

Merleau-Ponty, M. (1989), *Phenomenology of Perception*, trans. C. Smith (London: Routledge).

Nagel, T. (1986), *The View From Nowhere* (New York: Oxford University Press).

O'Brien, L. (1995), 'Evans on Self-Identification', *Nous*, 29: 232–47.

O'Shaughnessy, B. (1980), *The Will: A Dual Aspect Theory*, 2 vols. (Cambridge: Cambridge University Press).

—— (1989), 'The Sense of Touch', *Australasian Journal of Philosophy*, 67: 37–58.

—— (1994), 'The Mind-Body Problem', in Warner and Szubka (1994), 204–14.

Parfit, D. (1987), *Reasons and Persons* (Oxford: Clarendon Press). (First published 1984; the corrected 1987 reprint is referred to in the text.)

Peacocke, C. (1979), *Holistic Explanation: Action, Space, Interpretation* (Oxford: Clarendon Press).

—— (1983), *Sense and Content: Experience, Thought, and their Relations* (Oxford: Clarendon Press).

—— (1989), *Transcendental Arguments in the Theory of Content: An Inaugural Lecture delivered before the University of Oxford on 16 May 1989* (Oxford: Clarendon Press).

—— (1991), 'Demonstrative Content: A Reply to John McDowell', *Mind*, 100: 123–33.

—— (1993), 'Intuitive Mechanics, Psychological Reality, and the Idea of a Material Object', in Eilan, McCarthy, and Brewer (1993), 162–76.

Pears, D. (1984), *Motivated Irrationality* (Oxford: Clarendon Press).

Penelhum, T. (1970), *Survival and Disembodied Existence* (London: Routledge & Kegan Paul).

Perry, J. (1994), 'The Problem of the Essential Indexical', in Cassam (1994), 167–83.

Rosenberg, J. (1986), *The Thinking Self* (Philadelphia: Temple University Press).

Rovane, C. (1987), 'The Epistemology of First-Person Reference', *Journal of Philosophy*, 84: 147–67.

Ryle, G. (1994), 'Self-Knowledge', in Cassam (1994), 19–42.

Sartre, J.-P. (1989), *Being and Nothingness: An Essay on Phenomenological Ontology*, trans. H. Barnes (London: Routledge).

Savile, A., and Hopkins, J. (1992) (eds.), *Psychoanalysis, Mind, and Art: Perspectives on Richard Wollheim* (Oxford: Basil Blackwell).

Schaper, E., and Vossenkuhl, W. (1989) (eds.), *Reading Kant: New Perspectives on Transcendental Arguments and Critical Philosophy* (Oxford: Basil Blackwell).

Sen, P. K., and Verma, R. R. (1995) (eds.), *The Philosophy of P. F. Strawson* (New Delhi: Indian Council of Philosophical Research).

Shoemaker, S. (1984a), 'Personal Identity: A Materialist's Account', in Shoemaker and Swinburne (1984), 67–132.

—— (1984b), 'Persons and their Pasts', in Shoemaker (1984c), 19–48.

—— (1984c), *Identity, Cause, and Mind* (Cambridge: Cambridge University Press).

—— (1994a), 'Self-Reference and Self-Awareness', in Cassam (1994), 80–93.

—— (1994b), 'Introspection and the Self', in Cassam (1994), 118–39.

Shoemaker, S. and Swinburne, R. (1984), *Personal Identity* (Oxford: Basil Blackwell).

Snowdon, P. F. (1990), 'Persons, Animals, and Ourselves' in Gill (1990), 83–107.

—— (1991), 'Personal Identity and Brain Transplants' in Cockburn (1991).

Spelke, E., and Van de Walle, G. (1993), 'Perceiving and Reasoning about

Objects: Insights from Infants', in Eilan, McCarthy, and Brewer (1993), 132–61.

Strawson, P. F. (1959), *Individuals: An Essay in Descriptive Metaphysics* (London: Methuen).

—— (1966), *The Bounds of Sense: An Essay on Kant's Critique of Pure Reason* (London: Methuen).

—— (1974a), 'Imagination and Perception', in Strawson (1974d), 45–65.

—— (1974b), 'Self, Mind and Body', in Strawson (1974d), 169–77.

—— (1974c), 'Perception and Identification', in Strawson (1974d), 85–107.

—— (1974d), *Freedom and Resentment and Other Essays* (London: Methuen).

—— (1985), *Skepticism and Naturalism: Some Varieties* (London: Methuen).

—— (1987), 'Kant's Paralogisms: Self-Consciousness and the "Outside Observer"', in Cramer, Fulda, Horstmann, and Pothast (1987), 202–19.

—— (1988), 'Perception and its Objects', in Dancy (1988), 92–112.

—— (1994), 'The First Person—and Others', in Cassam (1994), 210–15.

—— (1995), 'Quassim Cassam on Transcendental Self-Consciousness', in Sen and Verma (1995), 416–18.

Stroud, B. (1982), 'Transcendental Arguments', in Walker (1982), 117–31.

Van Straaten, Z. (1980) (ed.), *Philosophical Subjects: Essays Presented to P. F. Strawson* (Oxford: Clarendon Press).

Walker, R. C. S. (1982) (ed.), *Kant on Pure Reason* (Oxford: Oxford University Press).

Walsh, W. H. (1975), *Kant's Criticism of Metaphysics* (Edinburgh: Edinburgh University Press).

Warner, R., and Szubka, T. (1994) (eds.), *The Mind-Body Problem* (Oxford: Basil Blackwell).

Wiggins, D. (1980), *Sameness and Substance* (Oxford: Basil Blackwell).

—— (1992), 'Remembering Directly', in Savile and Hopkins (1992), 339–54.

—— (1995), 'Substance', in Grayling (1995), 214–46.

Williams, B. (1973), *Problems of the Self* (Cambridge: Cambridge University Press).

—— (1978), *Descartes: The Project of Pure Enquiry* (Harmondsworth: Penguin).

Wittgenstein, L. (1958), *The Blue and Brown Books: Preliminary Studies for the 'Philosophical Investigations'* (Oxford: Basil Blackwell).

—— (1961), *Tractatus Logico-Philosophicus*, trans. D. Pears and B. McGuinness (London: Routledge & Kegan Paul).

—— (1978), *Philosophical Investigations*, trans. G. E. M. Anscombe (Oxford: Basil Blackwell).

—— (1979), *Wittgenstein's Lectures: Cambridge, 1932–1935*, ed. by Alice Ambrose from the notes of Alice Ambrose and Margaret Macdonald (Oxford: Basil Blackwell).

INDEX

Abstraction Argument 12–21, 76, 160
Acquired Ability Argument 82–3
action 84–5, 189
act-object conception of experience 98, 106–7
alien limb examples 65
Allison, H. 17–18, 21, 96 n.
Ameriks, K. 21 n.
Anscombe, G. E. M. 135 n., 147, 148 n.
anti-sortalist accounts of individuation 137, 138 n., 143, 145
apenetrability 83–5
apparent presence in the world, three grades of 58, 87–8
Aquila, R. 46 n., 80–1, 85
Armstrong, D. M. 62 n.
awareness of the self as a physical object 1–9, 21–7, 30–1, 34, 44–5, 50, 51–6, 60–1, 68–73
  broad versus narrow senses of 71–2
awareness of the self *qua* subject 4–5, 24–5, 56–61
Ayers, M. R. 2 n., 7 n., 10 n., 32 n., 35 n., 57, 64 n., 65 n., 73, 75 n., 109, 136 n., 137 n., 138 n., 173 n.

Baldwin, T. 72 n.
belief-independence of perceptual content 31, 140
Bell, D. 56
Bennett, J. 195
Berkeley, G. 82
Bird, G. 16 n.
bodily self 57–8, 72, 73–6, 142
  see also body/Body distinction; bodily self-awareness; core-self
bodily self-awareness 51–6, 57, 60, 63–8, 71, 77, 136–50
body blindness 80–9
body/Body distinction 52
body-image 84–5
body-ownership 63–7
  idealism about body-ownership 63–6
  realism about body-ownership 66–7
Brewer, B. 53 n.
bundle theory of the self 1, 10
Burge, T. 131 n.

(C1) *see* Objectivity Argument, concept version
(C2) *see* Objectivity Argument, intuition version
Campbell, J. 15 n., 78, 127 n., 130 n., 135
Carruthers, P. 83 n.
Chisholm, R. 3 n.
circularity argument 22–5
cognitive dynamics 145, 189, 191, 194–6
Cole, J. 81 n.
Concept Acquisition Argument 81–2
Content Argument 84–7
core-self 73–6
Cottingham, J. 4 n.
criteria of identity, constitutive/evidential distinction 123–4
  see also empirically applicable criteria of subject-identity

(D1) *see* Identity Argument, concept version
(D2) *see* Identity Argument, intuition version
demonstrative reference 68–9, 74–6, 104, 108–9, 136–40, 145–6, 150, 166
dependence thesis 99, 105, 107, 110–11, 113
Descartes, R. 3–4, 8, 10, 75, 88, 125, 126, 141, 183
descriptive metaphysics 51 n.
Discrimination Principle 84
discrimination requirement 121, 125, 126, 136, 156, 157
Dispensability Objection 54–5, 76–89
dualism, Cartesian 4, 7–8, 12, 14, 46, 127, 129–33, 134, 152, 155
dualism, post-Kantian 14
Dummett, M. 123 n., 124 n., 126 n.

Ego *see* transcendental Ego
egocentric spatial content of experience 45, 52–3, 56–61, 66, 73–4, 78–9, 80–1, 84–5
elusiveness of the self 1–6
empirical criteria requirement 119–20, 123–4

transcendental subject 13–18

Unity Argument 26, 29, 91–116
unity of consciousness 26, 36–7, 91–116,
180–3, 196–8
unity requires objectivity (URO) argument
90, 91
  see also Unity Argument

van de Walle, G. 151

Walsh, W. H. 11
Wiggins, D. 12 n., 44, 123 n., 136, 137,
143, 145, 175, 191 n.
Williams, B. 168–9, 183, 186
Wittgenstein, L. 7, 12, 18, 19, 60, 67, 105

zero point 53, 54, 59